ARRESTED

What to Do When Your Loved One's in Jail

Wes Denham

CHICAGO
REVIEW
PRESS

Library of Congress Cataloging-in-Publication Data

Denham, Wes.

Arrested : what to do when your loved one's in jail / Wes Denham.

p. cm.

Includes index.

ISBN 978-1-55652-834-7

1. Prisoners' families—United States. 2. Prisoners—Family relationships—United States. 3. Prisoners—United States. I. Title.

HV8886.U6D46 2010

362.82'9—dc22

2009042270

Cover and interior design: Visible Logic, Inc.
Cover image: © Veer Incorporated

Published by Chicago Review Press, Incorporated
814 North Franklin Street
Chicago, Illinois 60610
ISBN: 978-1-55652-834-7
Printed in the United States of America
5 4 3 2 1

It costs you less to live intelligent and free than stupid and confined.

—Frank Lloyd Wright

CONTENTS

1. **Star Light, Star Bright, Get Me Out of Jail Tonight!**
    Those Terrible Telephone Calls. 1

2. **The Golden Road to Samarqand** Preface to Freedom. 6

3. **You, the Gumshoe** How to Get Critical Information. 21

4. **Toss Your Crib, Car, and Computer** An Urgent Priority. 32

5. **Going to the Big House** Jail Visits 39

6. **"Give Your Hearts to Jesus, Boys . . ."** Life in Jail. 43

7. **Sick, Confused, and Crazy** Medical Care and Mental Illness. 55

8. **Bureaucratic Heroin and Black Holes** Commissaries and Jail Phones 60

9. **How Chancroid Saves a Twink** Sex in Jail. 68

10. **As the Worm Turns** Drug Addiction 74

11. **Does the Elevator Go Up to the Top, or Not?**
    Homo Chaoticus, Unsocialized Man 80

12. **Hitting Bottom** How to Recognize a Readiness to Change 89

13. **Why Gung Ho Is Good** The Character Factories. 93

14. **To Help or Not to Help?** Rating Defendants. 103

15. **The Tickle of the Trocar** Bail and Bail Bonds. 117

16. **How a Wino Saved the Sixth Amendment** Public Defenders, Plea Bargains,
    and the Caseload Gorilla 124

17. **The Pin-Striped Mafia** Fee Whores, Voodoo Doctors, Dodo Birds,
    and Other Legal Vermin. 132

18. **Crackerjack Private Attorneys** How to Find the Prize in the Box 142

19. **Show Me the Work, I'll Show You the Money** Getting a Quotation
for Legal Services and Fees. 152

20. **Negotiating a Contract for Legal Defense** Getting the Bang for Your Bucks 170

21. **How to Help the Defense** Getting Busy In Jail and Out. 173

22. **Money! Money! Money!** The Budget 179

23. **Outdoor Jail** Probation and Parole. 190

24. **To Snitch Is a Bitch** Cooperating with Police and Prosecutors 202

25. **Your Personal Witness Protection Program** Blowing the 'Hood. 206

26. **The Family Management Plan** Making a Difference for Your Defendant 209

27. **Why Are So Many People in Jail?** Juking the Stats in the Crime-Crazed U.S.A. . . . 220

APPENDIXES

A **Library of Forms and Letters**. 236

B **How to Dispute Attorney Credit Card Charges**. 243

C **The Dictionary of Crime and Punishment**. 245

Index. 253

1

STAR LIGHT, STAR BRIGHT, GET ME OUT OF JAIL TONIGHT!

Those Terrible Telephone Calls

IT STARTS WITH A phone call, almost always at night.

"I'm in jail! I can't stand this. I didn't do what they said I did. You've *got* to get me out of here. Please, *please* . . ."

You mutter, "I love you." You say, "I'll stand by you." But what else? Is there something you *should* be saying?

Now your loved one—the defendant—is begging, sobbing, yelling. In the background there are shouts, hoots, jeers, in English, Spanish, Hindi, and Chinese.

A mechanical voice cuts in. "Reminder: This call is being recorded. This call will terminate in 15 seconds."

"Please, please . . ."

Click.

Each night, thousands of people like you receive phone calls like this. Your family member, friend, or loved one has been arrested and is in jail. Even before you put down the phone, you realize that *your* life will also be upended and that this nightmare has only just begun.

In your home, things get crazy. Lights go on. Doors slam. People mill around and start talking all at once. Children start to cry. And what's up with the dog? How do you make decisions? How do you even *think* amid such an uproar?

What, you wonder, will it take to procure freedom or a shortened prison term? The defendant mentioned bail. Should you throw on some clothes and grab your checkbook and credit cards? Should you call relatives and ask them to get *their* credit cards and checkbooks? Should you all pile into a car and rush to a bondsman's office in the dead of night?

No! Absolutely not. That's a sucker play. I'll explain why shortly.

During the first call, here's what you do. First, *get the defendant to read his or her jail number to you*. It's probably on a plastic wristband. Write it down. You can't send mail easily or find out anything from police, jails, or courts without it. You have limited time on jail calls, so emphasize these important points:

1. Tell the defendant *not to talk* to police, prosecutors, or probation officers without an attorney present.

2. Tell the defendant *not to talk* to other inmates, who will snitch.

3. Tell the defendant *not to sign* any statement without an attorney present.

4. Tell the defendant *not to waive the right to an attorney*, no matter what.

5. *Promise* help and support.

6. *Do not promise* to bail out the defendant or hire a private attorney. Not now. Not yet.

The defendant will be stressed. It will be difficult for him or her to remember what you say. Make the defendant repeat each important point back to you. *Not talking* is the most important advice in criminal law. An O.J.-style Dream Team will tell you this for $5,000 an hour; a public defender will give you the same advice for free. The shock of jail makes people nuts. They babble; they snitch; they confess to *other peoples' crimes*. Cops take advantage. A certain amount of trickery and deceit during interrogation is legal—that's right, legal. If your defendant has difficulty understanding this important concept, try the short version: "Shut the f#*@ up!"

Everybody understands this.

As soon as the phone call is done, cut out the Stick 'Em Up pages from this book and pin them near the phone. They're checklists. You'll need them. Next, get the mailing address of the jail. Cut out the first Jail Mail on the next page, which *repeats* the crucial information above and explains it to the defendant. Scribble a personal message on the back, then fold, stuff, stamp, and seal. Write the defendant's jail number clearly on the envelope. Corrections officers may not deliver mail without it. Drive to the central post office—yes, in the dead of night—and drop this first letter into the box for the early A.M. pickup. Hopefully the defendant hasn't confessed or signed a statement. Hopefully your words got through the emotional walls, the confusion, and the noise. Jail Mail #1 will reinforce what you said.

Do you know what most defendants wish for, deep down in the guts where even psychopaths don't lie? Mostly they wish to get free *at once* and to get back to balling, banging, and boning, or whatever they were doing that got them arrested in the first place. They also want a hat trick—bail bond, private attorney, and a jury trial. And they want you to pay for it. And damn the expense.

The jail's holding pen will disabuse them of any idea that there is an easy fix. The hosing down jocularly referred to as a shower, the jellied finger up the anus and vagina, the jumpsuit, the flip-flops, and the endless rules will emphasize for even the most dimwitted

Jail Mail

PROTECT YOUR RIGHTS. STAY SAFE!, Page 1

(This information is from a book called *Arrested*.)

1. **Do not** talk about your case to other inmates. They'll rat you out for a deal.

2. **Do not** talk to police, probation officers, or prosecutors without an attorney present.

3. **Do not** sign any statement without an attorney present.

4. **Do not** waive your right to an attorney, no matter what!

5. Eat the food. It's not tasty, but you need to keep up your energy and stay healthy.

6. Make an appointment with the nurse or physician's assistant. Staying healthy is important. It will take time to get prescriptions. See if you can get aspirin or Tylenol. You'll need it later for caffeine withdrawal headaches.

7. Don't drink jail wine. The stuff can be poisonous. Inmates pee in it to get it started.

8. Don't use jail dope. It is poisonous. You'll be charged with more crimes.

9. Get a haircut. You want to look neat and tidy for the judge.

10. Bathe and shave. Get your toiletries every week. Judges don't like body odor.

11. Cut your fingernails. Long "pimp" fingernails annoy judges. If you can't get a nail clipper, bite your nails off.

12. Don't spit on corrections officers. Because of AIDS, spitting is a felony.

13. Don't touch or hit corrections officers. More crime means more time. Ignore insults.

14. If inmates bug you for details about your arrest, just say the whole thing makes you crazy and you can't stand to talk about it.

15. Avoid sex with other inmates. Too many diseases.

16. Sign up for free Bibles or Korans. You need something to read.

17. Sign up for all classes, religious services, lectures, etc. No matter how cornball, they're better than staring at flaking paint.

18. Get as many envelopes, sheets of paper, and stamps as you can. Call your family. Ask them to mail you an address list with phone numbers for all your friends and family members.

19. Get trade goods, such as candy and chips, out of the jail store or commissary. This helps make friends.

20. Wash your hands when you're around other inmates who are sick. But be careful about it—don't do it in a way that disrespects other guys. That could get you a beating.

21. Drink coffee and tea if available. If you go off caffeine cold turkey, you'll get a splitting headache.

22. Don't get jail tattoos. You can get seriously ill from infections. Jail tatts make judges nuts.

Jail Mail

23. No gambling. This wastes your commissary allowance and gets you a beating if you can't pay up.

24. Don't talk about your commissary allowance. This invites theft and shakedowns.

25. All laws apply in jail. Drug use, assault, and battery are still illegal!

26. Do not argue with corrections officers. Make complaints in writing through the jail's complaint procedure.

27. **Do not** "show out," or challenge, corrections officers. Disciplinary and incident reports can be sent to prosecutors to make your sentence longer and lessen your chances for leniency, probation, or diversion. The Man's got you. Get used to it.

28. Do not buy stuff from inmates running "cell stores." You'll have to pay off debts with sex, your own commissary allowance, or a beating.

29. Stay off radar screens. Concentrate on your legal defense and your life after jail. Don't become a problem for corrections officers. They can make your life more unpleasant than it already is.

30. Don't get into fights with other inmates. If you are reclassified as a violent inmate, your life will be more miserable. Avoid "stare parties" and walking with the "pimp roll," which challenge other inmates.

31. Don't try to break up fights. When the Blue Horde arrives, you don't want to be swept up in the crowd. Pepper spray and TASERs really hurt!

32. **Read** jail rules and orientation pamphlets and handouts. These are the rules. They tell you how the game is played.

33. Don't accept favors or an offer from another inmate to be your "protector." Protect yourself by doing your time quietly, working on your legal defense, and avoiding challenges to officers and inmates.

34. Take legal advice from attorneys, not inmates. If other inmates knew anything about criminal law, they wouldn't be in jail.

35. If another inmate claims to have been appointed to "supervise" you, don't believe it. Corrections officers are the supervisors in jail. Everyone else is just a prisoner.

PERSONAL NOTE

_____

_____

_____

_____

defendant that life, forever more, will be different.* In a big-city jail, inmates quickly discover that no one is in any particular hurry to do anything about them. Why should they? Once inside, prisoners aren't going anywhere anytime soon.

Time drags. Drunks puke into the drains, first the booze, then the yellow stuff, then the red. The air stinks. Curses and shouts ring out. Madmen babble to their demons, scratch sores, or masturbate astride the steel toilets. Sometimes the cold concrete and the cold steel, the din, and the humiliations will stimulate defendants to think new thoughts and ponder some changes. It takes time for jail to work its mental magic. But in jail, time is something that inmates share. It abounds. It overflows.

Jail is the Time Machine.

---

* During processing, jail inmates undergo body cavity searches for drugs and weapons such as tape-covered razor blades and shivs. They are issued flip-flops because shoes can be used as bludgeons and shoelaces as garrotes and hanging ropes.

2

THE GOLDEN ROAD TO SAMARQAND
Preface to Freedom

FOR A DEFENDANT LANGUISHING in jail, freedom, which once was taken for granted, now seems exotic and unreachable. Someone incarcerated for the first time has the sense of being swept up by a whirlwind and deposited on the other side of the Earth. It is a place as mysterious as the trans-Eurasian steppe. Everywhere there are unknown people, many speaking languages difficult to understand.

On the horizon far, far away, there appears an Asiatic city. Is this the city called Freedom? How peculiar are the blue-tiled minarets and the golden domes! Even at great distance, behind jailhouse bars, the air imagined carries the faintest hint of pomegranate, lemon, and rose. Fountains burble there, and when the wind shifts, there comes a murmur as the sunset prayer rises heavenward.

From jail, freedom is as strange as Samarqand. The gray painted line that must be toed twice daily at roll call is the beginning of the golden road to get there. It is a long and treacherous path. Robbers lurk, and vultures hover. Through steep passes, the broad highway narrows to a thread that can part in an instant and precipitate the defendant into bottomless gorges. But prisoners must walk this road. It is the only way to freedom. Their families can help.*

This book is your guide. This chapter details what's in it and how to use it.

WHAT THIS BOOK WILL NOT GIVE YOU

Legal strategies and legal advice are not to be found here for a simple reason: I'm not a lawyer. That's a good thing, because it means I can talk freely about how criminal defense attorneys earn, or fail to earn, their money. I'm fortunately not subject to regulation by fuddy-duddy bar associations, whose main rule seems to be:

---

* By "family" I don't mean a nuclear family with a mother and father living together in marriage. Most people in jail have never known such an arrangement. That's a big reason why they're in jail. More likely you're an ad hoc family. You're a grandmother, aunt, cousin, sister, spouse, girlfriend, brother, son, daughter, or best buddy. You don't all live together, and you've been brought together because you're the only loved ones the defendant has.

Of attorneys,
As of the dead,
Let nothing but good
Be said!

In any case, there are excellent books on criminal defense written for laymen. I particularly recommend *The Criminal Law Handbook: Know Your Rights, Survive the System*, by Paul Bergman and Sara J. Berman. It's well written. The authors even manage a mild witticism now and then—not bad for two esquires writing *pro se*.

Also, I will not discuss at any length the appalling disproportion of African Americans and Hispanics in jails and prisons. This is not an oversight on my part. Entire libraries have been written on this subject. In my first book, *Arrest-Proof Yourself*, Dale Carson and I wrote about the practical matter of why minorities are more available for arrest than white people. However, at this point none of that matters, because your loved one is *already in custody*.

Claims of racism are extraordinarily difficult to prove. Even blatant racism may not be grounds for dismissing charges. Racism may make police and prosecutors liable at most to civil damages, and many states have statutory limits on how much you can win in civil actions against government. In my state, it's $100,000. That prize will not attract big, contingent-fee law firms. During a major trial, they spend more than that for coffee and Danish.

Courts consider three things. First, they weigh the facts. Did defendants do the crime? Second, courts will consider matters of law. Were defendants properly charged? Were searches made properly and evidence obtained legally? Are the charges provable beyond a reasonable doubt? Lastly, courts will hear mitigating factors that may merit leniency. Notice that race, ethnicity, gender, and sexual preference are not on this list of judicial priorities.

Note also that among the government employees who compose the criminal justice system, minorities are *overrepresented*. Anyone who has spent time in a courtroom has heard defendants rage against the system's alleged bias against minorities. Defendants never seem to notice that the arresting officer may be black, the prosecutor a woman, the public defender Hispanic, and the judge Chinese. In every courtroom, there are moments of mirth.

Many African Americans harbor deep resentment against white people. If you feel this way, get over it, at least for the time your loved one is in jail. Resentment hinders, not helps. Take that chip off your shoulder and stow it in the closet for the duration. Don't be angry; be effective. You can fight for racial justice once your defendant is free.

Finally, I will not discuss the juvenile justice system, except in passing and for an absolutely important reason. The major recommendation of this book concerns *importing into the adult system some of the practices of the juvenile system.* In juvenile justice, families are players. As legal guardians of minor offenders, their status is mandated by statute. Families stand up with the defendant in court. Judges look to them for answers—and, more importantly, for solutions. "What," judges ask, "can you do to get this kid straightened out?"

Juvenile judges encourage non-prison punishments with heavy emphasis on education, work, rehabilitation, and drug treatment. Frequently they advise getting the juvenile a mentor. This is an interesting word. "Mentor" means, literally, a thinking instructor. Above all, kids need guidance in how to think. They need to think about how to become a citizen,* and how not to become a lowlife criminal.

Adult defendants are independent of their families, but only in the legal sense. When it comes to money and to understanding how the system works, they're often ignorant and frequently dependent, like grown-up children. I ought to know. I've spent so much time in jails and prisons with these poor people that I have nightmares about gray navy surplus paint and steel doors.

WHOSE SIDE YOU'RE REALLY ON

In criminal cases, the interests of judges and the defendant's family are similar. Judges want justice to be done and the public to be protected. They also want, if possible, for the defendant to be transformed into a citizen. This last is, or should be, your interest. You want the inmate's freedom, yes, but freedom as a citizen, not as a thug. Defendants' interests are different. They want to get out of jail *right now.* They want to beat the rap, or if that isn't possible, to minimize the consequences, regardless of the costs.

Freedom, of course, costs plenty. Expenses include inmate fees, jail phone bills, commissary fees, fines, victim restitution, probation fees, drug-testing fees, and drug treatment costs. Years later, there will be additional fees for sealing or expunging criminal histories and restoring civil rights. Most defendants depend on their families to pay some or all of these costs.

You will also spend hours driving, with cash and checks in hand, to jails, courtrooms, bail bond offices, probation offices, dingy drug-testing labs and fly-specked classrooms and treatment centers. You will spend many hours at home deciphering police reports, legal filings, and endless forms. You and the defendant will feel as if you're conjoined at the hip like two maniacal twins named Crime and Punishment.

The criminal justice system is like the toughest game of baseball ever played. The count is forever no balls and two strikes, and the defendant is always at bat. On the mound is The Man, throwing hundred-mile-an-hour fastballs, strange curves, weird sliders, and now and then a knuckleball that flutters like a hummingbird and stings like

---

* "Citizen" is one of the all-time great cop words, as it neatly encapsulates the qualities of morals, manners, work ethic, and long-term goals that socialized people have and people in jail do not.

a bee. The base run to freedom requires the defendant to hit the ball every time, because in this game, it's one strike and you're out.

Finances will be strained; tempers will snap. Some friends and family will become estranged. Always there are those god-awful—and god-awfully expensive—jail calls. Having to nag probationers and parolees to attend meetings, take drug tests, and complete legal paperwork is utter aggravation. If they reoffend and go back to jail, your heart breaks. All your efforts become worthless, and all your money is lost. You rolled the emotional and financial dice for someone you love, and the cubes came up snake eyes.

For some, however, freedom happens effortlessly. In many criminal cases, charges are dropped. Perhaps the police work was sloppy or the charges trivial or unprovable. Perhaps the prosecutor was overwhelmed with cases and decided to "nol-pross"* a few charges to clear the caseload and go home at five o'clock for a change. In my city, Jacksonville, Florida, 30 percent of people arrested are released within 72 hours because charges are dismissed or not filed. If this happens to your defendant, hallelujah. Time to celebrate. Give this book to some forlorn person waiting outside your local jail.

That person will need it.

A Big Mistake Loved Ones Make

Families make bad decisions when they confuse their interests with those of the defendant. It's easy to get caught up in the drama—lawyers, judges, courts, dustups with inmates and guards, the thousand petty treacheries and insults of jail life. All this can be weirdly exciting. Your urge is to rescue your loved one, no matter what. Unfortunately, unless you have a seven-figure bank balance, there's always a "what." The money you spend on criminal defense may mean that there will be no new home and no new car this year or for many years to come. Health care, education, even food and utilities may take hits. The time you spend on the defendant is time not spent on your own education, personal life, and career. Spending time and money on a loved one in jail often means *not* investing in other family members who may be more deserving.

The advice of this book is *always to put family first*. This means you don't get stampeded into draining every cent you have *at once* for bail bonds and private attorneys. Peruse the following chapters, work through the Stick 'Em Up checklists, and think about your options. There's the full ride: bail bond, private attorney, private investigators, and financial help through probation and parole, appeals, and restoration of civil rights. Then there are lesser degrees of support, such as no bond, a public defender, and help with

---

* Short for *nolle prosequi*, Latin for a decision not to proceed. Most attorneys mangle Latin, so the term comes out as "nol-pross." Nonetheless, attorneys love this ancient and elegant language because it confirms their position as keepers of the mysteries. Fortunately, most state legislatures deep-sixed the use of Latin in government, courts, and contracts years ago—because legislators didn't understand it either. *Ignorantia legis non excusat*!

jail costs and probation. Lastly, there's the zero option—cards and letters, the occasional magazine, and fervent prayers (or execrations!) for the accused.

Take a few days to weigh the possibilities. Defendants are in jail, after all, and aren't going anywhere. In fact, this book will show you how to use jail to persuade defendants to make changes. It will show you how to test defendants to see whether they are worthy of financial and legal support.

Is your defendant hard-core, someone who will not, or cannot, leave the badass lifestyle? If so, put your wallet back into your pocket or purse. Don't waste your money.

Nonetheless, about 30 to 40 percent of inmates hit bottom psychologically while in jail. They're ready to change. These you should help. You should also assist first-time offenders,* those who are truly innocent, and those who are mentally ill and should never have been locked up in the first place.

Deciding whether, and how much, to support a criminal defendant is a huge decision fraught with emotional pain. Emotional pain is worse than physical pain. Compare the most excruciating physical pain you have ever known with the emotional agony of a divorce, a family fight, or a breakup with a lover. Physical pain is limited; emotional pain can go on for years. So it's tempting to make your decision based on emotion, to act just to make that pain go away.

Emotional decisions are easy to make, but in matters of criminal justice, they're often wrong. This book presents tools that help you drain emotion from the decision-making process and apply reason and sound judgment instead. These help you break up big decisions into small components.

EVERYBODY LIES

The first step is to gather information on the case. This is not a simple undertaking, because in criminal justice everybody lies, shades the truth, or doesn't tell you everything. Expect defendants to forget to tell you that a gun was used, or that they have been charged with a sex crime, or that they have prior convictions you know nothing about. Expect them to tell you what you want to hear, that it's all a frame and that the police have the wrong guy. Expect cops to tell you untruths or partial truths to get a statement from you or to search your house. Expect what cops tell you to differ from what they said in the arrest report they submitted to the prosecutor. Expect forensic evidence to be inconclusive, or lacking, or ignored. Expect witnesses to lie or change their stories. Expect loose ends that will never make sense. Expect to be told, over and over, that somebody else, charged with similar crimes, got a better outcome.

---

* The exceptions are first-time offenders who are gang members. These guys regard their first arrest as a rite of passage. The police have "popped their cherry," and now they're government-certified hoodlums! In any case, gang members have already chosen to make the gang their true family. So let the gang finance their defense!

Players in the criminal justice system are used to this. They are comfortable with imperfect information. Don't let this imperfection make you crazy. In our Administrative Society, we deal too much and too often with bureaucracies. People expect every matter to be handled exactly the same way, with exactly the same outcome, every single time. Forget this! The criminal justice system has no such expectation. The system provides a reasonable prosecution and defense, which reasonably protects both society and the rights of the accused, and that's all. The defendant with a million dollars for legal defense will get a better shake than your inmate. That's a guarantee. The system does not provide perfect justice.

God does.

Nevertheless, information is out there that can help you to make better, more informed decisions. In chapter 3, you'll discover how to obtain that information over the phone, over the Internet, and in person. You'll discover the names of essential documents so you can ask for them. You'll find out how to get local jail rules so you and the defendant can avoid being distracted by jail mini-dramas and concentrate on defense and freedom. Most of all, you'll discover how to use this information to test your defendant for truthfulness and willingness to change.

It is also useful to find out what the defendant was up to in your home. In chapter 4, I'll show you how to toss your own house and car, and search for guns and drugs before the cops do. And when *La Poli* bang on your door, flash the buzzer, and ask, "Do you mind if we have a look around?" I'll tell you how to lawyer up in advance and say, "Yes, I do mind"—sweetly—to kick-ass cops and detectives. I'll also advise you when to drop a defendant like a radioactive rock and save yourself.

JAILS VS. PRISONS

Although the terms are used interchangeably in casual conversation, and confused constantly by television scriptwriters, jails are *not* the same as prisons. Prisons, operated by the states and by the federal government, are facilities where convicted felons serve sentences of one year or more. Prison inmates are no longer defendants but "convicts." Often they are referred to as "offenders."

Jails, operated by cities and counties, are *pretrial* detention facilities. Jail inmates have, in general, not yet been convicted of crimes. Inmates are, legally speaking, "detainees." This distinction is absolutely clear to everyone inside the criminal justice system and absolutely unclear to everyone else. The difference is muddied by the practice of having offenders convicted of misdemeanors, whose sentences are one year or less, serve time in local jails.

Jails are intended to hold defendants so that they can be conveniently produced at hearings and trials, interrogated at leisure, and served as needed with charges, indictments, and other documents. Jails keep defendants from hotfooting it out of sight or over state lines. Jails are, essentially, holding pens, and except for misdemeanor convicts, they are not intended as places of punishment—legally speaking, that is.

Tell that to *elected* sheriffs, *elected* judges, and *elected* mayors, who have a tough time dedicating their lives to public service election after election if the jails are not stuffed to bursting. Most elected officials and members of the public consider jail incarceration a form of *pretrial punishment*. In this way of thinking, if defendants are acquitted or released without sentences, at least they will have served some good old jail time and received a certified kick in the fanny from The Man. You may have thought this way too until—Omigod!—your loved one got hustled into the hoosegow. *Pretrial punishment has no basis in law.* It is a legal and moral outrage, and it happens tens of thousands of times a day in every state in the union.

Jails are operated on a strictly no-frills basis. You'll be dismayed to discover that for jail inmates, there generally is no school, no drug treatment, no radio, no television, no work, and nothing to do except wait, and wait, for judicial processes to conclude. That's the bad news.

The good news is that inmates in local jails are constantly moving in and out as their cases are disposed of and they leave for prison or freedom. This means that inmates in jails are less able than those in prison to clique up in racial, ethnic, and gang groups and wage war on one another. Jail inmates are usually better behaved than prison inmates, because they have not yet been sentenced and have not lost hope of freedom or leniency. With few exceptions, jail incarceration lasts one year or less. Rape and murder are less frequent in jails than in prisons. Prisons are hard time; jails are mostly boring.

With a loved one in jail, you'll be spending much time visiting your local lockup, so chapters 5 through 10 devote considerable time to exploring this locale. You'll learn how to conduct yourself during jail visits; how your loved one can stay out of trouble behind bars; how the jail's medical, commissary, and phone services work; and how sex and drugs factor into the jailhouse experience.

Jail Mail

The first thing that strikes you about jail is how difficult it is to communicate with an inmate. In many cities, inmates are allowed only one or two visits per week, and if a cousin, neighbor, or even some lowlife sex partner shows up first, you're out of luck—no meet this week. Inmate calls *from* jail are usually collect calls at phone-porn rates, and they'll drive you to the poorhouse. You cannot, of course, call *into* jail. E-mail in jail? Not! The solution is good old snail mail, delivered even today with renowned assiduity by the U.S. Postal Service. This book includes several tear-out, preprinted pages of Jail Mail so you can get essential information to your loved one quickly. These letters are also useful trade goods on the inside.*

---

* In jail, inmates trade mail, food, snacks, soap, paper—anything—to make friends and avoid getting beaten up.

UNSOCIALIZED MAN

Once you've got a clear picture of your defendant's case, it's time to make that terrible decision—whether to offer financial and legal support. The analysis must begin with an understanding of the criminal mind. Criminals are profoundly different from citizens. Having interviewed hundreds of inmates as an investigator, I'm convinced that even cops and judges don't always grasp the vastness of the disparity. The difference is not physiological but moral and mental.

First the moral. Many criminals have no morality at all. They're not *amoral*, meaning that they ignore moral laws. They're often not *immoral*, meaning that that they choose to violate moral laws. They're *premoral*, like humans raised completely outside society.

Mentally, they lack a thought process I call the "values check." Before taking an action, they don't pause for a split second to check the contemplated deed against values, laws, and long-term goals. They can't. They don't have any. There's no *there* there! Most people in jail act via stimulus-response. If it feels good, they do it. That's why most of them are incarcerated. There's a weird innocence about it all.

This mentality is hard to detect because it manifests only at the moment of decision. I've interviewed murderers and found some of them quite personable, even funny. Just ordinary Joes, one thinks. Of course, out in the world, if you chat up their girlfriend for a second too long, they might cock a Glock and put a nine-millimeter slug through your skull because you annoyed them.

Lack of values and stimulus-response decision making are why most people offend and stay perpetually in trouble with cops. As the family, your challenge is to impart, however belatedly, the socialization that alone can transform *Homo chaoticus* into a citizen. Tough love is the only tactic that works. During the past 50 years, everything else has been tried. Nothing else gets results. Jails and prisons do not reform; they merely punish. Only family members have the time, resources, and means to socialize criminals.

Socialization is crucial. Why? Because the feasibility of socialization is a key factor in your decision to spend, or not to spend, your money on criminal defense. Is your defendant capable of becoming a citizen, or a hopeless thug and lowlife? Tough love can get defendants straightened out and headed toward citizenship. It protects you against lies, self-delusion, the quick grift, and the long con. It will prevent your being bled out financially and emotionally by vampire defendants.

Chapter 11 will discuss the premoral mind, and chapter 12 will show you how to recognize whether your loved one is ready to mature and leave all that behind. Chapter 13 explains why military service, if an option for your defendant, is an ideal path to socialization. In chapter 14, you'll find worksheets that help you judge whether your loved one is worth defending. You'll weigh positive and negative factors and consider red-flag behaviors that put defendants at high risk of reoffending. There's no way to sugarcoat this. So take it step by step, one check-off box at a time.

If your judgment is yes, then gather funds, friends, and family members to help. Succeeding chapters will show you how. If your judgment is no, then so be it. Save your money.

BAIL BONDS

To rework some doggerel from the Protestant Reformation, bail bonds may be summarized thusly:

> As soon as the coin
> In the coffer rings,
> The soul from county jail
> Doth spring!

Bail bond offices surround most jails. Their neon lights, which wink night and day with the promise of freedom, produce madness. Defendants will demand bond. They will yell. Some will threaten suicide if you don't bail them right here, right now. But bail doesn't resolve legal problems, and bonds aren't cheap. They devour family funds that often could be better used to pay private counsel and to finance the years of probation fees, restitution, and court and jail costs that surely will follow defendants all the days of their lives if not paid in full. In chapter 15, I'll advise you when to post bail, and when not to.

I'll discuss particular situations in which you may find bonds useful, and I'll alert you to sucker plays, such as paying a bond when the charges are due to be dropped the next day anyway, and a second pitfall, called "Bond and Bust," in which the defendant is released then immediately rearrested at the jailhouse door on new charges or outstanding warrants. In both these situations, you lose your bond payment without your defendant being freed.

If you live in a state that allows bondsmen to mortgage your house, I advise caution. Before you take that drastic step, which can get your house foreclosed and you and your belongings dragged to the curb by a sheriff's deputy, wait a bit. Take a trip to think about it, preferably a cruise around the world on a slow boat.

THE PIN-STRIPED MAFIA

Next, almost all inmates will ask you to hire private counsel for their defense. This seems straightforward. It's not. Criminal law is the most unregulated and incomprehensible area of American commerce. It's extraordinarily difficult to know exactly *what* criminal defense attorneys are supposed to do to earn your money and how much defense should cost. It's easier by far to make an informed purchasing decision about witchcraft.

Attorneys, inclined by nature and training to talk, to argue, even to declaim, are strangely silent on two paramount issues:

1. Are private attorneys worth the money they charge?

2. Is the family paying for legal services that the defendant could get for free from the public defender?

On these points the learned profession is wordless. Not a phrase is to be found in legal tomes. Nary a Web site can be Googled, and even in the eternally nattering nebula of the blogosphere, no word is heard. Lawyers argue endlessly about everything else, but when it comes to money, they stand mute, pinstripe to pinstripe.

Chapter 16 discusses the history of public defenders, and why their services are frequently all a defendant needs to negotiate a standard plea bargain. Chapter 17 describes the tricks and scams private attorneys use to fleece the unwary, including subcontracting the entire defense, a practice so vile it would make a buzzard vomit. You'll learn things known heretofore only to insiders—the business end of criminal defense.

Chapter 18 will reveal what good lawyers actually do to earn their fees. A Stick 'Em Up worksheet will help you distinguish good attorneys from bad and legal saviors from legal stick-up artists. Chapters 19 and 20 will explain how to get a quote for legal services and how to negotiate the final contract. You'll discover how to use structured payments to give attorneys a financial incentive to mount a thorough defense, which helps you avoid getting billed thousands of dollars for a five-minute plea deal.

In chapter 21, you'll find out how you and the defendant can assist the defense. Even if you pay for private legal representation, the defendant, not the family, is the client. The defendant ultimately decides whether to accept a plea bargain or proceed to trial. Lawyers are prohibited from disclosing privileged discussions of legal strategy to the family unless the defendant specifically authorizes such release, generally in writing. Your job is not to backseat-drive the defense; rather, it is to make sure that private counsel is mounting a tough defense and doing something more than endorsing your check.

WHAT PRICE FREEDOM?

Exactly how much does freedom cost? Few in the criminal justice system know, because everyone works in compartments. Astonishingly few attorneys and cops know what probation and parole cost. Even some judges don't—for shame! One thing is certain: freedom will cost more than you think.

Foremost, freedom costs money—five-and six-figure money, generally over many years, even if the defendant is represented by a public defender. Chapter 22 provides a Stick 'Em Up worksheet to help you prepare a budget. With a telephone and the Internet, you can quickly fill in the numbers and add them up. I'll also outline the best—and worst—ways to finance these expenses.

Freedom also takes time. After jail and prison, your loved one generally will face years in the "paper handcuffs" of probation or parole. At this stage, any infraction is disastrous. One last burglary* for old time's sake; one boozy drive that a cop notices; one party where weed gets smoked; one noisy fight with a spouse or lover; one hearing, meeting, or class missed; or one form not notarized and filed in a timely fashion, and jail, prison, or probation start all over again. Chapter 23 will help you guide your loved one through the demands of parole or probation, lest he or she be whisked away once again into the Time Machine.

SAVE YOURSELF!

For some defendants, their only hope for freedom is to cooperate with police as a confidential informant or witness. I'll discuss this dangerous situation in chapter 24. If you live in a no-snitch zone, where police cooperators get morning wake-ups in the form of 7.62 mm armor-piercing rounds, you'll need to consider whether the defendant, and you, need to blow town.

You yourself may have dangerous and creepy encounters with criminals. If you're scheduled to be a witness, you may receive threatening calls or grim knocks on the door. If your defendant runs up drug and gambling debts in jail, he or she may sic the sharks on *you* for payment. Chapter 25 will help you plan a swift getaway.

☠ THE DANGER SIGN

The most ominous graphic in this book is the Danger Sign. The skull and crossbones signals situations that put your defendant, and you, at risk of being arrested, injured, or killed. All Danger Sign information is as deadly serious as the threats discussed.

---

* People use the words "burglary" and "robbery" interchangeably in conversation, but they are distinct crimes. Burglary is theft from an unoccupied dwelling or vehicle. Robbery is violent theft from a person. Robbery is by far the more serious offense.

FAMILY MANAGEMENT, FAMILY INTERVENTION

In the adult justice system, families are peripheral. Because 90 percent of cases are plea-bargained and never go to trial, family are only infrequently called as witnesses or asked for statements. If criminal justice players think about families at all, they think of them mostly as human ATMs, useful mainly for producing cash. The only parties with legal rights are the state, the defendant, and, increasingly, the victim. Family members have no rights, only obligations.

This is a stupid state of affairs. Jails are full to bursting. Nobody knows what to do with all these perps—except families. More and more, judges will consider what families can do to socialize adult defendants. However, because families have no statutory role, they have to organize and *insert themselves* into the process. This is not easy. Most attorneys are narrowly focused on matters of bond, charge reduction, case dismissal, plea, or trial. Nonetheless, there are specific points in the judicial process at which families can influence decisions for leniency. These are hearings for bail and bond reduction, pretrial intervention (also called "diversion"), and sentencing.

In chapter 26, I will show you how to organize a proposal for defense counsel called the family management plan. I'll explain how to round up education and military records, photographs, witness statements, character references, and employer and clergy letters to make the case for leniency. This chapter is "Let's Make a Deal" with the judge. The family management plan is the climax of the book.

THE BIG PICTURE

In chapter 27, I'll present important numbers that will give you a larger picture of how a theory of policing called zero tolerance, backed by recent laws passed by Congress and the state legislatures, has affected criminal justice.

Nothing is more extensively studied than crime. So well developed is crime reporting that scarcely a candy bar gets swiped from a gas station without a blip appearing on some computer screen. The number of crime researchers is astounding. Universities and think tanks have phalanxes of them. State governments fill entire buildings with cohorts of crime-stat-crunching civil servants. The federal government deploys vast legions of crime statisticians in bureaus that stretch from Washington, D.C., to West Virginia. In your mind's eye you can see these researchers nestled in gray cubicles and almost hear the electrons hum as they buzz numbers through spreadsheets and ponder the subtle mean deviations that separate a rapist from a mere fornicator and a batterer from a drunken lout.

Everyone studies what government does about offenders, which is to arrest and incarcerate them. Nobody researches how families deal with offenders. Government, of course, gives out research grants, fellowships, and jobs. Families don't.

When a loved one is in jail, things get hectic fast, so on the next page you will find a bullet-point synopsis of the most important points made in this book. As soon as you get busy working your plan, things will seem less crazy and less hopeless.

You'll feel more confident and more competent—because you are.

ARRESTED BULLET POINTS

A quick summary of the book's main points, so you can get what you need right now.

- ► Make decisions in the best interest of the entire family, not just the defendant.

- ► Use checklists and worksheets to calm down, think, and make good decisions. Do not rush off and spend money willy-nilly on bonds and attorneys. Get the facts first.

- ► Search your house and car for drugs, guns, and stolen goods. Dispose of same. Search your computer for illegal, i.e., underage, pornography. Secure-erase any you find.

- ► If police question you, or want to search your house without a warrant, state that an attorney will speak for you. Use the public defender's name if you don't have private counsel.

- ► Evaluate whether your loved one is worth defending. Can the defendant live lawfully and peacefully?

- ► Lack of socialization and a chaotic mentality are the reasons most defendants are in jail and prison. Freedom requires emergency "middle-classification."

- ► Post bonds only after a bond reduction hearing.

- ► Hire private attorneys only when they commit to specific legal work above and beyond negotiating a plea.

- ► Ask the public defender or private counsel how you can assist them. Do not try to backseat-drive your loved one's legal defense.

- ► Insist that the defendant work on his or her defense while in jail or out on bond.

- ► Involve the defendant in defense budgeting and get a commitment for repayment of legal expenses.

- ► Probation and parole are criminal sentences, not freedom. They are long, hard, and expensive and are filled with pitfalls.

- ► Formulate a family management plan.

- ► Insist that the defendant pursue actions that make the case for leniency while in jail or out on bond.

- ► Take immediate action to protect yourself and family members if you are threatened.

3

YOU, THE GUMSHOE
How to Get Critical Information

GUMSHOE IS ONE OF the great terms from crime fiction and film noir. It means "private investigator," and it refers to the soft-soled shoes that PIs once wore to silence their steps as they pounded the pavement in search of clues. You'll do plenty of pavement pounding yourself to get essential information about your defendant. This chapter will tell you what to look for, why you need it, and how to get it.

SERVICES AND SUPPLIES

High-Speed Internet
Much basic information is available on the Web sites of your local jail and police department, the county court, state government, the public defender, private attorneys, and the FBI. You'll be going to all these places. The Internet is a huge time saver; it beats shoe leather and the telephone every time.

If you already have high-speed service, great. If you don't but it's available in your area at an affordable price, order it immediately. Most services have tiered pricing, depending on how fast you want Web pages to load. Download speeds of 1.5 megabytes per second or higher will do for the purposes of this book. Dial-up Internet is too slow to connect to many Web pages, and in any case, it ties up your phone line.

If you do not have a computer with fast Internet access, get a friend or relative to help or use the computers at your public library. Call the library first to check whether the staff will allow you to print out the documents you are researching. I recommend against doing research in an Internet cafe. These establishments are notorious for lax Internet security. I was an investigator in a case in which an Internet cafe's owner skimmed financial and personal information from his customers' online transactions, then robbed them blind!

Once you're online, you can google the sites you need fast. For example, to find jail info for New York City, type "Jail, New York City" into your search engine. Keep in mind that jails are run by the *city* or *county* department of corrections. Prisons are run by the *state* department of corrections.

Office Supplies and Stamps

Number 10 envelopes, 9-by-12-inch envelopes, paper, file folders, and a staple gun are the minimum supplies needed. Get lots of stamps and an inexpensive scale to weigh heavy letters. The U.S. Postal Service Web site will calculate postage for heavy or oversize envelopes. *Don't use postcards.* Other inmates will read them. Also get several labels and return postcards for certified, return-receipt-requested mailings. You may need to send certified notices in emergencies.

Quarters

The criminal justice system snacks on quarters—quarters for the parking meter; quarters for cell phone lockers; quarters for soft drinks, pay phones, the hot dog guy; and, of course, quarters for everyone else asking you for quarters around the courthouse and jail. Get several rolls from your bank.

Alarm Watch

Courthouse and jail parking lots swarm with meter readers and tow trucks. Get an inexpensive alarm watch that will tweet 15 minutes before your parking meter dies and the hook goes on.

INFORMATION YOU NEED

Charge Sheet

This is the bare-bones listing of the charges against your defendant. It's the first piece of information you should obtain. Most police departments post these on their Web sites. If you can't locate the charge sheet by name, search by the defendant's jail number. It's critical to get this number during the early phone calls.

The illustration that follows is an actual charge sheet. It is loaded with important information:

1. **Jail number:** This number has to be written on all envelopes addressed to the defendant. Otherwise, mail may not get delivered. Many names are misspelled on criminal records, which is why getting your defendant's jail number is so important.

2. **Location.** This indicates where the defendant is being held. Most big cities have multiple jails. In my city, "PDF" refers to the John E. Goode Pretrial Detention Facility, a.k.a. the main jail.

3. **Description.** Physical information like height, weight, and hair color lets you know whether this person is your defendant. In large cities, an aston-

Sample Charge Sheet

Doe, John D.
Jail Number: xxxxxx   **JSO ID: xxxxxx**

Inmate Information

Housing Location: PDF

Race: B **Sex:** M

Height: 508 inches

Hair: BLACK

DOB: 09/08/1988

Age: 19

Weight: 140 pounds

Eyes: BROWN

Arresting Agency: JACKSONVILLE SHERIFF'S OFFICE

Arrest Date: 11/12/2007

Admission Date: 11/13/2007 01:56 AM

Expected Release Date: N/A

Next Court Date: 07/17/2008 09:00 AM , COURTHOUSE, CRA

Length of Sentence: N/A

Payment Required for Release: Not Eligible for Bond

Pending Unsentenced Charge(s): Yes

Visitation Information: 8:00 AM to 10:00 PM, Friday (Visits are limited to 1 visit per week for maximum of 2 hours.)

Charge Information

Charge Statute	Charge Description	Charge Type
S893.13(1)(A)1	POSSESS / SELL CONTROLLED SUBSTANCE NAMED IN FS 893.03 (1A;1B;1D;2A;2B)	FEL
S812.13(2)(A)	ARMED ROBBERY-FIREARM OR OTHER DEADLY WEAPON	FEL

Sample charge sheet, with the name of the accused changed and identifying information erased.

ishingly large number of inmates have the same name. Even if your defendant's name is something unusual, like Thelonious Knockwurst, there may be someone else in the lockup with a similarly unfortunate moniker.

4. **Next court date.** This is important if you plan to attend the hearing. Since calendars are subject to frequent change, check the date with the staff of the clerk of the court. Clerks of the court are the administrators of the courts. They maintain hearing and trial calendars, case files, and legal records. They also collect fines, fees, and court costs.

5. **Bond.** This is usually a preliminary bond amount. It's not set in stone. Your defendant should request a bond reduction hearing.

6. **Charge information.** This is a brief outline of the crimes with which the defendant is charged. On the sample sheet, the charge type "FEL" indicates a felony.

7. **Visitation.** This is crucial. Note that in this jail, only one visit per week is allowed. Nothing is more annoying than showing up in your best clothes, with a carload of children and relatives, only to be told by a corrections officer that your defendant has already had a visit for the week. That's the reason you should always make essential communications by mail or phone. Jails don't take reservations for visits. They're not hotels.

Arrest Report

This is a detailed description of what police did at the time of arrest. It may contain witness names and statements, and descriptions of evidence recovered or property seized. It may reveal, or hint at, the case the state has against the defendant. Generally, arrest reports are obtainable from the police department for a fee. They may also be posted on the department's Web site.

Use the arrest report to truth-check your defendant. A blatant lie, such as a defendant failing to mention to you that a firearm was recovered during the arrest, is cause for grave concern. On the other hand, comparing the defendant's story with the arrest report's narrative may reveal the familiar pattern of police overcharging.

Arrest reports sometimes name witnesses. Defense counsel may want to take their statements to check for inconsistencies or investigate them prior to cross-examination. Take both the charge sheet and the arrest report with you when you consult private attorneys so they can more accurately determine how tough the case is and what to charge and can give you an informed opinion about specific motions and strategies. Otherwise, they'll have to talk in generalities.

Arrest And Booking Report
Jacksonville Sheriff's Office
Jacksonville Florida

ADULT

Yr: **2007**	Incident #:	Amend #:
Jail #:		File Direct: **YES**
JSO ID #:		Court: **Circuit**
SSN:	OBTS #:	

Arresting Agency: **Jacksonville Sheriff's Office**

Day/Date/Time Arrested:

Name. **Doe, John D.**
Aliases:

Sub-Sector of Arrest: **K2**

Nickname(s):

Subject's Home Address: *Apt./Lot #:*
City: **JACKSONVILLE**   *State:* **FLORIDA**   *Zip:*

Sub-Sector of Residence:
OC deployed prior to/during Arrest: **NO**

Race: **BLACK**   *Sex:* **Male**   *DOB:* **9/8/1988**   *Age:* **19**   *Eye Color:* **BROWN**
Hair Color: **BLACK**   *Complexion:* **DARK**   *Height:* **5' 8"**   *Weight:* **140**   *Build:* **Thin**
Drivers License #   *State:*   *Subject's Resident Type:* **CITY**
Hm Phone #   *Bus. Phone #*   *Phone Ext.*

How long in Jax.

Arrest Made On: **OV**

Subject's Residence Status: **RESIDENT**   *Armed With:* **HANDGUN**
Distinguishing Marks: **TATTOO ON FACE**
Employer: **NONE**   *Place of Birth:* **JACKSONVILLE DUVAL FLORIDA**
School Last Attended: **UNKNOWN**

US Citizen: **YES**

Domestic Violence Involved: **NO**	*Children under 18 Present:*	*If No is it Domestic Related:* **NO**

Day/Date/Time of Incident-From: **Monday**   *Day/Date/Time of Incident-To:* **Monday**
Incident Address: **7071 103RD ST**   *Apt./Lot #:*
Offense Location Type: **Hotel / Motel**   *Interviewed by:*
Where Arrested: **7071 103RD ST**   *Apt./Lot #:*
Involved in Traffic Accident: **NO**   *Injuries from Accident:*   *Is Incident Gang Related:* **NO**   *Is Arrestee a Gang member?* **NO**

Statute or Ordinance Number(s):
#1   *Statute No:* **S812.13(2)(A)**   *Degree:* **F1**   *UCR Code:* **120A**   *Attempt Code:* **Commit**   **11/13/2007 - 00:58**
ARMED ROBBERY – FIREARM OR OTHER DEADLY WEAPON

Citation #	SA#	Warrant Type: **Not Applicable**
Capias/Warrant #	Case #	No. of Counts:
Jurisdiction:	CT. Location/Div.:	
Bond Amount: **$.**	Date of Issue: Date of Return: Judge:	
Disposition:		Disposition Date:

#2   *Statute No:* **S893.13(1)(A)1**   *Degree:* **F2**   *UCR Code:* **350A**   *Attempt Code:* **Commit**   **11/13/2007 - 00:58**
POSSESS / SELL CONTROLLED SUBSTANCE NAMED IN FS 893.03 (1A;1B;1D;2A;2B)

Citation #	SA#	Warrant Type: **Not Applicable**
Capias/Warrant #	Case #	No. of Counts:
Jurisdiction:	CT. Location/Div.:	
Bond Amount: **$.**	Date of Issue: Date of Return: Judge:	
Disposition:		Disposition Date:

Blanket Bond:

ADDITIONAL INFORMATION **1**   *Reporting Officer:* **XXXXXX**
On XXX at approximately 2000, Detectives XXXXXXXXXXXX **were posing as drug buyers at (7071 103rd St.) the Hospitality Inn.**
They made contact with the listed defendant at the rear of the motel. Detective McCoy had $40.00 of marked JSO funds in his hand. The defendant snatched the money out of detective XXXX hand and an unknown black male handed detective XXXX (2) pieces of crack cocaine. After the transaction was made, the defendant pulled out a gun and racked it. Detective Bowen pulled out her service weapon and shot the defendant twice in the stomach area. The unknown black male fled on foot in an unknown direction. The takedown units arrived at the scene and the defendant was laying on the ground. Detective XXXX handcuffed the defendant. Rescue #52 arrived at the scene and transported the defendant to Shands Hospital. Det. XXXX rode in the rescue unit to the hospital with the defendant.

Note that this arrest report has far more detail than the charge sheet. A private attorney can see at once that this is a tough case. The defendant sold dope to undercover officers, pulled a gun, and was shot. To find out what else happened, see this defendant's *second* arrest report.

Arrest And Booking Report
Jacksonville Sheriff's Office
Jacksonville Florida
ADULT

Yr: **2007**	Incident #	Amend #
Jail #		File Direct:
JSO ID #		Court: **Circuit**
SSN	OBTS #	

Arresting Agency: **Bond Company** ⬅

Day/Date/Time Arrested:

Name: **Doe, John D.**
Aliases:

Sub-Sector of Arrest: **A1**

Nickname(s):

Subject's Home Address: Apt./Lot #: **120**
City: **JACKSONVILLE** State: **FLORIDA** Zip: **32210**
Race: **BLACK** Sex: **Male** DOB: **9/8/1988** Age: **19** Eye Color: **BROWN**
Hair Color: **BLACK** Complexion: **DARK** Height: **5' 9"** Weight: **140** Build: **Thin**
Drivers License # State: Subject's Resident Type: **CITY**
Hm Phone # Bus. Phone # Phone Ext.
Subject's Residence Status: **RESIDENT** Armed With:
Distinguishing Marks:
Employer: Place of Birth: **JACKSONVILLE DUVAL FLORIDA**
School Last Attended:

Sub-Sector of Residence:
OC deployed prior to/during Arrest: **NO**

How long in Jax.
Arrest Made On:

US Citizen: **YES**

Domestic Violence Involved: **NO**	Children under 18 Present:	If No is it Domestic Related: **NO**

Day/Date/Time of Incident-From: **00:00**   Day/Date/Time of Incident-To: **00:00**
Incident Address: Apt./Lot #:
Offense Location Type: Interviewed by:
Where Arrested: **500 ADAMS ST E** Apt./Lot #:
Involved in Traffic Accident: **NO**   Injuries from Accident: Is Incident Gang Related: **NO**   Is Arrestee a Gang member? **NO**

Statute or Ordinance Number(s):
#1 Statute No: **S812.014(2)(C)6** Degree: **F3** UCR Code: **2400** Attempt Code: **Commit**   **11/20/2007 - 16:19**
GRAND THEFT - MOTOR VEHICLE (LESS THAN $100,000)

Citation #	SA#	Warrant Type: **Bond Surrender**
Capias/Warrant #	Case #	No. of Counts:

Jurisdiction: **Jacksonville Sheriff's Office**   CT. Location/Div.:
Bond Amount: **$10,003.**   Date of Issue: Date of Return: Judge:
Disposition: Disposition Date:

Blanket Bond:

ADDITIONAL INFORMATION **1**   Reporting Officer: **B.B.BONDSMAN 9460**
**BIG DADDY BAIL BONDS, INC., SURRENDERS THE BOND ON THE DEFENDANT AS HE WAS SUBSEQUENTLY
ARRESTED ON ADDITIONAL CHARGES AND FAILED TO APPEAR IN COURT ON 11/13/07, VIOLATING HIS BOND
CONTRACT.**

**DATE OF ORIGINAL ARREST: 08/10/07
JAIL NUMBER: 2007034395
CHARGES: GRAND THEFT - MOTOR VEHICLE
CASE NUMBER: 2007-CT- 1111 -AXXX** ⬅
**DIVISION: A
NEXT COURT DATE: 11/27/07**

DUE TO HIS FAILURE TO APPEAR AN EWARRANT WAS ISSUED, CONTROL # 1241

The second arrest report tells an astonishing tale. The defendant, only days after being gut shot, made bail, jumped bail, swiped a car, and got busted by a bounty hunter. Family members who posted bond will lose their money and may have their collateral seized. One can assume that Johnny Doe won't get a private attorney this time around and can expect to stay in prison for many years. Note that this report includes a case number, an important piece of information discussed in the next subsection.

Case Numbers, Names, Addresses, and Phone Numbers

From the defendant, the arrest report, or the clerk of the court, get the case number, which is assigned by the courts to your defendant's legal proceedings. You'll need it to discover when hearings are being held and to locate court documents that are public.

Next get the telephone number for the jail shift commander and the telephone number and address of the jail administrator. Get contact information for the public defender, the clerk of the court, and private attorneys. You'll need these in case of an emergency or a threat to your inmate.

Jail Rules

The defendant received a copy upon admission, but you need one as well. Get it from the Web site of the city or county department of corrections. If you cannot access the rules online, pick up a copy at the jail or at police headquarters. The department may also publish a detailed orientation document for inmates, explaining how they must behave, how health care, commissary, and complaints are handled, how inmates are classified, and how infractions are punished.

Attorney Information

Regardless of whether you ultimately hire private counsel, the defendant will probably be represented by a public defender during initial hearings. The office of the public defender, which is funded by your state, generally publishes information about its services and who qualifies for them. Like jail information, it's available online or at the public defender's office. Get two copies and mail one to the defendant.

Information about private attorneys may be available online or in a pamphlet or brochure. Get copies for yourself, but *do not* mail them to the defendant, who may consider such a mailing to be a promise to pay for private counsel.

Other Records

Round up educational records and graduation certificates. Get military records, especially descriptions of service specialties and the type of discharge. Don't forget decorations. Valor under fire merits favorable consideration from many judges.

Get employment verification in writing if applicable. Make copies of professional licenses, such as CDL (commercial driver's license), chauffeur, electrician, plumber, health care worker, insurance, financial, real estate. If the defendant is a member of a union, make a copy of the union card. Immediately call the local to see if the defendant is covered by legal insurance. Ask employers the same. Defendants rarely know these things. If the defendant was arrested pursuant to a traffic stop, check whether automobile insurance or American Automobile Association (AAA) insurance will cover private attorney fees or bail.

This takes time. Be patient but politely persistent, especially when requesting information from government officials.

Probation Report

This document, prepared by probation officers working for the court, lists a few reasons why the defendant should, and many reasons why the defendant should not, receive leniency. It always includes a rap sheet and outstanding warrant information. Probation reports can be prepared at any time prior to the sentencing of defendants who go to trial. They may or may not be prepared for defendants who take a plea bargain. Practice varies. Check with defense counsel to discover how the reports are compiled in your jurisdiction.

Many defense attorneys, for tactical reasons, waive the report, because it is usually prejudicial to the defendant. You will want to see it anyway, because as the family, you are evaluating the defendant for the long term. Besides, you may decide to counter the probation report with a little whiz-bang paperwork of your own: a family management plan.

Rap Sheet

A defendant, unfortunately, may have not one rap sheet but many, spread across multiple legal jurisdictions. Lists of prior arrests made in your city or state are available to you fairly quickly through the police department and the state agency responsible for criminal data collection. Usually there is a small fee. Arrests, outstanding warrants, and convictions in other states and U.S. territories may be recorded by the FBI in its National Crime Information Center (NCIC) database. The prosecution and judge will have access to NCIC data, and you and your defendant may or may not be able to look at it in the probation report.

You need to obtain this data for two reasons:

1. There may be incorrect information. Challenging the errors is time consuming and wearying, but if they are left unchallenged, they will haunt the defendant in later years and occasion unnecessary police questioning and traffic stops.

2. Local, state, and federal rap sheet information trickles in to the prosecution at uneven rates. Government databases are not updated instantly, and much reporting still occurs through paper reports mailed in to the FBI. Charges pending in other states can cause an offender who completed a sentence to be rearrested and extradited to another jurisdiction, where the process starts all over again.

You want to know how much trouble the defendant is in everywhere in the United States. It is sometimes possible to get charges dropped or warrants quashed in other states as you deal with the current arrest. Your goal is to get everything dealt with, now and forever.

Your defendant may wish to request his or her own copy of the NCIC information directly from the FBI. Given the vagaries of government, and the routine waivers of speedy trial, it may arrive sooner than the court's information. This is known in the trade as a "556 request," which refers to the fact that the attorney general's order enabling the records request was number 556. Naturally, if you say you're making a "556 request," some of that snappy FBI cool will rub off on you.

To simplify things, you'll find a downloadable version of the required rap sheet request on my Web site, www.wesdenham.net. Make sure the return address is *your* address, not the inmate's jail address. Don't forget the $18 money order. Never send personal checks to agencies in the criminal justice system. Most will refuse to accept them because of the high incidence of check fraud.

The defendant, not you, must make the request and must submit a full set of fingerprints. The FBI will not send this information to third parties, even family members. Fingerprints must be submitted on a "228." This is the FBI form number of the standard fingerprint card. To get your defendant's prints, first ask the jail staff.* The jail has fingerprint supplies, of course, and perhaps a fingerprint scanner. Staff will not, however, be accustomed to an inmate's making a 556 request, and they may refuse reflexively because they think something fishy is going on, perhaps an identity swap. They have reason to be suspicious. Forcible breakouts from modern jails happen rarely. Most escapes occur through bonehead clerical errors and mistaken identification that allow inmates to sashay out the door unchallenged. When this happens, jail officials and the police chief get a major media burn, complete with uncomfortable grilling and very comfortable posturing by city commissioners and a delighted, crazed press.

If you manage to persuade them, give them a copy of the request letter and a stamped envelope addressed to the Department of Justice with the money order enclosed. Ask them to roll the prints then insert the card into the envelope and mail it themselves.

If they refuse, have the defendant request that defense counsel seek a judicial order. If that doesn't work, you can roll your own. Download the fingerprint form from the FBI database at www.fbi.gov/hq/cjisd/fprequest.htm, get an inkpad, and take the defendant's prints yourself. This is easy when the defendant is out on bail—he or she can even have a private firm take the fingerprints. It's tough if the only time you can see your loved one is during court appearances or through bulletproof glass during visitation.

---

* A word of sympathy is appended herewith for corrections officers, bailiffs, clerks, prosecutors, public defenders, and their staffs. These are the long-suffering, not overly well-paid public servants of the criminal justice system. They will often be brusque or unsympathetic when you encounter them. Remember that day in and day out, they process criminals. Their jobs are frequently boring and occasionally terrifying.

The hardest part will be persuading your defendant to cooperate. Most inmates don't want to know, and don't want to be reminded of, every arrest and every conviction. They'll think you're testing them.

You are.

Web Sites

Bookmark the Web sites for your local jail, the state department of corrections, FBI criminal history requests, the state probation department, and the court. Don't forget basic computer chores such as exporting your bookmarks to a separate file and backing up files and bookmarks to an external disk or drive in case your computer crashes.

ESTABLISH A MAILING ADDRESS

Many defendants have no fixed address. On the outside they bunk with women, hang out with buddies, and wander from sofa to sofa. Every day when I walk my pooch, I hear people shouting to each other, "Where you staying at?" Once arrested, many defendants give false addresses because they have something to hide or they think it's cute. It's not. It's dumb.

Criminal justice is a long, long process that operates mostly on paper. In jail, of course, corrections officers serve legal notices on defendants. Nonetheless, one of the first things you should do for defendants is to establish a permanent mailing address. Immediately file the defendant's change of address with the U.S. Postal Service. In addition, mail the change-of-address notices, with the inmate's jail and case numbers, to the jail administrator, the clerk of the court, the office of the public defender, probation or parole officers, bail bondsmen, the prosecutor's office, and to private counsel, if there is any. Don't forget to mail the defendant's change-of-address notice to utilities, banks, credit card companies, insurance companies, and the department of motor vehicles. Bad addresses cause no end of legal and financial headaches to defendants, probationers, and parolees. Establishing a permanent address is a tremendous service.

MEDIA ATTENTION

If your defendant's case has attracted media, avoid them like plague. Say nothing, not even "no comment," to the yammering horde. Ignore phony empathy from ambitious reporters. Always remember that what the media truly want from you is free programming content around which to sell ads.

Do not summon the media yourself because you feel you deserve 90 seconds of airtime. Here's an example of what can happen. One of my neighbors, who shall remain nameless, was burgled. She called local TV and gave the reporter a televised tour to show *exactly* how the thief broke into her condo. This, of course, was a how-to lesson to every other burglar in the neighborhood. Some people are born stuck on stupid.

Statements to the media can cause you to be subpoenaed as a witness. The recorded statements you give may contradict later testimony you make under oath. This can lead to your indictment for perjury. Worse, local TV will show your face. If your defendant decides to cooperate with police in return for leniency, no-snitch hit squads will know what you look like and where you live. They'll be revving the Death Cab and ramming ammo pans into the AK-47s before the commercials end.

Not talking with the media, and staying away from photographers and videographers, keeps your defendant's options open. It keeps you from contradicting testimony you may give later and avoids tipping off the prosecution about the defense plan. Most importantly, it keeps you, your family, and the defendant safe.

4

TOSS YOUR CRIB, CAR, AND COMPUTER
An Urgent Priority

IF THE DEFENDANT LIVED with you or used your vehicle and computer, you should immediately search all three. This serves two purposes. First, it will help you truth-check the defendant. Second, you will avoid going to jail yourself for possession of contraband. You can't assist a defendant when you're in an adjoining cell.

Act fast, before search warrants are issued and items in your home become evidence. It is important to distinguish what you suspect from what you know for a fact. Words are critical. You do not know, and do not want to know, *as a fact*, that certain substances could be illegal drugs or that certain merchandise could be stolen. What you're searching for, officially, are things that don't belong in your home.

PHYSICAL SEARCH

The House

Houses are tough. To do a truly thorough job, you have to wreck the place. If your defendant was handy with tools, you'll have to work harder and be alert to hollowed-out hiding places.

1. First, get the proper tools. You'll need a screwdriver that accepts multiple tips and a *large* box of tips from one of the home stores. These contain the TORX and star tips used in automobile fasteners and the square tips used for furniture screws.

2. Wear *leather* gloves when you're poking around in dark spaces. Getting cut by knives and razor blades is dangerous. Getting stuck with needles contaminated with HIV or hepatitis can be fatal.

3. Search all cabinets, drawers, shelves, and storage areas in the house, garage, and shed. Feel around under the drawers. Check all plastic containers.

4. Poke a stick into powdered stuff such as sugar, coffee, laundry detergent, and flour to feel for anything hidden underneath.

5. Look behind furniture and pictures. Poke into picture frames that are inset and have deep, boxed mats.

6. Look under beds and appliances, and in the spaces *underneath and above* cabinets.

7. Check the fridge and the freezer. Unwrap all freezer packages.

8. Check tool and fishing tackle boxes. Look behind perforated tool-hanging boards.

9. Raise ceiling tiles and peek around with a flashlight.

10. Check pet carriers and pet food bags and boxes.

11. Look under cushions and mattresses. Don't rip them up—that's TV cop stuff.

12. Give closets close attention. Open boxes and containers, including those for toys and board games.

13. Computer towers contain mostly empty space. Unscrew the back and peek inside.

14. Examine luggage and book bags.

15. Take bags out of trashcans. Look underneath the cans themselves.

16. Look under lamp bases. Go underneath tables and look at the undersides.

17. Pull up area rugs and bathroom mats.

18. Check the toilet tank and the space behind it. Poke into the space underneath cabinets by removing the footboard. Look into medicine cabinets. If a medicine cabinet is not secured to the wall, pull it out and check the space behind it.

19. Look underneath dishwashers by removing the footboard. Look behind and under the refrigerator and stove.

20. Flip through books and open all CD and DVD cases.

21. Check pots and pans.

22. Check flowerpots, planters, and fertilizer and topsoil bags.

23. Check the garage, especially overhead racks, tool racks, and cabinets, and along garage door tracks.

24. Check around and behind TVs, stereos, and computers.

25. Check loose boards and the space underneath staircases.

26. Look underneath the house if it's raised on joists.

27. In the attic, poke around blown insulation with a stick. Poke into any torn areas of paper-backed or foil-backed insulation. Be careful to wear gloves and long sleeves—insulation makes you itch. Don't forget to shine a flashlight around roof trusses and the junction of the trusses and the top plates of the walls.

28. Be alert to incongruities. If you find a bar of soap in a bedroom, pry with a knife to see if it was hollowed out.

29. Remove access panels from hot water heaters and peer inside with a flashlight. Check behind air conditioning filters, air conditioning vents, and heating registers.

This will take several hours. Do the best you can. Don't beat yourself up thinking you might miss something. If your defendant was fiendishly clever, you won't find the contraband, and neither will police.

The Car

Vehicles are easier than houses. Only professional criminals go to the trouble and considerable expense of building secret hiding places and installing phony gas tanks. For details and photos, see my first book, *Arrest-Proof Yourself*, or go to www.wesdenham.net.

1. First, put on your leather gloves.

2. Poke underneath seats. Go all the way to the back.

3. Examine the glove box and all storage areas. Pull out rubber cup holders.

4. Take out the ashtray and check for residue. Wash the ashtray thoroughly.

5. Check the trunk, the tire well, and behind seats where the tire tools are stored.

6. Crawl under the vehicle and look around with a flashlight.

7. Open the hood and remove the air filter.

8. On pickup trucks, unscrew the bed liner and pull it back for a look. Check the space surrounding tie-down hooks. Look into the space between the truck bed and the cab.

9. Poke around underneath and behind bumpers.

10. Feel around under the dash and shine a flashlight into the air conditioner vents.

11. Pull out removable radios and stereos.

12. Check the side panels in doors for scratches around the screws. If you see any, remove the panels.

When You Find Weird Stuff

Always wear gloves around substances you suspect but do not actually know to be dope. You don't want residue recovered from your skin and clothes. You don't want to leave fingerprints on syringes, bongs, pipes, and baggies. When quantities are small, get rid of the stuff. Place everything in plastic bags and smash syringes and bongs with a hammer. Your own trash can or dumpster is subject to warrantless search, so carry suspected dope hidden in a garbage bag to your car so nosy neighbors won't see the stuff and rat you out to cops and dope dealers. Drive to a secluded dumpster and toss. Do not use dumpsters in shopping malls, which have video surveillance cameras.

If you find large quantities, such as wrapped kilo blocks of what you suspect, but do not know for certain, may be cocaine, heroin, or hashish, or large bags of what you suspect may be marijuana, you have two problems:

1. The cops could find the stuff and arrest you.

2. The owners of the drugs could beat or kill you to get their merchandise back.

You need legal advice—fast. Hire a defense attorney for yourself to get an opinion of your legal jeopardy. Attorney-client communications are confidential and cannot be coerced by police. If counsel advises you to surrender the suspected drugs to police, ask for counsel to be present at the handover. *Important:* Have a camera ready and take photos of the suspected dope *with police in the photograph.* You may need to prove to drug dealers that cops have the drugs. If dealers think you stole their merchandise, they may kill you.

Guns are trickier than dope. Consult an attorney at once when you discover a weapon whose registration, ownership, and evidentiary status you *do not know*, and, frankly, do not want to know. For heaven's sake, don't leave your fingerprints on the thing. If you are not familiar with firearms, do not try to unload it. The best advice is to pay a criminal defense attorney to have a staff member or private detective give the weapon to police. This process will be expensive and annoying, but by surrendering the weapon, you will have done your civic duty. Because attorneys and their staffs cannot be made to talk, you will also have effectively shielded your identity from police and avoided being entered into police computers as a subject of interest.

If you find merchandise that you suspect but do not know for a fact to be stolen, get rid of it, no matter how valuable. Don't even think of pawning this stuff, hustling it at flea markets, selling it online through craigslist or eBay, or peddling it around the neighborhood through what is jocularly referred to as the Hoodlum Shopping Network. Doing so creates paper trails and witnesses who will lead police to you.

Keep your lip zipped forever, and I mean *forever*, about what you find. Neighbors and "friends" will rat you out to get a deal when they're arrested or to gain favor with drug dealers and gunrunners. Do not—repeat, *do not*—keep, use, or sell suspected drugs, guns, and stolen goods that you find.

COMPUTER SEARCHES

Erase all e-mails. Erase browser histories. Dump the cache and clean the cookies. Lastly, check bookmarked Web sites and erase any bookmarks to sites that raise red flags. Now start searching for files that you suspect but do not know for certain may be illegal pornography, which is to say photos depicting sex acts with minors.

If you find pictures of unknown provenance that you suspect, but do not know for a fact, to be illegal pornography, you've got a serious problem. Possession of such images is a federal crime with harsh, mandatory punishment. Here's what to do.

1. Erase any suspected illegal porn you find. Using a disk utility, wipe the free space, overwriting each hard drive block 7 to 15 times with zeros and ones. Don't forget to search CDs, DVDs, memory sticks, floppies, and external drives, which are also used to hide porn. This can take many hours. Do not take your computer to a store or technicians and ask them to erase it. Techs are required by their employers to notify law enforcement agencies whenever they encounter illegal porn. Most keep the feds' numbers on the speed dial.

2. If you don't know how to do this stuff, execute plan B: Remove the hard drive and hit it with a hammer until it is in many, many small pieces. Now go back and smash DVDs, CDs, external drives, and memory sticks. Bag and toss the chunks in a dumpster far, far away.

On the way back, buy a fine new computer from an electronics store near you. America needs the economic stimulus, and you need to be able to sleep at night.

In your own bed.

SOME PRACTICAL ADVICE—OFFICIAL AND CONFIDENTIAL

It is illegal to destroy evidence, so characterize your actions thusly:

► Do you know for certain that the powder, pills, liquids, crystals, and leaves you found were illegal drugs? No, you don't! You're not a chemist, and you don't have a state-certified analytical laboratory in your spare room. Officially, all you know is that you found some nasty, disgusting substances that you disposed of immediately.

► Ditto unusual goods. Are they stolen? Who knows? The only thing that's certain is you found stuff that wasn't yours and you trashed it at once.

► As to suspected computer porn, you're not an attorney. Can you recite the case law that creates the fine distinctions that make *Cum-Slut News* illegal pornography and *Playboy* an award-winning "general interest" magazine? Of course not! All you know, officially, is that you found and deleted some annoying files that were taking up valuable hard-drive space.

Do not quiz your defendant. A search will show you what was going on, but you do not want to elicit confessions or specific knowledge that may implicate you in crime.

☠ WHEN THE POPO COME

When police knock on your door and start questioning you, it is an emergency. They are trained in interrogation; you are not. They are allowed to use trickery in questioning; you are not allowed to use deception in answering. You can be arrested for lying to police officers or for perjuring yourself later under oath. You can be charged if police search your house and find drugs, weapons, or stolen merchandise.

Shut down interrogations and attempts to search without a warrant by using the following techniques:

1. Do not allow police inside your home. Speak to them outside. Allowing them entry might be construed as a consent to search.

2. You are required by law to tell police your legal name, as it appears on your birth certificate or your marriage license. So tell them. You are not legally required to tell them anything else.

3. Hand police officers the defense attorney's business card or a piece of paper with the public defender's name on it. Say the following: "My attorney will speak for me."

4. Say no more! Do not argue with police over your constitutional right to silence. Just exercise your right by staying quiet and gently closing the door.

5. Notify defense counsel about an attempted interrogation or search.

6. Police may try to search your house in your absence by gaining consent from an unwitting child, family member, or visitor. Instruct everyone in the house not to talk to police or allow them entry.

Now relax. Take a breath. A hot-tub bath and an adult beverage in moderation would not be uncalled for. You have just dodged a *big* bullet. Besides, having read this chapter, you've long since tossed your crib, car, and computer and vanished any weird stuff.

5
GOING TO THE BIG HOUSE
Jail Visits

To INMATES, VISITS ARE more important than you can imagine. Remember, however, that inmate visitation is not a legal right. It is a privilege that can be revoked at any time. Visitation is subject to rules and limits—lots of them. So before your first visit, check the jail rules (see chapter 3, p. 27) and follow them explicitly. It's difficult enough to get into a jail for a visit. If you break the rules, you might find it even more difficult to get out!

Here are some pointers that are applicable nearly everywhere:

1. Find out which jail is holding your inmate. Most cities have several.

2. Be sure to visit on the correct day. Any other day, you'll be denied entry. If you're coming from out of town, phone the jail to see if they can accommodate your schedule.

3. Don't take more family members than allowed. Check rules regarding children. If you take too many people, some will have to stay behind and pound the linoleum in the jail lobby.

4. Take plenty of quarters for parking meters and lockers.

5. Make sure your car has current tags, is street legal, and contains *no drugs, guns, or contraband*. Jail parking lots swarm with cops, meter maids, and tow truck spotters. It's no fun to emerge from a jail visit and find that your car has been towed, and liberally ticketed, in your absence. It's less fun to get busted.

6. Use the restroom in the lobby before you go inside. A full bladder on the jail floors, where often there are no bathrooms for visitors, can be agonizing. Demand that children use the restroom whether they need to or not. You know the drill.

7. Don't even *think* about taking a gun, a knife, a sharp object, or narcotics into jail. This includes penknives carried on key chains.

8. Ditto for cell phones, iPods, PDAs, Walkmans, laptops, radios, Game Boys, computer memory sticks, cameras, and all other electronic gizmos. Stash these, along with your purse, in the jail lobby coin lockers.

9. Toss all food, drinks, gum, and tobacco before entering.

10. People think that dressing hot and sexy for an inmate is a treat. It's not. It's a treatment—for you. Jail staff will deny you entry or make you cover that hottie outfit with a XXX-sized T-shirt. Jails are full of young men and women who are so horny that their eyeballs are popping out. In the corridors, corrections officers practically skate on jizz as it is. The last thing they need is for you to get inmates more jacked up than they are already. So, women, wear your church clothes. No bare bellies, tight jeans, pop-up boobs, or stiletto heels. Men, leave your muscle shirts and skin-tight, package-displaying dance pants in the closet. Cover the chest fur, the muscles, and the gold chains. Drop those gold and cubic zirconia–studded grills into a water glass at home.

11. No hats! Jail staff want surveillance cameras to get a good look at you. They know about all the little nasties that can be hidden under a lid. If you're wearing a wig or toupee, you may be asked to lift that rug and give it a shake.

12. No gang colors, please.

13. Leave the phony Louis Vuitton, Gucci, and Hermès handbags at home, along with any other fake designer merchandise you bought from your friendly neighborhood street vendor. Cops can make an issue of these things when they want to.

14. If your jail allows you to supply your inmate with clothes and personal items, bring only those allowed. Anything on the banned list will be seized. Bring items in an open shopping bag. If you bring luggage, corrections officers may deny you entry or cut your bag to ribbons.

15. Give corrections staff your inmate's jail number for positive identification. Otherwise, you might visit the wrong defendant.

16. You are subject to personal search and must pass through a metal detector before entering. If you have artificial joints, embedded shrapnel, or metal screws, pins, and rods in your bones, you're going to set off the alarm. Bring along your prosthesis card to show to staff. They may ask to see the surgical scars. Don't be angry. They're doing their job. So just hike up the pants legs, or drop that skirt a bit, and show the incision. If you have artificial limbs, you

may have to take them off and have them searched. Yes, people have tried to smuggle drugs and weapons into jails inside artificial legs.

17. Be courteous with jail staff. Do not engage in idle chatter, and *do not* discuss the legal details of your loved one's case with them. Their job is to preserve the health and safety of inmates, staff, and visitors and to produce defendants safely in court. They are not attorneys and cannot advise you on legal matters. But if you're nice, they can help in other ways. They know the system; you don't.

18. Jail staff are generally professional and courteous, but they will not tolerate infractions of rules. Do not raise your voice or argue with them. Don't forget, you're already in jail! You're surrounded by law enforcement officers who can, with a touch of a button, lock down the floor and arrest you. If you feel that you or an inmate has been treated unfairly or in a manner not in compliance with department of corrections rules, discuss it with an attorney or file a complaint using the jail's complaint procedures.

FAMILY INTERVENTION

Remember the main message of this book: you should not *unconditionally* offer financial support to inmates. Of course they want private attorneys. Of course they want a fat deposit to the commissary account. Of course they want bail, bail, and more bail. When you visit, they can't wait to tell you that the food sucks, the corrections officers are beasts, and the other inmates are—*egads*—crooks!

So what?

Keep your heart soft but your head hard. Sooner rather than later, your visit needs to become an intervention. To keep sane, you will need to express your sadness and anger at the damage the inmate has done to your family. Tell the inmate how hellishly hard it will be to finance a defense and reentry into society. Just say the words. Don't yell them.

If you don't have money for bail and private attorneys, just say so. If you do, don't promise at once to start paying. Ask your inmate these questions:

▶ What are you going to do, beginning right now, to live lawfully and peaceably?

▶ What are you going to do, beginning right now, to live without drugs?

▶ What are you doing to assist counsel in your legal defense?

▶ How are you going to pay back all or part of your family's money?

If you get lies and evasions or insincere lip service, don't waste your money. Let the inmate know he or she has to earn your money with effort and good behavior. If you get questions like "What can I do?" that's good. Now you can get busy. Now you can use your visitation time purposefully and for great effect.

Keep asking probing questions until you get detailed answers and definite commitments:

► What school will you enroll in? What church will you attend?

► Which branch of the military will you join?

► Where are your educational, employment, and military records?

► Have you received your medications? Did you sign and mail the medical power of attorney?

► Do you have addresses for friends and family?

► Do witnesses need to be located and their addresses supplied to defense counsel?

Make jail visits work time rather than gab time. This will keep you sane. It will keep inmates focused on their future and thinking about themselves as future citizens, possibly for the first time in their lives.

6
"GIVE YOUR HEARTS TO JESUS, BOYS . . ."
Life in Jail

THE TOUGHEST THING FOR inmates to grasp is that The Man has got them. Temporarily, they're toast. They've moved from a life of willy-nilly to a life of rules, from a life where nobody's in charge to one where somebody absolutely, without question, is in charge.

The jail is run by The Man—that is, the government—and The Man and his corrections officers run it their way for their reasons and do not ask inmates for comments or suggestions. There are daily lineups, counts, and toeing the painted line with the toes— not the heels, not the insoles, the toes. Inmates eat when The Man says eat; they sleep when he says sleep. When they get wild, they get sprayed with stuff that turns tears into molten lava. When they get crazy, they'll be strapped into a restraint chair and left to howl until the pills go down or the shots kick in.

Inside, they have to do things The Man's way—period. In the immortal words of an unknown Marine Corps drill instructor:

> Give your hearts to Jesus, boys,
> 'Cause your *ass* belongs to me!

This makes inmates nuts. They challenge, they defy, and they shout and shriek. Resistance, as they say, is futile. It also wastes time, which, even in the Time Machine, is not infinite. Many inmates don't understand that jail is temporary. Prison or freedom or the purgatory called probation will follow in one year or less.

You and your defendant should both avoid getting caught up in jail dramas, jail humiliations, jail games, and jail idiocies. Your most important service to defendants is to keep them focused on a future life outside jail and keep them busy with their legal defense. This is astonishingly difficult. Most inmates never think of the future—that's one of the reasons they're in jail in the first place.

What works in jail is to surrender. In The Man's world, inmates should do it The Man's way. The trick is to give it up without seeming cowardly, which will earn a beating from other inmates. In jail you keep your dignity by living the life that counts, deep down, where only you and God know the truth.

What helps is for you and your defendant to understand what jails are: they're giant pens designed to keep inmates somewhat orderly, somewhat healthy, and somewhat fed, so that they can be produced as required in courtrooms, where judges and juries will decide their fate, where lawyers will argue about it, and where you, the family, may get in your two cents.

That's it.

Jails were never meant to educate or to reform. But they can transform, or more accurately, inmates can transform themselves, using jail's indignities to their advantage. One of life's ironies is that wealthy people actually pay to get locked up in rehabs and fat farms, there to be starved, barked at by exercise instructors, and regimented morning, noon, and night. Jail can be a poor man's retreat.

DRIFTING THROUGH THE TIME MACHINE

What works in jail is to concentrate on what's going to happen in the courtroom and afterward, so that obeying the rules and avoiding confrontations with authorities and other inmates will become easier. A future focus means that what happens now, in jail, is not emotionally important. Here's how it's done.

Stay Off the Radar

Getting noticed means getting hassled. Jails have classification systems. Violent and crazy inmates get treated differently. Things can always get worse. Corrections officers know the system. If your defendant becomes a PITA (Pain In The Ass), infractions will be reported to prosecutors to increase charges.

Ignore Insults

Despite the best efforts of jail administrators, there are always a few sadists and control freaks among corrections officers. They will use taunts and insults to get inmates to "show out," that is, to challenge their authority. When all else fails, they will use racial and ethnic slurs—"nigger," "kike," "wop," "spic," "chink," "mick"—to get a reaction. If inmates refuse to rise to the bait, the tormentors will move on to others who will.

Respect Other Inmates

Defendants should keep their mitts off other inmates' stuff and stay out of their space! In the miniature world of jail, pitiful possessions—letters, paper, legal files, toothpaste, books, magazines—assume outsized importance. Tensions run high. Inmates should be polite but not subservient, friendly but not overly familiar. They should *never, ever* question other inmates about their cases or their activities. Being branded a snitch can be hazardous to health.

No Fighting

No trying to stop fights. Once the buzzer sounds, the Blue Horde will rush in. Getting zapped by pepper spray, TASERed, and beaten and kicked by guys who can bench-press a moose really hurts.

Respect Local Pecking Orders

Many jails house inmates in groups in areas called dormitories. Your inmate should ask others in his area "How do things work here?" It's smart to pick up on problems and note other inmates' sensitivities.

FATUITIES OF THE FUNHOUSE

Jail is a place of idiocies innumerable. Advise inmates to avoid all of the following.

Stare Parties and the Evil Eye

Inmates obsess over the pecking order. Because they are at the bottom of the social ladder, they get frantic to climb up one rung. Many will stare at other inmates in order to establish dominance.

Spitting

Inmates have this weird idea that laws do not apply in jail. They don't realize that fighting, especially with corrections officers, merits real-world assault and battery charges. Ditto spitting. Because of AIDS fears, most states have passed laws that make spitting on corrections officers a felony.

"Supervisors"

This is a game in which one inmate will approach a newbie and declare that corrections officers have put him in charge of new inmates. This is absurd. Inside jail, The Man rules. Everyone else is a prisoner. The right answer to this assertion is "I'm sure that corrections officers will let me know about that when they come by."

"Protectors"

In this ploy, an inmate will sidle up to a new arrival and whisper ominously that there are lots of bad people here, lots of bad stuff going on! Fortunately, this guy knows his way around and will be your inmate's protector. In jail as elsewhere, nothing is free, so protectors expect to get paid with the protectee's food, commissary goods, phone time, and possessions, and as much sex as the protector wants. The proper response? "I'll ask the corrections officers for their opinion."

Protection Rackets

This is the violent form of "protector." When this happens, inmates have to pay the protector weekly to avoid beatings. The best-run jails shuffle inmates between floors and wings to break up this sort of extortion. Should your inmate be extorted, he or she should request an immediate move to another part of the jail. Follow up with a request of your own sent by fax and telephone, then by certified mail, return receipt requested. Advise defense counsel.

Snitches

They're everywhere. Sometimes they rat out another inmate in return for a proffer. More often, they snitch to guards about rule infractions. Some are just born quislings. Others are bored and enjoy the uproars that occur when corrections officers show up with manacles and leg irons and hustle some rule breaker off to the hole. Any inmate who is insistently and overly friendly is probably a snitch.

Crooked Guards

Even the best-run jails have one or two. These are the guys who mosey up to inmates, make buddy-buddy, and offer to bring in things from the outside. The preferred merchandise is drugs, cigarettes, lighters, food, condoms, cell phones, personal lubricants, and porn. These procurers cannot be paid with commissary credits, only cash, for which they will approach you, the family. Don't pay them! They're criminals.

Cell Stores

These are cells filled with commissary goods, which inmates resell at a markup to other inmates. Unlike actual commissaries, which distribute goods several times a week and are paid with credits from funds deposited by families (see chapter 8, p. 62), cell stores are open all day. Cell stores are run by enterprising criminals who have access to cash.

Given that commissary goods are expensive to start with, cell store stuff is fantastically overpriced. Cell store proprietors sell on credit, which has to be repaid with a stiff vig* added. When inmates are unable to pay with their own commissary goods, or phone time, or sex, proprietors often satisfy the debt with a good ol' Brooklyn stomping, some teeth cracking, and a little head smacking against the concrete wall.

Jail Wine

O, for a draught of vintage! That hath been
Cool'd a long age in the deep-delved earth.

---

* Short for "vigorish," which is crook slang for the usurious interest charged by loan sharks.

Who doesn't need a drink in jail, a sweet taste of the soft life, of better times, with a promise of brief oblivion? There is no legal alcoholic beverage on the inside, only jail wine. This stuff is made from fruit juice or Kool-Aid. Inmates pee in it to get it started. (Most of them have some sort of yeast infection.) Then they let it ferment in plastic bags kept warm between their legs.

Jail wine bubbles with bacteria, spirochetes, and noxious protozoa numberless and unknown. It can be poisonous. It can also inebriate. Inmates don't need to be high, or to lower their mental defenses—ever. Guys go nuts on this stuff. They fight like fiends, then get worked over by guards, tossed into the hole, and prosecuted for new felonies.

Jail Tatts

Jail tattoos are applied with needles made from document staples that are straightened and jammed into plastic razor handles. Inmates make the ink by melting plastic chess and checker pieces or razor handles in their jail bongs. How they get lighters and matches into no-smoking jails is one of the continuing mysteries.

Jail tatts can cause horrific skin infections. I've seen abscesses the size of golf balls oozing pus and blood. Even worse, jail tatts mark defendants for life as crooks and give police yet another easy way to identify them in the future. Judges, by the way, do not enjoy seeing "Fuck You" tattooed across a defendant's forehead or knuckles.

Gambling

Nothing causes more violence in jails than gambling. Many jail commissaries, unhelpfully, sell playing cards. Inmates are adept at making dice from toothpaste mixed with toilet paper. They use pencils to mark the dots. There's no penny ante here, since there aren't any pennies. The stakes are soap, toothpaste, phone time, and commissary goods. All this sounds innocent, just a bunch of guys hanging out in their jail dorm enjoying a game of cards or a roll of the bones. It's not.

Jails, lacking discretionary goods and services, have warped economies. Being down two bags of chips in a card game is a serious problem. Winners demand repayment with a stiff vig. Losers may have to drop their pants and take it up the tunnel or get the living daylights beaten out of them. Naturally, everybody thinks everybody else in the game is cheating. Usually, they are.

Since inmates cannot possess cash, they develop artificial currencies. In federal prisons, the most common currency these days is foil packs of cheap, oily mackerel, called "macks," purchased from prison commissaries. Most inmates don't eat the stuff, which is more akin to fish bait than food. They just use macks as money.

Rumors

Jails are full of tough guys who gossip like hens. In addition to the usual urban myths (AIDS was invented by white people to eradicate blacks; aliens are on ice in Area 51 in Nevada), there are constant stories about inmates who got a better deal than anyone else. With dark hints, inmates will insinuate that some sharp lawyering got done, some judges and juries got bribed, an outside fixer was brought in, etc. Your defendant will insist, until you are absolutely demented, that someone else with the same charges got a better deal.

Ignore this stuff. If someone else really did get a better deal, so what? Since when has life been fair? Mostly this is wishful thinking. Inmates never know the details of one another's cases, the points of law at issue, what evidence the government has and whether it will stand up in court, and whether cooperation with police occurred.

If inmates understood criminal law, they wouldn't be in jail. If they understood cops, they would obey laws, drive within the limits, come to a full and complete stop at signals, and smile sweetly and speak softly to law enforcement—just like I do.

Bust-Outs

Modern jails are secure. Daring helicopter escapes and dashes through dynamited walls occur frequently in movies but rarely in life. Tell your defendant not to get involved in wild escape schemes. Jail is temporary. Why bother?

Help your inmate stay focused. Working on the defense, writing letters, and reading books and magazines takes plenty of time. Of course, human companionship is essential. Everybody hangs out with other inmates and shoots the breeze. Nonetheless, tell your inmate, as often as necessary, to avoid foolishness and violence. When trouble or craziness start, your inmate should fade—fast.

 **THE JUDAS RAT**

Welcome to the lowest rung of hell! Your inmate has been running a criminal enterprise from jail, or gambled and lost, or bought drugs on credit, or gotten leaned on because of some witness testimony. Your inmate has ratted you out to criminals on the outside, and the bad guys are turning up the heat. Here are the signs:

► Your inmate calls you from jail on a cell phone. Cell phones are not allowed in jail. Cell phone calls mean something illegal is going on.

► You've been asked to dramatically increase your payments to the jail commissary. You've received vague excuses like "I've got a few things to take care of."

► You've been instructed to deposit money in a bank account, or to wire it to persons unknown, or to leave it under a rock.

► Loan sharks knock on your door demanding payment.

► You get threatening phone calls.

► You're told you're in a no-snitch zone and that you'll be killed unless you refuse to testify or use your influence to get someone else to refuse to testify.

► You're asked to pick up a package on the outside and hold it for a while.

► You're asked to meet with a corrections officer outside the jail.

► You're asked to drop off a package of food, snacks, cigarettes, or other goods to a corrections officer, a stranger, or a work detail outside the jail.

► You're asked to buy drugs or guns and deliver them to persons unknown.

► You're told to perjure yourself or give false statements to police.

If this happens, immediately do the following:

1. Cut off money, phone calls, and mail. Cease payments to private attorneys. Call the cops. Give a statement to police and write a letter to the judge and the jail administrator outlining any threats you've received. This animal has sold you out for drugs or money. He needs to be dead to you. Otherwise, you'll be dead to him, really dead.

2. If threatened, read the section on witness protection (chapter 25, p. 206), then vanish.

JAIL FOOD

What's to say? It's bland, and it's meager—white bread or cornbread; mystery meat and goo; bologna, not too green, on Wonder Bread; and sawdust cereal for breakfast. Hot dogs are mostly cornmeal. Beanie weenies and mushy veggies round out the diet. The hottest items on the menu are the pats of margarine on paperboard squares. These are used as a lubricant for jail sex.

Ignore food complaints from your defendant. The stuff won't kill anybody, and inmates should eat the food, like it or not, to keep up their health and mental faculties. Occasionally the cornbread has weevils and the beans have bugs. So what? Eat up! Jail food is always thoroughly heated, and bugs have vitamins.*

Most jails serve special meals to inmates who declare themselves Orthodox Jews or Muslims. Contrary to common belief, inmates in most states do not have a legal right to special diets. Jails provide them as a convenience. This cuts down on bellyaching, jailhouse petitions, and other annoyances. Don't expect the food purveyor, Low Bidder, Inc., to be too scrupulous in these matters. There won't be an imam or rabbi in the kitchen, and at the wages they pay, do you really think the cooks will know that mackerel is kosher but catfish is not? What happens in real life is that when the mystery meat is pork, the kosher and halal guys get something different. Of course, under that omnipres-

---

* When I interviewed Armando Valladares, a Cuban poet who survived 22 years in Fidel Castro's horror-house prisons, he told me his health actually improved after he added snakes, cockroaches, and spiders to his diet. Cuban prisons make American lockups look like the Ritz Carlton—without the chocolate on the pillow, of course.

ent brown goo, the special meat could be fricasseed rat. Who would know? Or care? In any case, Jews and Muslims have religious dispensation to violate their diets in wartime or in prison. If these guys were truly pious, they'd know that.

Most jails serve meals that total less than 3,000 calories daily. So when inmates go in tubby, they come out trim if they stay long enough in these taxpayer-subsidized fat farms. Commissary snacks have an outsized importance in quieting hunger pangs and alleviating boredom. Commissary food, alas, is mostly junk. In the commissary inmates can ask for Darjeeling, hot, with a whole grain muffin, but they won't get it. They won't get petits fours, either.

MAIL

Mail is crucial. To get it delivered, you must put the inmate's full, legal name and the jail number on the envelope. Rules vary by city, but in general you cannot send pornography, or material downloaded from the Internet, or material about jail-breaks or bombs, or instructions on how to kill cops or commit crimes. Scratch that hate literature. Interestingly, my book *Arrest-Proof Yourself* is banned from our jail, which the jail chief thinks is hilarious. Cops, quite naturally, regard arrest-proofing as a metaphysical impossibility.

Most jails allow magazines and paperback books to be mailed, but only by the publisher. This reduces the entry of drugs, tobacco, and weapons into the jail. Remember that the overwhelming experience of jails is boredom. Send books of crossword puzzles and other amusements if your defendant enjoys such things. They're also useful trade goods. Jails that limit the number of books an inmate can have at one time will often make exceptions for religious literature. So send a Bible, Koran, Torah, Book of Mormon, Kitáb-i-Aqdas, Bhagavad-Gita, or other religious text. Corrections officers can be hazy on world religions, and their Arabic, Hebrew, Sanskrit, and Persian may be rusty, so a cover letter explaining that the book is a religious text can be helpful. Check your jail's rules for details.

JAIL GEOGRAPHY

It matters where on the Fruited Plain your inmate was arrested. States and cities vary tremendously in how they manage jails. In New York City, inmates can get visits every day. Families can bring them clothes, food, books, magazines, and lots of goodies. Allowing inmates to wear their own clothes emphasizes their status as detainees, not convicted criminals. In my city, the choices are more limited. There are red jumpsuits for violent inmates, orange for the mentally ill and suicidal, and green for everybody else. All feet are shod with soft foam flip-flops, which cuts down on stompings.

In Los Angeles, world center of movies and television, inmates can give interviews to the media in special jail studios and indulge in the new national pastime, trial by media.

They also can appear at preliminary hearings via closed-circuit TV and thus avoid being transported in irons to the courthouse. This makes sense in L.A., which houses, on average, 20,000 inmates daily. Without the video hookup, they'd have to hold hearings in the Rose Bowl with judges on the 50 yard line.

Franklin County, Pennsylvania, has the snazziest jail I've ever seen. Inmates gather in a lobby that would grace a resort hotel, there to drink coffee—ah!—and read uplifting periodicals and watch the many educational offerings of our television networks. Sunlight floods in through a crystalline atrium. There are work details galore, and opportunities to be outside all day to trim the grass and prune the roses. Inside, there are 12-step groups to exorcise addiction demons, prison society visitors, music, and mail. Vendors deliver goody boxes of chocolates, meats, and a fine selection of cheeses. School is in session every day. They probably give cha-cha lessons. For one mad moment, I wanted to rush up to Chambersburg, slap a cop, and join the fun.

Nonetheless, many inmates get a rude shock when they commit crimes outside their home states. I've interviewed defendants who hail from New York, Massachusetts, and California but run afoul of the law right here in Jacksonville. "What about the Second Chance Initiative?" they ask. "When is the New Directions Program going to kick in?"

"What?" I reply. "No programs like that in this town."

Then I pop their bubble thusly: "Important Inmate Message: You're not back home. You're in jail in the Bible Belt. Down here, Jesus Christ is Lord, and when you break His laws, He's gonna kick your ass."

They've got more shocks coming. In Florida, three-time losers get routed into habitual offender courts that hand out *triple* sentences. These are staffed by state attorneys and judges so tough they think walking barefoot on nails is a foot rub. My advice to young Florida thugs who lust for a life of crime is to head north toward the Georgia line and don't stop going for a thousand miles or until they see snow.

SOFT JAILS, HARD JAILS; GOOD JAILS, BAD JAILS

Soft jails provide inmates with creature comforts, good food, unrestricted family contact without glass separators, and the opportunity to wear their own clothes and to enjoy care packages brought by families or purchased from vendors. Such jails emphasize that nonsentenced inmates are pretrial detainees and not convicts. For those inmates who are serving short sentences, they provide educational classes, work release programs, drug counseling, and job training.

Soft jails inevitably allow greater entry of drugs, alcohol, and tobacco. They inadvertently allow easier communication with criminal confederates on the outside and greater opportunity to manage criminal enterprises from the inside. With smuggled cell phones, witness intimidation and contract killings become simpler to arrange.

Hard jails emphasize pretrial punishment. Their purpose is to make jail itself so tough that, regardless of guilt or innocence, regardless of what judges and juries decide, each inmate gets a good kick in the fanny from the taxpayers. The most notorious are Sheriff Joe Arpaio's Maricopa County jails in Phoenix. There the food consists of surplus green bologna on day-old bread, at a cost of 30 cents per inmate per day. About 2,000 inmates are housed in Tent City, which consists of military-surplus tents surrounded by stun fences, guard dogs, and machine gun towers so inmates can get the full benefit of Arizona's dry air and 120-degree summer heat. Interestingly, the recidivism rates of cities with hard jails are no lower than those with soft. Even butt-kicking sheriffs can't make citizens.

Good jails balance inmate comfort with security and safety. Their administrators run them tough and tight but do not add gratuitous harassments and humiliations. They understand that their job is inmate detention and care, and that justice comes from judges and juries, not jailers.

Bad jails? They're all alike and all horrible. Inmates and corrections officers beat, kill, and rape. Guards roam the halls selling drugs, tobacco, and booze for payments of cash or sex. Officers sell phony release papers or arrange escapes. Nowadays, most of these hellholes are in small towns where corrupt sheriffs plumb the depths of human depravity amid tall corn, swaying wheat, and fluffy cotton growing under blue skies and God's golden sun.

Rural America has its limitations.

☠ DEATH IN CUSTODY

If your inmate dies while in custody, either from beatings by corrections officers or from failure to receive treatment for a serious illness, you may have cause for civil litigation and criminal prosecution. Emphasis is on "may." Here's what to do:

1. Do not talk to the media. Not a single word.

2. Do not sign any releases or other legal documents without advice of counsel.

3. Immediately seek advice from attorneys specializing in accident and injury cases. If you do not have substantial funds for legal fees—which is to say five- and six-figure money—seek a contingent-fee attorney. These lawyers advertise heavily in the phone book and on television.

If the inmate died because of failure to treat an illness, of great importance will be written notification, prior to the inmate's demise, informing jail administrators of the illness and its seriousness. Hopefully this notification was posted certified mail, return receipt requested, or delivered by a process server. These delivery methods are the gold standards of legal notification.

If the inmate died of natural causes or was killed by other inmates, or if jail staff rendered reasonable health care, you probably will lose.

If corrections officers murdered your defendant or were negligently responsible for the death, expect paperwork to disappear, e-mails to vanish, telephone call recordings to be irrecoverable, surveillance tapes to have "technical difficulties," and memories to quickly and opportunistically fade.

You'll need a team of legal hardboys, the kind who eat broken glass for breakfast, to subpoena evidence and to break through statutory liability limits. To get corrections officers fired, arrested, and charged for their crimes, you'll need the cooperation of the police internal affairs department and the office of the prosecutor. Let your attorney guide you.

Expect this process to be hellish and to take years. If this happened to your defendant, you have my deepest sympathy.

We expect better from our country and our government.

7
SICK, CONFUSED, AND CRAZY
Medical Care and Mental Illness

In jail, health care is frustrating to schedule, slow to arrive, and utterly vital. Many inmates are admitted to jail in less than tiptop shape. They have pneumonia, infections and oozing abscesses, diabetes and heart disease, headaches, diarrhea, rotten teeth, K-9 bites, gunshot wounds—and that's just for starters. Many are mentally ill, more are drunks, and a high percentage are addicted to narcotics and will undergo acute withdrawal in jail.

It's important to understand the objective of jail health care. The goal is *not* to bring inmates to the rosy peak of health. The goal is to keep inmates *healthy enough* to stand up in front of a judge in court hearings and understand the proceedings. That's it. When defendants drip pus and blood in the courtroom or spit out a molar in front of His Honor, someone will call maintenance.

If inmates are acutely ill, they will be taken, heavily guarded and in irons, to the public hospital. This is dangerous and expensive because of the risks of flight and of assault on hospital staff. Inside the jail, health care will be provided by Low Bidder, Inc. Rarely will your inmate see an actual doctor. Most health care is provided by nurses and nurse assistants. Inmates are lucky if they are treated by a physician's assistant, because in most states PAs can write prescriptions.

Even so, inmate health care is enormously expensive. When inmates have serious and expensive illnesses, they will get "compassionate release." This means they will be freed and unceremoniously shoved out the front door where, blinking in the unaccustomed sunlight, they can arrange, or not, for their own medical treatment. This sounds harsh, but does the sign on that jail say "Free Bad-Boy Health Care"?

It does not.

YOUR HEALTH CARE RESPONSIBILITIES

Your duty as a family member is to inform the jail of the defendant's medical conditions:

1. Fax the watch commander or jail administrator a medical and psychiatric information form. You will find this form in appendix A (p. 236).

2. Mail a copy via certified mail, return receipt requested. Send another copy by regular mail to defense counsel.

Do not, when you receive phone calls from your inmate complaining about health problems, run down to the jail and start pounding on the administrator's door. Don't holler at jail staff on the phone, send threatening letters, or make ominous noises about hiring lawyers. This last is futile because government employees have sovereign immunity from personal liability for actions taken pursuant to their jobs. Translation: you can't sue them unless they do something truly egregious, and that better be on videotape.

What you should do is calm down and review your jail information package regarding health care. Normally, inmates have to fill out a form to request a nurse visit. Then they have to wait. Everything in jail takes forever because everything is so time consuming and labor intensive. To merely move an inmate from point A to point B, multiple corrections officers have to operate the electric door controls, accompany the inmate, watch moves on video monitors, and log all movements into the jail database. (Some high-tech jails let inmates move, unaccompanied, by remotely unlocking and locking doors. Inmates scoot through the maze like rats.)

If your inmate has prescriptions, these have to be filled at an outside pharmacy and transported to jail. To get the drugs inside, health care providers must have their medical kits searched and need to pass through metal detectors. Once inside, they have to wait until corrections officers bring the inmates. All this takes time, much time.

Occasionally, corrupt nurses will smuggle Schedule II and III narcotics* into jail and sell them to inmates, who then pressure family members to pay up on the outside. *Do not* let yourself get pimped out to stethoscope-carrying crooks. Write a letter of complaint to the jail administrator and send it certified, return receipt requested. See the "Judas Rat" section on p. 49 for warning signs of jail scams.

Instruct inmates to follow the procedures and be patient. Until medicine arrives, they're going to have to tough it out. If after several days your inmate has not received medications, do the following:

1. Call the jail administrator's office and make a *polite* complaint. Ask for help.

2. If this doesn't produce results, the inmate's attorney should seek a court order directing the jail administrator to provide care. Smart defense lawyers will push the issue by filing emergency motions for dismissal on the grounds that the defendants are too ill, or too confused, to participate in their own defense. This will generally result in medical care being pro-

---

* Schedules are groups of drugs defined by the U.S. Controlled Substances Act (21 U.S.C. § 801 et. seq.). In Schedule I are illegal drugs with no medical use, such as heroin, X, psilocybin, marijuana, LSD, etc. Schedule II and III drugs have medicinal use but are addictive and require a prescription. Examples are most amphetamine-derived stimulants, tranquilizers, and sedatives. (Consult *Arrest-Proof Yourself* to see how to avoid getting busted when your sleeping pills, or Junior's Ritalin, fall between the car seat cushions.) For a detailed list of scheduled drugs, go to www.wesdenham.net.

vided or your defendant being freed on recognizance (that is, no bond) or freed because charges get dropped. NOTE: If your defendant has diabetes, remind the attorney that both low and high blood sugar levels caused by this disease can profoundly diminish mental capacity.

3. If all else fails and the illness is severe, suggest that your inmate complain of chest pain, shortness of breath, and pain radiating from the chest to the left arm. These are the symptoms of heart attack, and they usually will get your inmate taken to a hospital. Make sure he or she actually is seriously ill before you recommend this ploy. The inmate also needs to be over 30. This doesn't work for teens and 20-somethings.

You may need to obtain a medical information power of attorney,* or confidentiality waiver, from the defendant. This is a document that empowers you to obtain prescription and medical information and send it to the jail health service. For a sample, see appendix A (p. 236). Federal law prohibits health care professionals from disclosing information to you unless you provide them with such a document.

The problem with powers of attorney is that they have to be notarized. This simple procedure is astonishingly difficult in jails. Most jails have notaries on staff, but they may refuse to notarize any documents other than those required by the judge or defense counsel. Call jail staff and ask their advice on how to get a power of attorney notarized. You may have to bring a notary into jail as a visitor, which is not easy. The public defender's office or your private attorney may be able to send in a notary without you being present. Complicating things is your inmate's lack of ID, which was, of course, seized at the time of arrest. Jail and defense counsel notaries will accept the inmate's jail number tag or bracelet as sufficient I.D. Private notaries probably won't.

MENTAL ILLNESS

The closure of state mental hospitals is a shameful episode in our history that is not over yet. Today, in every town, the stand-in for the mental hospital is the local jail. Mentally ill inmates are at risk of harming themselves and others and are frequent victims of beatings and money scams. If your defendant is mentally ill, do the following:

1. Telephone the jail watch commander or administrator and inform him or her of the mental illness. Immediately fax to the jail's watch commander or administrator a letter informing this individual of psychiatric conditions. Attach a medical and psychiatric information form, which you will find in

---

* "Attorney" here merely means that you have the right to act on behalf of another person. Don't get the idea that with a few sheets of paper you have suddenly become a lawyer and can march into the courtroom and orate to judges and juries.

appendix A (p. 236). Make copies before you fill it out—you may need to update the form as new information becomes available.

2. *Do not* discuss in your letter any impending charges against your defendant. Limit yourself to medical information only. Keep a copy of this letter for reference. If your inmate is transferred to a different facility, you will need to fax and mail this information again.

3. Ask that that your inmate be moved immediately to special facilities for mentally ill inmates. Jail staff will be familiar with such requests. Gather all medical records specific to the illness. If you need a confidentiality waiver or medical power of attorney agreement to get information, move heaven and earth until you get these documents signed and notarized. Make sure to mention your need for a notarized document to the jail staff.

4. Communicate the mental illness at once to defense counsel. Send counsel a copy of the medical and psychiatric information form you sent to the jail. Send additional medical records as soon as possible. Inform counsel if your defendant has a mental illness restriction on his or her driver's license. This is clear evidence of diminished mental capacity. Counsel may recommend that an independent psychiatrist examine the inmate.

5. If the defendant has medical insurance, get the group number and policy number, the name of the insurance company, and the telephone and fax numbers. You will need these to pay for independent medical evaluation and treatment.

Contrary to what you see on TV, acquittals by reason of insanity are uncommon. Far more likely, but still quite advantageous, is diversion into treatment. "Diversion" means that your defendant is released from jail and placed in a treatment program. The judicial process is essentially put on hold. If your defendant completes treatment and other release conditions successfully, he or she will not be convicted of a crime and can truthfully swear to the same in writing on future job applications or under oath in future legal proceedings. This is extremely important.

If you're fortunate, your city will have specialized jail facilities for mentally ill inmates. In California, there are mental illness courts that facilitate treatment and diversion out of the criminal justice system. If you live with the defendant, or if you are a legal guardian, you stand a chance of having the defendant released into your custody, hopefully on recognizance and without bond. The important thing is to get mentally ill defendants out of jail ASAP.

They don't belong there.

☠ SUICIDE THREATS

If your inmate threatens suicide, immediately do the following:

1. Telephone the jail's watch commander and relay the suicide threat. All well-run jails have procedures for this problem.

2. Fax a medical and psychiatric information form to the jail if you have not done so. See appendix A (p. 236). Fax with it a letter requesting that the inmate be removed to suicide watch facilities and examined by a psychiatrist.

3. Send copies of the letter and form via certified mail, return receipt requested. Notify defense counsel by phone or fax. Send copies of the letter and form by regular mail.

Suicide watch facilities are grim. Inmates may be shackled and placed in leg irons. They may be housed in special cells without furniture or toilets other than a floor drain. They may be made to wear special uniforms with colors that identify them as suicide risks. They will have privileges curtailed. If they're fortunate, they will be transported to a locked psychiatric floor in the county hospital.

Expect your defendant to be angry, then resentful, then furious. When he or she is returned to the general population, expect abusive phone calls and insulting letters.

Inmates threaten suicide for two reasons. Either they're truly mentally ill or they want to manipulate you into posting bond. If the threat was made to force bond, this is beneath contempt. Cut off all communications, and money, until the defendant can pull it together and act like an adult. A few days in irons in the Wacko Hole will focus the mind and stimulate rational thought.

An American jail is no fun, but compared with the horror houses of Africa, the Middle East, Latin America, or Southeast Asia, an American jail is a fairy princess's palace. Never forget this.

When defendants start whining and complaining, and tricking and gaming, give them a dose of Momma's favorite medicine: tough love.

8

BUREAUCRATIC HEROIN AND BLACK HOLES
Commissaries and Jail Phones

THE GREAT THING ABOUT money is that it has universal purchasing power. It is, to use the technical term, "fungible"—your $20 bill is worth exactly as much as my $20 bill and can be used to buy the same things. But when money has to be spent according to a rigid budget, that universal power is destroyed—each dollar may be spent only for the specific use to which the budget allocates it. In government agencies, such as jails, the problem is acute. If the pen-and-pencil budget gets maxed out, administrators can't buy any more writing implements, even if other budget lines, like computers, are brimming with funds. In government it's insanely difficult to get money transferred from one budget line to another. Sometimes it takes legislative approval. At the very least, it requires memos, meetings, and obsequious requests to superiors—prefaced, preferably, with a few salaams and "Your Excellency's." Many law enforcement agencies are managed by outstanding civil servants, and budgeting makes them nuts.

In jails, however, certain sources of funds are not constrained by the budget. They instead produce bonanzas of *unallocated funds*. Administrators can, within reason, spend the money collected from these sources on anything they want—no memos, no meetings, no "But, sir's." To heck with the budget, just cut the check! Anything's possible—a new prisoner transport van, some high-def TVs for the employee lunchroom, perhaps some stereo computer speakers for long-suffering, music-deprived watch commanders. Why not one of those fancy, high-tech "butt scanners" that zap inmates' mouths, anuses, and vaginas with microwaves and detect metal objects? And what self-respecting jail wouldn't want a few .50-caliber hand cannons in case a rhinoceros gets loose in the cells?

In government, an unallocated dollar is worth 10 times its budgeted counterpart. Its value is like gold, but its effect on administrators is like heroin. I don't refer here to street stuff cut with baking soda and roach powder. I mean clear, sparkling, pharmaceutically pure junk mainlined to the cerebrum with a fire hose. That's how good it is. In jails, the bulk of this magical money comes from jail phones and commissary fees. To indulge their addiction, administrators set these fees high. They'll stay high forever.

JAIL PHONES

Outgoing calls made by inmates are always collect calls. They are billed at steep rates, similar to those of phone sex lines. If you have a landline telephone, the call begins with a recorded message that you are receiving a call from an inmate at your jail. Do you want to accept? If so, you press the designated button on your telephone and the conversation, and the billing, begin. On cell phones whose networks do not allow collect calls, the procedure is different. Typically the jail will contract with a third party that you pay in advance for jail phone time over the telephone or through a Web site. You buy so much time, and when it's done, that's it. No more calls until you buy more minutes.

The jail phone is a vital communications medium, especially in jails that limit visits. For families, the phone is how they get information on threats to the defendant, on health care problems, and on case progress. For inmates, the jail phone brings in the voices of loved ones and the sounds and concerns of the outside world, which are so alien to jail life.

The jail phone is also a black hole for money. It is not unusual for families to incur jail phone bills of hundreds of dollars a month. Unpaid jail phone bills can cause your credit scores to crash. This will make it difficult for you to get loans and can also trigger increases in interest rates on outstanding loans and credit card balances. Aimless chats on the jail phone burn up money better used elsewhere. Funding to assist defendants should go instead to legal fees and jail and probation costs, because these speed the transition to freedom.

Jail calls need to be managed. Inmates' immediate emotional needs are less important than their long-term freedom and socialization. You should advise other family members of the high costs so they can decide how to manage inmate calls. Once that's done, and you've told the defendant that calls must be made within limits, you should mail a list of telephone numbers and addresses of all other family members and friends who want to communicate by mail or telephone with the defendant. (Remember that everything the inmate had at the time of arrest was seized. So any address books, or cell phones with preprogrammed numbers, are locked away in the property room.)

Some inmates will ignore your instructions to limit phone calls. Many will call when you are not at home and talk for hours with children, friends, and relatives. This is a serious betrayal of your trust. If you see it occurring, cancel your landline telephone service *at once*. Use only a cell phone for future communication so you can place a strict dollar limit on jail calls. In fact, consider dropping support for defendants willing to ruin you financially just to get some feel-good time on the phone.

NOTE: *All jail phone calls are recorded.* Stop your inmate from discussing details of the case or confessing to other crimes. Recordings released to prosecutors can precipitate add-on charges and new indictments. In addition, keep in mind that jail phones are located in general population areas. If other inmates overhear confessions or discussions of cooperation with police, your defendant could get beaten, stomped, or shanked.

THE COMMISSARY

One of the things that relieves the tedium of incarceration is the commissary cart coming by the cells and delivering snacks, stationery and stamps, chess and checkers sets, and other necessities and frivolities. Some commissary operations are contracted to large national companies. Others are run by that leading corporate citizen, Generous Contributor, Inc., whose controlling shareholder is known for replenishing local campaign funds early and often and who can always be counted on to find a place on the payroll for otherwise unemployable nieces and nephews of elected officials.

Needless to say, quality varies. Prices never vary. They're high. Commissary goods are marked up to generate not only a profit for the contractor but also a generous contribution to the unallocated funds of the corrections and police departments. Complaints about commissary prices are futile. They are what they are.

Your job is to manage an inmate's use of the commissary and to be alert to requests for sharp increases in commissary payments, which could indicate that your defendant is gambling, buying on credit from a cell store, or being shaken down in a protection racket. Be aware that many jails charge inmates fees to help cover the cost of their incarceration—arrest fees, booking fees, and any other fees that jail administrators can get approved—and these will be deducted from any commissary payments you make. Check with jail staff for details; if all of your initial payment is applied to fees, your inmate won't be able to get snacks.

JAIL SCAMS

Jails are, by definition, full of crooks, with time on their hands and imaginations fired by boredom. They run all sorts of scams on one another and on citizens on the outside. These range from simple grifts like three-card monte to long cons that can take weeks to relieve the mark of funds. Don't be a bunny! Avoid the following scams.

Cell Phone Calls
Cell phones are banned from jails and prisons. If you get a cell phone call from jail, hang up at once. No good can come of this.

Three-Way Calls
Many jail phone systems have design flaws that allow three-way calls. Never participate in a three-way call unless it is organized by defense attorneys using their phone system. Three-ways are used by criminal confederates on the outside for no good purpose.

*72 Scams

There is a nationwide plague of scams that derive from a design flaw in some jail phone systems that allows call forwarding to be enabled. Scammers call other inmates' loved ones and purport to be corrections officers. They declare that your inmate has been injured! To be transferred to the jail health service, they tell you, just dial the following numbers. . . . The numbers inevitably include *72 or the numbers 1172. Once you dial these call-forwarding codes, the scammers can make unlimited long-distance calls, all of which will be billed to you, perhaps at ruinous jail phone rates!

Disable *72 call forwarding for the duration. Scammers often will call your home until they can speak to children, who can be more easily conned. Often they will pretend to be phone company representatives and will ask children to push buttons as part of a "line integrity test."

Getting the charges from a jail phone scam cancelled by the telephone company is difficult, time consuming, infuriating, and sometimes impossible. Will your city government refund money to you? No! An enormous phone bill can result in telephone service being cut off and a negative credit bureau report that tanks your credit score.

Mystery Callers

You may get calls from strangers who purport to be friends of your defendant. Remember, anyone can get an inmate's name and charge sheet on the Internet in order to learn details of the case. They may ask you to send money to outside bank accounts or payment services, or log on to Web sites, or give them your e-mail address, or call a 900 number, or arrange meetings with strangers. All of these are ways to tap your cash.

Internet Rip-Offs

Bad guys can load key loggers and root kits onto your computer through Web sites and e-mails. These will transmit your account numbers and personal identification information so crooks can assume your identity and squeeze you dry. When you're on the Internet, log on to service vendors, such as jail phone services and inmate payment services like JPay, *only* from the jail's own Web site. Lookalike sites are phonies that will tap your cash. Never click on a link that appears in an e-mail. Always go directly to the service and enter the site by using your user ID and password.

If the defendant lived with you prior to arrest, or was familiar with the way you use the Internet, change all passwords *at once*. Make careful notes so you do not forget the new codes and get locked out of important Web sites and services. Use high security passwords. In general this means a password that has six or more characters, some of which are numbers and at least one of which is a symbol. The password should also have both capital and lowercase letters. To reduce confusion, use the same high security password for all your accounts. Direct your computer not to "remember" passwords after they're entered.

Run your antivirus and spyware removal programs frequently. Activate a firewall to keep bad guys from learning your computer's serial number and IP address. Better yet, get an Apple Macintosh computer. They are, so far, immune from most viruses and spyware, although they do need firewalls. If you keep passwords, account numbers, social security numbers, and dates of birth in a computer document, encrypt the file. I use encryption even the Pentagon can't crack. The program cost me less than twenty dollars. (Always buy encryption and antivirus software *in stores* from reputable companies. The programs you download from obscure Web sites are often written by hackers, mostly Russian, working for bad-boy Internet companies in Mauritius, Nevis, and Cyprus. The "security" programs they sell are jam-packed with viruses and spyware.)

Credit Card Security Problems

If your inmate is an authorized user of *your* credit card, have his or her name removed *at once* from the account. Call the credit card company and request a "security closure" of your account. The bank will then issue you a new card on which the account number, expiration date, and security code on the signature strip have been changed. Even when inmates are honest, they can be beaten or pressured to draw money from, and make charges to, your credit card. They can even have a balance transfer check for the available credit line sent to an outside address. As long as inmates are authorized users, this is legal and you have no—repeat, no—recourse. Don't think you're safe because banks are unlikely to accept jail calls. Scammers will send account numbers, names, and passwords to outside confederates who can siphon off the money through untraceable "burner" phones.

When you make Internet credit card payments to jail telephone services or third-party jail payment services such as JPay, always use a "virtual account number." This is a one-time-use number created by the bank's computers that will charge your account only up to the maximum amount you specify (see chapter 22, p. 184, for more details). This will protect you from automatic monthly charges that are hard to stop. It will also prevent fraud by inmates and their criminal confederates who might extract your personal identification number and customary passwords from the defendant. Another option is to use only prepaid debit cards from Wal-Mart.

Bank Account Security Holes

If your defendant knows your bank account number, have it changed at once. Get new checks. Don't forget to change out the debit card. Never hand over a voided check, for "account set-up purposes," to someone *outside the jail* who purports to be a jail official. Most jails don't accept personal checks anyway. Bad guys can clean out your account if they know your account number, bank routing number, and personal identification information.

The Verification Grift

You may receive a phone call and hear a chirpy customer-service voice saying something like this:

"Hi! I'm Clarisse from JPay. I see you're interested in making payments to your inmate's account. I'm calling today to verify the information you gave us to make sure it's correct. Could you give me the full, 16-digit account number of your credit card?

"And the expiration date?

"And the three-digit security code on the end of the signature strip?"

A variation would go like this:

"Hello. I'm John from the pretrial detention facility. I see that you have a relative in jail with us and will probably want to visit him. As you know, we require identification for you to enter the jail visitation area. Could you verify your social security number for me?

"And your date of birth?"

Whenever you receive verification calls, or calls alleging fraud, or calls with alarming news about your inmate, hang up and call the jail watch commander. Remember, you are not an inmate. Jail personnel have no need for your personal identification information and account numbers.

The Pigeon Drop

This is a classic scam that has innumerable variations. All involve calls or visits by people claiming to be law enforcement officers who ask for your help in catching some evildoer. The assistance requested always involves handing over your money or a credit card to trap the bad guy. It doesn't seem to occur to people that law enforcement agencies have *their own cash* to use for investigations. Here's how these scams go:

"Hello. This is John Smith, Special Agent in charge of the Public Corruption Unit (PCU) of the FBI. I understand you have a relative incarcerated in the local jail. Is that correct?

"The FBI believes that one of the corrections officers is stealing inmate commissary funds. There's nothing worse than a law enforcement officer who's a crook. We've been surveilling this guy for weeks, and we'd certainly appreciate your cooperation in catching him.

"I want you to get $1,000 in cash and bring it down to the jail. Outside the front door you'll meet an undercover FBI agent. She'll be reading a newspaper. Go up to her and ask for her badge number. She'll answer, '12653.' That's the code word. She'll take the money. She'll give you in return a U.S. Treasury check in reimbursement of the $1,000 because we have to keep the actual currency as evidence.

"Of course, you will receive a personal thank-you letter from the director that will have the FBI shield stamped in brilliant gold foil and will be suitable for framing."

Naturally that "treasury check" will bounce. You're the pigeon, and you've just dropped your money.

Corrections Officer Scams

If a corrections officer asks to meet you outside the jail, refuse. No officer has any business reason to do so. COs engage in two types of scams. The most common is to bring in clothes, food, tobacco, and drugs to inmates in exchange for lots of money. In the second, the CO will tell you he has a computer password that allows him to gain access to prosecutor files and court case records. He tells you he can create documents that will drop charges and allow your defendant to be released. With so many cases pending, who will ever know!

These are serious crimes. When caught, the CO will rat out your defendant, who will probably face new charges. If you agree to any of this foolishness, a prosecutor, if sufficiently annoyed, may order you arrested as an accomplice.

Avoid getting conned. You can end most of these games by simply saying, when asked to do something shady, "Let me talk to the watch commander and see if that's OK." That usually ends the discussion.

BLACK HOLES

The criminal justice system can be a black hole for your money, especially if you fall victim to scams or do not budget and control costs. Remember, wheels turn slowly in criminal justice. You almost never have to pay for anything *right this minute*. Things can wait until you have time to ask questions, check things out, and proceed with caution. Do not allow your defendant, and especially strangers, to stampede you into making unconsidered payments. Keep updating the Budget Stick 'Em Up from chapter 22 as new information becomes available on the total long-term costs of criminal defense and assistance. Don't allow your defendant to lay a guilt trip on you when you have to say no.

Proceeding calmly, purposefully, and slowly is the *quickest* way to assist your defendant to eventual freedom.

☠ SO YOU WANT TO SCAM THE MAN?

Wouldn't it be fun to pay jail and commissary fees with forged or no-good checks or stolen credit cards? Some fake ID, you think, will cover your tracks. Why not? The Man has jailed your loved one and cost you money, time, and humiliation. This is payback! Just imagine how annoyed some city employee will be when that check bounces and that fake ID you made with your computer leads nowhere! Ha, ha, ha!

Wrong! Those humble jail clerks and those overburdened or bored corrections officers work for the po-leece. Cops are not unaware of check kiting, check forging, unauthorized use of credit cards, cloning and counterfeiting of credit cards, identity theft, stolen IDs, counterfeit IDs . . . have I left anything out here? Not only do cops know about these things, but they also take training classes to stay current with the latest scams. Many enjoy busting bad check artists and credit card thieves, who are smarter than the average crook, tell amusing and complex lies, and give cops a break from busting corner boys, prostitutes, and drunks, which can be boring.

Jails have a few tricks of their own. Most do not accept credit cards. Why pay the discount, tolerate the disputes, and eat charge-backs from banks? They don't have to accept them, because government agencies, like the jail and police department, are monopolies. They don't have competing lockups across town advertising lower prices, softer beds, two-for-one sales at the commissary, and 12 months credit same as cash.

Many jails hold checks before crediting payments to inmate accounts. My jail, for example, holds checks, including cashiers' checks and money orders, two entire weeks. That's long enough for a check to clear by carrier pigeon from Madagascar. Families who pay by check will, as a special bonus, get treated to two weeks of inmate whining about no chips, no stamps, no cinnamon toothpaste, and no cards.

When you hand over a rubber check, the clerks might attempt an instantaneous electronic clearance. Hmm! When you slide over that phony driver's license, they might log on to the state department of motor vehicles database to verify the license and the photo. Heck, they might even ask you to pop your mitts down on an optical fingerprint scanner. This gizmo will flash a warning that you—*gasp*—aren't you!

Corrections officers can push a button and lock down the building. If you run, or get crazy, they can push another button and summon the Blue Horde. When it's over, you'll be facing a long list of charges and will look like you passed through a wood chipper. So don't take a stupid pill.

Pay The Man. Use cash. Don't forget to smile!

⑨

HOW CHANCROID SAVES A TWINK
Sex in Jail

RAPE IS LESS COMMON in jails than in prisons. Jailed inmates are always moving on to freedom or prison. While in the custody of well-run jails, they are moved from area to area, floor to floor, to break up conspiracies and cliques and to protect threatened inmates. Jails use classification systems to prevent young and first-time offenders from being housed with violent repeat felons. The system, however, is not perfect. Jails are filled with sexually deprived young men and women, and in jails, unlike some prisons, there are no conjugal visits. Here's how you and your defendant should confront the risks.

RAPES, BEATINGS, AND KILLINGS

If your defendant is threatened, he or she should immediately ask to be moved to another area of the jail. You should contact the jail administration and make the same request. Back it up with a letter sent certified mail, return receipt requested.

The objective when threatened with rape is first to avoid being beaten or killed. Violent offenders sometimes will kill their victims so they cannot testify to rape. This is called, in prison slang, a hump and dump. The secondary goal is to avoid being infected by the assailant's semen, blood, or pus, which carry blood-borne viral and bacterial infections, such as AIDS, hepatitis, gonorrhea, and syphilis.

Once the assault starts, if your inmate cannot fight free, he or she should bargain with the rapist—in other words, give it up, conditionally. First, he or she should offer to masturbate the assailant. A hand job may prevent anal or vaginal penetration and lessen the risk of disease. Your defendant should try to keep the assailant's semen or vaginal discharges away from sores on the hands and the arms, which would facilitate infection.

If pressure continues, your defendant should tell a useful lie and claim to be infected with a serous disease. **Important:** your inmate *should not* claim to have AIDS. This disease, which now can be managed with oral medications, no longer frightens inmates. In any case, assailants will know such a claim is a lie if your inmate is not receiving daily doses of AIDS meds. Instead, your inmate should claim to have a disease that no one in jail has ever heard of. I suggest chancroid. This is an actual bacterial disease that causes chancres and pustules to form on the genitals. Your defendant should also claim to need a "monthly shot" to control it. This is not how the disease is treated, but who's going to know? Your inmate must have a way of explaining not receiving daily pills. The threat should go like this:

"Man, you don't want to do this. I got chancroid."

"What?"

"Chancroid, man. It makes your dick fall off."

"You're lying! You don't get no pills."

"I gotta have a monthly shot."

"Huh?"

"Tell you what, I'll get you off with a hand job. Feel better fast. What do you say?"

Yes, this is disgusting, but it's better than being beaten, raped, and killed. Things move slowly even in the best-managed jails. Your defendant may need this emergency strategy until he's moved.

Women in jail can be threatened into sex by corrections officers or by other inmates. If they're being threatened with a beating, or with being penetrated with bottles or sticks, they should bargain for a hand job also. They should use a variation of the lie but say that chancroid "makes your cunt or dick rot off."

Women being threatened by lesbian inmates should consider other options. If the assailants want forced cunnilingus or tribadism (rubbing the vulva against a partner), your defendant should consider giving in to avoid a beating. These lesbian practices are less likely than vaginal penetration to exchange blood and cause disease.

If your defendant gets raped, don't expect corrections officers to be shocked. If your defendant is crying, they might offer a tissue—that's it. The prosecutor may pile some extra charges on the assailant, but most of these inmates are facing a long stretch of hard time anyway. Unless the assailant happens to be a millionaire, your chance of collecting civil damages is nil. Suing the city won't go far either, unless your inmate was killed and the jail can be shown to have been grossly negligent. Gross negligence is tough to prove, especially against government. Nonetheless, you should notify defense counsel at once of threats or rapes. Counsel may be able to obtain an emergency order moving or freeing the inmate. Judges can make jail administrators jump like no one else.

Twinks, Sissies, Cheesy Whores, and Strawberries

One of the worst outcomes short of death is when defendants become "twinks," or "sissies," who are sexual slaves of a "protector." The other horror is defendants who lose all sense of dignity and prostitute themselves for drugs, cigarettes, and food. "Cheesy whores" are inmates who have bacterial infections that cause white or orange anal discharges with the consistency of cottage cheese. "Strawberries" have red, inflamed buttocks from anal gonorrhea. If you notice these symptoms in your inmate, or see oral discharges or difficulty speaking due to gonorrhea of the mouth and throat, alert defense counsel. Ask for a motion to grant compassionate release. The psychological damage caused by the collapse of self is worse than prison. It will take years of medical treatment and counseling to heal inmates who have fallen to such depths.

Rape by Corrections Officers

If rape threats come from corrections officers, the situation is dire. Notify defense counsel. If your local prosecutors are tough, they may agree to set up a sting to bust the officer. Don't get your hopes up. Try to get the inmate freed first.

One of the moral tragedies of the American penal system is how little punishment crooked corrections officers receive. This is due to several reasons. First, being a correctional officer is such a miserable job that it is extraordinarily difficult to attract, train, and retain officers. Bad apples tend to get fired rather than prosecuted in order not to demoralize other officers. Second, most corrections officers are members of unions, which can afford tough-as-nails defense attorneys who can and will drag prosecutors through trial hell. Third, corrections officers work for big bureaucracies that know how to protect themselves and limit financial, legal, and political damages. Lastly, it's difficult to find safe prisons for convicted corrections officers and cops. When incarcerated, they're at constant risk of being killed.

It's still a tragedy. Crooked cops and corrections officers deserve a special place in hell.

DEALING WITH THE DAMAGE

If raped or beaten, your inmate will need counseling and psychological care. Remember, however, that raped defendants have another, more immediate problem. They're still in jail! Most of them still face hard time in state prison. Keep yourself and your defendant working on legal defense and freedom. It's much easier to be healed psychologically when you're living on the outside with family than when you're locked in cages with crooks.

Protect Your Defendant and Yourself

If your jail allows it, you may be able to get condoms to your defendant. This is stopgap protection until your defendant can be moved. If you are the spouse or lover of the defendant, take precautions to protect yourself. When your defendant is freed on bail or released upon completion of sentence, insist that he or she be tested for sexually transmitted diseases before you have sex.

WHAT IF YOUR DEFENDANT LIKES JAIL SEX?

This happens. Some inmates get twisted about it; some don't. I have a friend who did a year in the local jail farm for drug possession. She had sex with women in jail, and since

SEXUALLY TRANSMITTED DISEASES, Page 1

Have defendants checked for all these diseases upon release from jail or prison, regardless of whether they tell you they engaged in sex. Many can be transmitted without sexual contact. Avoid squeamishness and shame. These are diseases, not moral curses or divine punishments. Most can be cured, treated, or prevented. If you are the spouse or lover of a defendant, avoid sex until both you and the defendant have been checked. Consult your physician about having yourself and the defendant vaccinated for hepatitis A and B. If you are a female virgin, consult your gynecologist about vaccination against human papillomavirus. Take these pages with you for reference during doctor visits.

BACTERIAL

Chancroid (*Haemophilus ducreyi*). Causes genital sores and chancres. Treated with antibiotics.

Chlamydia (*Chlamydia trachomatis*). Causes inflammation of genitals and, in women, the cervix, with white discharge. Treated with antibiotics.

Donovanosis (*Granuloma inguinale* or *Calymmatobacterium granulomatis*). Causes clear, painless ulcers on the genitals. Often mistaken for syphillis. Treated with antibiotics.

Gonorrhea, a.k.a. the clap (*Neisseria gonorrhoeae*). Causes discharges of blood and pus from genitals; swelling and inflammation of testicles, prostate, and rectum; and extreme, fiery pain during urination. Treated with antibiotics.

Nongonococcal urethritis (*Ureaplasma urealyticum* or *Mycoplasma hominis*). Same symptoms as the clap but easier to treat. Responds to antibiotics.

Staphylococcal infection (*Staphylococcus aureus*). This can cause infections in any part of the body. In its worst drug-resistant form, methicillin-resistant *Staphylococcus aureus* (MRSA), this disease can eat flesh from the bones and cause horrific internal tumors. Treated with oral and intravenous antibiotics.

Syphilis (*Treponema pallidum*). Until AIDS, this was the most feared venereal disease. Characterized by clear pustules and chancres on the genitals, red lesions of the skin, and ulcers. In secondary and tertiary stages, causes tumors, raised papules, and gross malformations of the face, hands, and limbs. In the central nervous system, it causes extensive neurological damage ending in insanity. Treated with oral and intravenous penicillin.

FUNGAL

Jock itch (*Trichophyton rubrum*). This fungus causes athlete's foot when it infects the feet, and ringworm when it infects other portions of the skin. Treated with topical antifungal drugs.

Yeast infection (*Candida albicans* and other fungi). Produces itching and inflammation of the vagina, anus, and thighs. In men, early stages have few detectable symptoms. In advanced stages, causes the white, gooey coating of mouth and genital mucosa known as thrush. Treated with antifungal drugs.

VIRAL

Cytomegalovirus (CMV, herpes 5). Spread by most bodily fluids, including saliva. Causes a form of mononucleosis, with lethargy, fever, and swelling of the throat and pharynx, and symptoms resembling those of hepatitis. Antiviral drugs are used for severe cases.

Herpes (*Herpes simplex*). Produces clear pustules on the genitals, mouth, and other mucosa. There is no cure, although some antiviral drugs reduce viral shedding and the risk of transmission.

Human immunodeficiency virus (HIV). Causes AIDS by destroying the immune system. Starts with fever, followed by weight loss and numerous symptoms of secondary infections by other viruses, bacteria, and fungi. There is no cure, but it can be treated with a combination of antiviral drugs.

Human papillomavirus (HPV viruses). Causes genital warts and cervical cancer. No cure. A vaccine can prevent the most common varieties of the virus. To be effective, it must be given in youth before the virus is contracted. Approved for young women in the United States and for young women and young men in the United Kingdom. May soon be approved for young men in the United States.

MCV (*Molluscum contagiosum*). Causes pearly, pink, domed-shaped genital lesions that spread to the skin. Patients usually self-cure within two years. Excessive and painful lesions can be surgically excised or removed by lasers or liquid nitrogen.

Viral hepatitis. Various related viruses that cause symptoms such as fever, vomiting, nausea, jaundice, blood in urine, and liver cancer.

PARASITICAL

Pubic lice, a.k.a. crabs (*Phthirius pubis*). These pinhead-sized insects can spread from the pubis to other parts of the skin, hair, and eyes. They cause itching and burning. Treated with insecticidal creams and shampoos.

Scabies (*Sarcoptes scabiei*). These microscopic insects burrow into the skin and cause painful itching. Treated with insecticidal creams.

PROTOZOAL

Trichomoniasis (*Trichomonas vaginalis*). Causes itching and burning of the vagina and male and female urethra, and a greenish yellow discharge. Appears in women and uncircumcised men. Treated with oral doses of metronidazole.

being released, she continues to have sex with both men and women. She thinks it's fun. Other inmates will get out and obsess: "Omigod, I'm gay!" Maybe they are; maybe they aren't. Sexual preference is not binary. Almost no one is 100 percent straight or gay. Sexual preference is a continuum, and a large percentage of the population have occasional sexual encounters with the same sex even if they are primarily heterosexual.

Sexual preference is also situational. Homosexual and lesbian sex is common throughout history in situations where men and women are isolated from the opposite sex, as, for example, in jails and in harems. In centuries past, many pirate crews were homosexual on the high seas and heterosexual in port. Were pirates gay, or was the situation more along the lines of "Help out a shipmate, here, will you?"

Do not go nuts or abandon defendants because they get off on jail sex. Concentrate on defense and freedom. Inmates' transformation into citizens who can live in freedom is *more important* than their sexual preference. Citizens can be gay, straight, or in between.

10
AS THE WORM TURNS
Drug Addiction

TWENTY-FOUR PERCENT OF jail and prison inmates are arrested for drug crimes; 70 percent have controlled substances in their bodies at the time of arrest.* Drugs are the problem, and they make all other problems worse. One of your biggest decisions is whether your defendant can live without them. If your defendant is granted probation instead of prison time, will he or she be able to live without going near drugs, without druggy friends, and without going to parties and getting into cars where the stuff is in the air?

These are crucial questions. They test whether your defendant merits financial help. If your loved one, while locked up in jail, cannot understand that drugs and freedom are incompatible, he or she suffers from a severe case of knucklehead-itis. How you confront drug problems depends on how your defendant uses drugs.

NONADDICTS

People are not addicts if they can stop using illegal substances without becoming ill with withdrawal symptoms. Stopping casual and recreational use has immediate and beneficial legal consequences. It takes the heat off.

During my misguided youth, I used drugs for two years and had several scary encounters with FBI agents and campus police. Even in those mad times, I had enough sense not to carry dope with me or in a vehicle, so I survived, unarrested and unjailed, to become a modestly productive citizen. Once I quit, and stopped hanging around dopers, the results were immediate. No more cops. For decades I never again encountered a police officer except for traffic tickets.

To complete probation or parole, however, it's not enough for defendants to get off street drugs like heroin, X, cocaine, and amphetamines. They have to avoid switching to other controlled substances, especially to Schedule II and III narcotics for which they do not have prescriptions. That means they can't pop little brother's Ritalin or gobble Momma's sleeping pills. Those will light up a urine test as fast as street drugs and violate the probationer right back into the joint.

---

* Doris James Wilson, *Drug Use, Testing, and Treatment in Jails*, U.S. Department of Justice, Bureau of Justice Statistics, May 2000, www.ojp.usdoj.gov/bjs/pub/pdf/duttj.pdf.

Do not engage defendants in arguments that certain drugs are not as bad as others, that certain drugs are legal in the Netherlands, or in Mali, or on the moon. Insist to defendants that what matters is that drugs are illegal, right here, right now, and if defendants continue to use them, they will be back in jail or prison in short order. Defendants have no slack in these matters. During incarceration, probation, and parole, they will be tested frequently. The only level of drug use that will preserve their freedom is none whatsoever.

This does not mean that defendants have to live in utter austerity. Most people require chemical assistance during their passage from the cradle to the grave. Have a frank discussion on this subject with defendants. Suggest that, like most Americans, they have a drink when they need to relax. Squelch arguments that alcohol is a drug, and can be addictive, so why not marijuana, cocaine, etc. Keep things blunt and easy to understand: as long as defendants do not drive while intoxicated, or violate public peace, alcohol is legal; drugs are not. With alcohol, in moderation, they relax and stay free. With illegal drugs, they relax themselves right back into prison.

If defendants are smokers, do not lecture them about tobacco and its ills. During probation or parole, and the hard process of becoming a citizen, they're going to need a smoke. The goal for defendants is not to live tobacco- and alcohol-free, or with a low carbon footprint, or to experience the virtues of organic vegetables, hyperbaric oxygen, and whole wheat. The goal is for them to be able to live in freedom in 21st-century United States under close scrutiny for years on end by government employees. This is a difficult proposition.

Cannabis Users

Those who partake of marijuana (or its rich, frat-boy derivatives hashish and kief) may be classified as nonaddicts by default, since marijuana is not addictive. Discontinuing use will not initiate withdrawal symptoms. Nonetheless, this is the favorite drug of the criminal justice system because its universal use makes possible millions of arrests and guarantees full employment for lawyers, judges, cops, corrections officers, and administrative staff. Cops in particular love weed because stoners insist on carrying it around in their vehicles and its stench makes detection easy.* Even better, marijuana users don't resist arrest. By contrast, drunks often fight. As for meth heads, they're so wired that TASERs affect them about as much as mosquito bites. Those freaks can take a magnum round through the left ventricle and still keep coming long enough to kill a cop. But stoners are limp and compliant when arrested. Sometimes they don't even *know* they're arrested. They think they're in a cab!

---

* Sublimated molecules of marijuana can penetrate glass, wax, and plastic. It's nearly impossible to block the odor. K-9s detect it instantly. After one scratch or woof, it's jail time!

My beef with marijuana is moral and medical. One of the effects of tetrahydrocannabinol is to extinguish ambition, drive, and focus. No one knows how long this effect lasts. I've often wondered whether use of the drug in my youth is in part responsible for the aimlessness of my adult life. Marijuana is also many times more carcinogenic than cigarettes. That's the reason that spliff tokers like Bob Marley die young of brain tumors. Big dopers usually survive lung cancers, if they survive, by having lobes of their lungs cut out. They have to whisper their way through life.

Marijuana-positive drug tests are the leading cause of probation and parole violations. Defendants on probation need to understand that they cannot even be in the same vehicle, or building, as dope smokers. One whiff and they're toast. Attorneys have been known to argue that violations were caused by "second-hand dope." Judges get a laugh out of that as they sign an order that remands yet another dopey defendant to the joint.

ADDICTS

The above advice is for defendants who can stop using drugs. The real problems are for those who cannot. Families need to understand addiction. If you're a former addict, you know. If not, this is how it is: For addicts, drugs are not merely a craving, they are all there is in life—period. Imagine having a huge worm inside you, extending from your eyeballs to your toes. If you don't feed this worm its drug of choice, it starts to turn, then to twist, until your whole being is one intolerable itch. The only thing you can think about is getting drugs right now, no matter what the cost. *Nothing else matters.* Family are ignored, friends are abandoned, work is missed, bills go unpaid, laws get broken. Everything is sacrificed until the worm is fed.

Most addicts are in wretched health. Cocaine snorters drip snot and have collapsed noses. Heroin shooters are covered with sores and have inflamed, infected veins. Crackheads don't eat and become "skels," with bulging eyes and droopy skin. X users destroy so many brain cells with each dose that they become retards within months. Glue and gasoline huffers melt their livers and scramble their brains so they puke bile while they babble. As for methamphetamine, currently the worst drug of abuse in the world, within months it will age a person by decades. Meth heads have skin that swells with dripping abscesses. Their hair and teeth fall out. They don't eat. Meth's addictive power is astounding. Mothers will sell their babies for a $5 hit of tweak.*

Drug addicts steal, cheat, and lie. Don't bother to ask them, "Will you please, pretty please, with sugar on top, cease being a junkie if I pay the attorney fees and the bail

---

* I recently walked into a supermarket moments after a meth head attacked a 74-year-old man at the cash register to steal his change. The old guy stabbed the kid in the face with his pocket knife and popped out an eyeball, which I skidded over on the way to the dairy aisle. Florida being what it is, the kid got busted, and the old man got a handshake and some attaboys from the cops. Me? I got nasty sneakers and sour milk.

bond?" All you get for that is "Yeah, yeah" and "Sure, sure." *Never, under any circumstances, post bail for drug addicts.* You'll be lucky to get one kiss on the cheek before they scamper off to score.

Getting clean has two stages. Physical withdrawal takes 3 to 10 days. At the end of physical withdrawal, addicts will no longer be ill without drugs. Contrary to common belief, which is stoked by endless movies and TV shows (beginning with Frank Sinatra's stunning performance in the 1955 film *The Man with the Golden Arm*), going cold turkey is not as horrible as commonly thought. Most drug addicts go cold turkey repeatedly, usually when they run out of money. That's why treatments that use substitute drugs, like methadone or tranquilizers, generally fail.

Moral development is more important than physical withdrawal. Getting clean requires hitting absolute rock bottom. It requires a profound disgust at what one has become. Addicts, like vampires, hate mirrors because they show the wretched reality that is masked by the illusions and thrills of drugs.

Never deny to your defendant that drugs are thrilling. They are, and that's the problem. On amphetamines or LSD, you feel as if your brain is atop a rocket headed for space. You fly higher and higher, bigger than life. You think you understand everything. Your brain is ablaze with endorphins.* Such pleasure . . . such clarity! Up ahead, just out of reach, is something profound. Is it an equation that unifies all physical forces? Is it the secret and all-powerful name of God? If only you could get one more hit. If only you had another $10. If only you had a vein. If only . . . The mirror reveals these Lords of Creation to be jittery, oozing skeletons, babbling nonsense.

Heroin and related opioids are different. They bathe each cell in softness and pleasure. The world vanishes as the brain falls airlessly into dreams and brilliantly colored visions. The clumsiest touch feels like the caress of some dreamed-of, endlessly desired demon lover. On heroin, having sex with a crocodile would be fun.

Fortunately, well-run jails make it difficult for inmates to get drugs. This provides a unique opportunity. Most addicts have multiple addictions. They smoke, gulp gallons of coffee, and take uppers and downers to counteract the side effects of their primary drug. In the joint, they're suddenly off *everything*, including coffee and cigarettes. (These days, most jails and prisons are smoke free, officially anyway.) Suddenly, they're having the Mother of all Withdrawals. Their heads explode from caffeine headaches. They twist and twitch. They tremble from nicotine willies. Sweat pours. Taking food is impossible because they're blowing their guts into the floor drain. Sleep? It's not even a memory.

This is when your jail calls will get crazy. It's when the screaming starts and when the suicide threats get made. Families need to toughen up while addicts tough it out. To kill the worm once and for all, addicts need to spend some nights with their teeth chattering

---

* Endorphins are natural brain chemicals that cause pleasure. Narcotics produce an endorphin rush.

in their heads and their feet drumming on the concrete. Perhaps, when it's over, while they're lying on the floor with their jumpsuits gritty with sweat salt, they'll do some very private thinking. Perhaps they'll decide, once and for all, to shove that addiction devil deep down in the hole. That's when you can help.

Not before.

DRUG TESTS AND DRUG BUSTS

Defendants who are not ready to give up illegal drugs obsess about drug tests. They talk about them, read about them, and research them for hours on the Internet. They know story after story about somebody who beat a test. They will recite arcane legal arguments, for example, a case in which the positive result of a random drug test was suppressed in court because drawing numbers out of a hat could not be shown to be mathematically random beyond a reasonable doubt. Most defendants, however, cannot afford constitutional challenges to drug laws, and in any case, the tests themselves are becoming more accurate and more sensitive each year. Training for lab technicians and law enforcement personnel also has improved, so that positive drug tests are tougher to beat than ever. Most strategies to beat drug tests are easily defeated by randomizing the test dates and, on occasion, using skin-patch and hair tests that detect drugs for up to three months after use. For details, see www.wesdenham.net for Laboratory Corporation of America drug test sensitivity information.

For the family, the issue is simple. The goal for the defendant is to live in freedom, which means, in practice, to live drug free—period. Defendants will argue with you ad nauseam about how *unfair* it is that so many people on the outside can use drugs recreationally without getting busted. Say this to stop that whining:

1. Citizens do not have to pee into government-supervised cups for years on end. Defendants do.

2. Citizens do not have the words "Narcotics Arrest" appear on police laptops during traffic or street stops. Defendants do. This means that for the rest of their lives, they can expect to have their vehicles and persons searched for drugs whenever they encounter police officers. Their rap sheets follow them everywhere.

To live in freedom, defendants have to give up not only drugs but also druggy-thuggy buddies, dope smoke–filled clubs, and wild doper parties. Most crucially, they cannot ride in vehicles with dope users. The reason is that during police searches, everyone routinely denies owning seized drugs: "Uh-uh, officer. That's not my stuff. I don't know nothing!"

Most state legislatures write the laws so that, legally speaking, seized drugs, guns, or stolen merchandise are considered to be the property of *everyone in the vehicle.* Cops love to stop cars full of young guys. There's almost always some dope to be found and some dumb probationer or dumber parolee to take the rap and get violated back into the pen.

Getting arrested changes everything. Defendants cannot live as they did prior to arrest and not expect to spend years in prisons.

11
DOES THE ELEVATOR GO UP TO THE TOP, OR NOT?
Homo Chaoticus, Unsocialized Man

Do I really look like a guy with a plan? . . . I just *do* things!
—The Joker, *The Dark Knight*

IN THE CHAPTERS THAT follow, you will finally make the crucial determination—whether to offer a defendant your financial support. This choice depends in part on whether you'd just be wasting your money, or whether the defendant can get socialized enough to stay out of jail and away from a life of crime. (Moral perfection, of course, is not necessary.) To help you assess your loved one's chances, this chapter will first explain the *unsocialized* behavior common to the majority of jail and prison inmates. Then, at the end of the chapter, I'll discuss why you, the defendant's family, are essential to the socialization process that alone can spare an inmate a lifetime of intermittent imprisonment.

Please note that the traits discussed in this chapter are *not* applicable to misdemeanor defendants who are law abiding most of the time but who slip up now and then, to inmates who are mentally ill, or to professional criminals who make a cool, calculated decision to pursue criminal enterprise because they like the life, the excitement, and the high profit margins.

I'm convinced, after spending so much time in jails interviewing defendants, that most inmates are profoundly different from middle-class people,* more so than sociologists—and even cops and judges—realize. The difference consists not of mental traits that are there but of some that are not. Unsocialized people lack morals, ethics, and personal objectives. They're missing the mental apparatus for checking contemplated actions and decisions against longer-term goals and values. They experience reality as an eternal present, with no ability to contemplate the future. All this is aggravated by

---

* My definition of "middle-class" is based on values, not income. It refers to people who work for a living in legal enterprise or, if they are blessed with independent means, still do useful things. It assumes values like respect for work, religious faith, a belief in education, civility and good manners, and the primacy of the family. It excludes able-bodied slackers, regardless of whether their subsistence comes from crime, a million-dollar trust fund, or a monthly check from Uncle Sugar. It excludes crooks, drunks, addicts, and those who are cruel or deceitful, regardless of tax bracket.

an obliviousness to social pecking orders and an inability to change behaviors to fit circumstances. This different mental arrangement produces *Homo chaoticus*, or unsocialized man.

ATEMPORALITY AND THE ETERNAL PRESENT

The ability to change presupposes the mental ability to project into the future and imagine oneself *as changed*—thinner, richer, happier, more successful, more God-fearing, more in love, etc. Socialized people set goals and objectives in the present to ensure a better future.

Unsocialized people, on the other hand, live only in the present. They have no goals. They mostly act on impulse. If they feel like it, they do it. So, if they're hungry, they eat. If they're sleepy, they sleep. If they're horny, they grab the nearest woman. If they're broke, they scrounge for money. For *Homo chaoticus*, life is not willed—it just happens.

Strangely, this life is never dull. The electricity and water are always being cut off, or there's a repo truck backing up to the car. There's always a party, a fight, a woman, a scam. Living minute to minute, through nonstop calamities, unsocialized people become the embattled heroes of their own mini-dramas.

Such people, of course, never think about the consequences of their actions. For them, there never can be a "What if?" There's only what *is*, forever different, forever new. As they say in the vernacular, "Shit happens, man!" That is the point precisely. For *Homo chaoticus*, life isn't lived; it just occurs. Chaotic people rarely wear watches—there's no need. They mostly work casual jobs or not at all, and there's always someone else, like Mom, or Grandma, or a girlfriend, or a probation officer, or a defense attorney's paralegal, to wake them up when needed.

This can be tough even for professional criminals. One of the most difficult challenges for middle managers in the drug trade is how to get corner boys to show up *on time*, day after day, to sling rock, weed, and crystal. The kids don't have alarm clocks, and they move from place to place. Often dealers have to troll the neighborhoods in the SUV and round up the chaotic little twerps. Even worse, they have to make these kids, who are hazy on arithmetic, keep accurate counts of the merchandise and make change, without stealing the cash or the dope. Now and then they have to shoot one.

This carefree attitude about time makes police and the FBI nuts when they schedule a bust. When detectives hear that a major deal is going down *at a specific time*, they have to requisition vehicles, get approval for overtime, then load up and roll to the stakeout. Too often, nobody shows up. It's not that the bad guys get wind of the takedown. Most of the time, they're just partying, or sleeping, or getting laid, or watching TV. Their customers always want drugs, so if they don't do a deal today, they can do one tomorrow—if something else doesn't come up.

One of the rotten little secrets of the drug trade is that for most of its foot soldiers, the pay is lousy. They could do better flipping burgers. Drug mules, cash couriers, and corner boys handle lots of money, but none of it sticks. The bosses hit them with a few C-notes now and then to keep them happy. When I talk to these guys in jail, I always ask them, "If the money's so good in the drug business, how come on the outside you're living in a roach box? How come every morning you're wading through pizza crusts and beer cans to go to the bathroom and every night you're boning some skank who's giving you diseases?" The answer is always the same: "Drugs are all there is."

Their inability to project thought into the future traps these guys in a hellish present. I tell them there has to be something else in life other than bling made of fool's gold, but chaotic inmates can't imagine another life. They are vaguely aware that outside their neighborhoods there are thousands of tidy homes with green lawns, nice cars, food galore, happy pets, air conditioning, and cable TV *with* HBO. They can't conceive of the work ethic, budgeting, and self-discipline required to have such things. To postpone gratification, to work for years before getting what you want, is unthinkable.

The impulsive existence causes other problems. It stimulates inmates to confess, because when they're under pressure of interrogation, that's what feels good *at the moment*. Where a socialized person would weigh the relief of confession against the waste of years in prison, inmates confess all the time to crimes they didn't commit just to get detectives to back off and leave them alone. Worse, they sign statements they can barely read, and scarcely understand, without an attorney present. This screws the pooch. Confessions and statements can be suppressed only through exclusionary hearings, which are complex, expensive, and problematic.

Living exclusively in the present also leads inmates to fixate on the jail experience, with all its annoyances and humiliations. They whine and complain to families, show out to corrections officers, scuffle with other inmates, and snitch to guards. They get written up for disciplinary infractions, have their privileges suspended, and often rack up extra criminal charges. They don't get it that jail lasts one year or less. They can't control present behavior for future benefit.

Finally, because jail preoccupies them, they stay distracted and can't cooperate in their criminal defense. It's extraordinarily difficult for them to write down details, get their story straight, think about the physical evidence, and advise about witnesses.

When you ask chaotic inmates about their plans and their dreams, you get a blank stare. They recognize the words, but such terms have no operative meaning. When you ask them where they expect to be five years from now, they mostly say, "I'll probably be dead." In part this is fatalism. The homicide rate among males 18–24 is high, but it is not 100 percent. This classic answer is, I believe, also due to their atemporal mode of existence. There's the present, or there's nothing.

I've always been amused when highly socialized people make overly sincere efforts to live "in the moment." When most people say they want to live more in the present, they merely mean that they want to take things easier and have a bit more fun. The real atemporal life of *Homo chaoticus* is something they will, blessedly, never know. It's a life without future and without hope inside a mental, moral, and spiritual jail.

OBLIVIOUSNESS TO SOCIAL STRUCTURE

Socialized people easily change behaviors to fit circumstances. They act one way at work, another way at home, and other ways with buddies, parents, preachers, etc. They always know when they're in charge and when they're not. In the presence of cops and judges, they naturally modify their behavior and get polite fast. They say, "Yes, Officer" and "No, Officer" and "Yes, Your Honor" and "No, Your Honor." They don't antagonize people who can slap them into jail.

Socialized people tolerate being second banana at times because doing so allows them to achieve their goals. For people who live completely in the present, getting ordered around is unbearable. Acting on emotions and impulses, they go wild around authority figures. The typical *Homo chaoticus* reply to cops' questions is "Fuck you, motherfucker!" This lyrical line is music to a cop's ears, because it presages at least a misdemeanor bust and maybe some fleeing, eluding, and resisting to boost the encounter up to a felony. Unsocialized people run from cops, which is unwise; assault cops, which can be painful; and occasionally draw knives and guns on cops, which can be fatal. They mouth off to judges, which is never advisable, and show out to corrections officers, who can make jail and prison life even more miserable.

Unsocialized people cannot tolerate insults. When somebody cuts them off in traffic, they explode into rage. When someone annoys them, they get abusive or violent. Without goals, there's no reason not to. This inability to find a place within social structures causes unsocialized people to have a tough time holding jobs. The minute they're stressed, they act out, mouth off, walk out, or get fired. Living without watches and calendars and being allergic to authority and resistant to paperwork cause unsocialized people to violate probation and parole. They can't even think about next week, much less mark a calendar and set an alarm clock to attend a probation or parole meeting.

Chaotic people value doing their own thing regardless of what society says. They refer to this as being "authentic." Mostly, this translates into acting on any and all impulses, saying whatever pops into their heads, and being oblivious to the needs of others. Socialized people act differently. They don't express everything they feel, so as not to offend or provoke. They sometimes act not to fulfill immediate personal needs but to further the objectives of a group, such as the family or the organization for which they work. They do so because they realize that, on balance, they also benefit.

PREMORALITY

The problem with chaotic people is not that they have bad morals; it's that they have no morals whatsoever. They are neither amoral, meaning that they ignore existing moral structures, nor immoral, meaning that they willfully choose evil. Both of these words presuppose an awareness of existing moral order. But everyone who spends time with criminal defendants notices a strangely innocent quality in many of them. They are not evil in the sense of actively planning evil deeds and intending to do harm, because they don't *plan* anything. Crime just happens.

Let me give you an example. I interviewed a young murderer once and found him whimpering about his deed. "I shot my cousin," he moaned.

"What happened?" I asked.

"We was playing cards," he replied.

"So why'd you shoot him?"

"'Cause he cheated me!"

He was astonished that I would ask. His cousin pissed him off, so *of course* he shot him. What else was he supposed to do? To *Homo chaoticus*, reacting immediately in response to an insult is the only conceivable behavior. It doesn't have any moral quality at all. It just happens.

Chaotic people are, in essence, *premoral*. I use this term to convey the strange, unworldly quality of so many inmates. More than once I've had the distinct impression that these guys were hatched in an incubator aboard some mother ship then beamed down to planet Earth.

THE VALUES CHECK: THE PAUSE THAT SOCIALIZES

The atemporal mindset, the inability to adapt to social circumstances, and the absence of a moral compass, which collectively are the personality of *Homo chaoticus*, are difficult to detect in casual situations. These guys appear so normal. Why, you wonder, are they always getting into so much trouble? The reason is that the chaotic personality only manifests *at the moment of decision.*

That's the moment when civilized people compare their contemplated actions with their internalized standards of behavior. Would this choice be right? Would it be smart? Would it further their goals? I call this momentary pause taken before actions or decisions the "values check."

Let's take a simple example. Almost everyone has been cut off in traffic and maybe even forced off the road by boneheads who swerve in front of your vehicle. This makes you nuts! You want to pull out a pistol and fire some rounds through their cars! You want to run them off the road then open up a size-large can of whup-ass! You want to stand on their bruised and bleeding bodies and shout, "Who's your daddy!"

But you don't do any of these things, for obvious reasons:

1. They're morally wrong.

2. They're illegal.

3. They're physically dangerous.

4. They're unproductive and would divert you from important objectives.

Civilized people do not interrupt their work and personal lives to trade fisticuffs with fools by the side of the road. To make the decision to pocket these insults, you compare your contemplated acts of mayhem with your higher values, then make the appropriate decision.

Many times a day socialized people make a values check before they do, or say, anything. The values check allows you to offer a cheery "Good morning!" to the bosses you hate rather than telling them to take this job and shove it. The values check allows you to ignore certain annoyances from your spouse or partner because you love that person and, in the long run, it's better to stay together than not. The values check allows you to patiently correct your children rather than whacking them on the head with a shovel when the little demons get out of hand. This behavior may not be "authentic," but it certainly is civilized.

Chaotic people, on the other hand, can't make a values check, because there aren't any values there. They make stimulus-response decisions. They get an urge; they act. Until that moment, however, these men and women seem like anyone else.

Unfortunately, that makes it easy for them to fool you, especially when they're talented. A famous example is the murderer Jack Henry Abbott, a skilled writer. His autobiography,

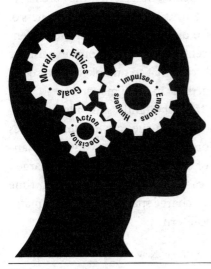

Civilized Man

Homo Chaoticus

In the Belly of the Beast, was praised to the skies by the *New York Times*. With the support of writers Norman Mailer, twice winner of the Pulitzer Prize, and Jerzy Kosinski, winner of the National Book Award, Abbott was released on parole. Within weeks, he got into a stupid argument with a waiter outside a New York restaurant, pulled a knife, and stabbed the guy to death. Even at his second murder trial, he gained the support of celebrities like Academy Award–winner Susan Sarandon. He was one charming rascal.*

MIDDLE-CLASS ALLERGY

Despite their ability to simulate normalcy, unsocialized people often find ordinary existence quite stressful. They can be allergic to middle-class American life. Schedules, rules, routines, watches, calendars, appointments—the whole shebang makes them crazy. One of my former brothers-in-law had this allergy in a bad way. Sadly, it became apparent only after he married my sister. As a skilled registered nurse, she earned more money than he did, and promptly acquired a neat home, with a real white picket fence, in the suburbs. This made him nuts.

During family visits, over polite chatter at the dinner table, my ex-bro would get so stressed he would rush out the back door to smoke a joint, fondle his pistol, and dream mad dreams. In due course he and my sister were divorced. He, at last report, had found the chaotic version of happiness out in the boondocks in a rusty trailer. There, in the red Georgia clay, he grows enough top-of-the line marijuana so there's always plenty to smoke and some to sell. Life is easy in the lounger as the hemp ripens in the warm sun.

But middle-class life is exactly what defendants must embrace if they want to get free and stay free, because the criminal justice system is governed by the standards of civilized behavior we call middle-class values. They are so fundamental, in fact, that they are never questioned and rarely discussed. Prosecutors, judges, and juries measure the heinousness of a crime and decide on the appropriate punishment based on to the degree to which defendants are, or are not, socialized. The justice system has centuries of institutional experience in dealing with chaotic behavior. During hearings and trials that to onlookers seem quite harum-scarum, the players make remarkably fine distinctions in these matters.

For example, recognizing that many crimes result from thoughtless impulse, the system categorizes as especially heinous those that do not. It punishes *premeditated* crimes more severely because they are *not* thoughtless reactions, but the result of advance planning and clear intent to do harm. Take the example of the card player. He was charged with murder in the second degree because his deed was not premeditated. Doing time for murder two is no cakewalk, but in my state the lesser charge spared him what inmates refer to as the Big Needle or the Ride on the Gurney to Eternity.

---

* Abbott spared his celebrity friends further embarrassment and the State of New York further expense when, alone in his cell, he hung himself by his shoelaces in 2002.

Inmates must understand that they are living in the Land of The Man. If they want to live in freedom and not like rabbits in a cage, their former, middle-class-allergic lives need to be over. They have to begin to look like, talk like, and act like the middle-class Americans who run and fund the criminal justice system.

In a more perfect society, this would not be so. As long as you obey the law, you should be able to dress and look as you please, to hip-hop and let your hair drop all the way down to your toes. But this is not happening in these United States. Because of computerized databases that instantly show police officers the records of defendants' arrests and convictions, defendants will receive extra police scrutiny for the rest of their lives. Until they are finished with the criminal justice system—and I mean *all the way* finished, through jail, prison, probation, and parole—some of their social privileges have been canceled.

LOVED ONES AND SOCIALIZATION

When offenders are free once again, it will take time for them to develop these middle-class values. To them, the values check that makes self-restraint possible is an alien form of thinking. It won't be perfected overnight. Fortunately, people learn best, and most quickly, from one another. The most important thing for unsocialized defendants is to live among law-abiding middle-class citizens. Many have never known households that are not in crisis, where people go to work each day, pay their bills, and work toward their goals. Defendants have to give up the thrills and craziness of the unsocialized criminal life. They have to learn the lower-key pleasures of family time, a job well done, money well earned, a life without catastrophe and drama, and regular routine.

They need to learn these things from *you*. You're their family. There's no one else. In jail and prison, all they learn is how to be a better crook. What's more, socialization takes years and immense investments of time and money. Only family have the will and the resources to devote to the task.

What about the tens of thousands of government and nonprofit programs to aid offenders in their reentry into society? All of them are successful in varying degrees at preventing recidivism. All of them are overwhelmed by numbers. In my city, we have several that have had outstanding results—with several hundred offenders per year. What the heartwarming press reports never mention is that in Jacksonville, several hundred is the number of people arrested *every day!* Most defendants haven't a chance to enter a program. There's no room. The same occurs with desperately needed drug treatment. There are long waiting lists.

There is a second reason why the aid of family is preferable to formal programs. In group settings, there is one leader for many offenders. This is a heavy caseload. With family, the ratios are reversed. There are usually several supportive friends and family members per offender. This means there are more people to encourage, lead, and help. There are also more people to scold, nag, and kick butt, which are equally essential.

In chapter 26, I'll discuss family management. This is the process of arranging the financial and administrative support that assists defendants in completing probation and parole. With the assistance of counsel, family management plans can be organized into petitions for leniency. Most importantly, with family management, you can show defendants how to live as citizens, without fear, and in freedom.

It will be the most important lesson of their lives.

12

HITTING BOTTOM
How to Recognize a Readiness to Change

THIS BOOK CONTRADICTS MUCH that is written about criminal defense. I have not advised you to move heaven and earth to get offenders out of jail at once. I've recommended that you, the family, use jail just like society does, to test your defendants to see whether they are capable of becoming citizens worthy of support.

Since it's unlikely that you and the defendants live together in a nuclear family, you probably have limited ability to influence their behavior. Your major hold over the defendants is, bluntly, that they want your money for bail and criminal defense. You have to decide *whether* help is merited. You *do not* want to become the Crime Co-Pay Department, a one-stop shop for financing defendants' reentry into thugdom.

That's why you have to use jail as a test. For inmates, the experience is a huge bop on the head and a big time-out from life. People react in different ways. The hard core, who have been arrested many times, know the drill. They trudge down the corridors and wait patiently for their uniform and toiletries. Mostly they're interested in getting some sleep so they can bear the drug withdrawal, cigarette willies, and caffeine headache that are on the way. They'll be in prison on and off until they hit middle age and can't run and gun anymore.

Some defendants are passive. They're lazy by nature and regard jail as a cheap motel with lousy food. Mostly they're glad that they don't have to work, pay bills, or listen to women nag. These slugs are as hopeless as the hard core.

Young gangbangers get excited by their first arrest. They've popped their cherry, so to speak, and become government-certified hoodlums! The gang life and the adrenaline rush of crime are all they know and all they want. They pimp-roll up and down jail corridors high-fiving their homies and *carnales*. It never, and I mean never, occurs to these guys that if all their buddies are in jail, the thug life may not be working out so well. Hard time in prison may change their minds later. It will spare them what else lies in store for them on the outside—a bullet.

With these three groups, reform is unlikely. When asked for financial support, double your money immediately by folding it once and putting it back in your wallet.

So whom can you help? You can assist those defendants who, emotionally and mentally, hit bottom. Until they do, you can't intervene successfully. Criminals are perpetrators, not victims. They made choices along the way that got them where they are. They can make other choices that lead them back to freedom—if they want to. A hard landing in jail makes some of them, about 30 to 40 percent, want to.

This contradicts the widespread notion that *society* is responsible for criminal behavior—that society, and not criminals, has to do something about crime. Society has to get busy and eradicate poverty, make fathers and mothers love each other and their children, give everyone a college education, etc. All of this will happen when the Messiah comes, if then. If I hear another bleeding heart say that poverty and joblessness are the reasons for crime, I'll toss my cookies. I have never, ever, heard a criminal say that he or she turned to crime because McDonald's and Wal-Mart wouldn't provide a job! Most crooks would rather jump into a box of rattlesnakes than work a straight shift.

Besides, victimology doesn't leave you, the defendant's family, with options. Are you going to eliminate poverty? When you embrace the reality that defendants *choose* the life they lead, now you can get to work. What defendants lack, for the most part, are not choices, but the values that allow them to make good choices. They can obtain values, but it will take time.

Defendants have four huge mental blocks. Until they get over them, they won't hit bottom. The first is an obsession I call "If only." Inmates spend days pondering why, this time, they got caught. If only that snitch hadn't ratted them out! If only they hadn't cheated on their girlfriend who dropped a dime in revenge! If only they had kept the auto tag current and avoided a traffic stop! If only they hadn't sold dope to an undercover police officer! If only the wiretap had been declared inadmissible! If only their pimp had encrypted the whore and john list on his stupid laptop! And so on.

As loved ones, you have to help defendants face hard realities. As long as they're hung up on "If only," their true interest is merely to become better criminals. You should insist that they get over this. They need to start thinking, every day, *How can I live in freedom?* This is a different question entirely.

The second obsession I call "But I got away with it!" Most criminals break laws frequently. They use and sell drugs and sex, steal cars, burglarize homes, shoplift, etc., day after day, sometimes for years. This engenders in them the attitude that police are incompetent, or corrupt, or just don't care. Defendants do not understand what everyone else in the criminal justice system knows: cops can't catch offenders every time, but they don't have to. To keep crime under control, they have to arrest offenders only *now and then*. Prison sentences are so progressive, especially with three-strikes laws and special courts for habitual offenders, that even occasional arrests will result in criminals spending most of their adult lives in prison. This is the iron arithmetic of law enforcement. You need to give your defendant a strong lesson in criminal justice math.

The third obsession I call "But it wasn't illegal." This applies to the 20 to 30 percent of defendants who are arrested, often repeatedly, in bullshit misdemeanor busts over loud parties, family squabbles, acting out in front of police, driving with suspended licenses, riding bikes at night without a light, etc. I personally believe that the use of arrest and incarceration instead of simple tickets and fines for such infractions is a national disgrace. Nonetheless, these laws are in place and they are enforced. They are also incredibly broad. For example, in Georgia, one of the legal definitions of disorderly conduct is acting in a "tumultuous" way. This can cover any behavior short of coma. Annoying behaviors, which get petty offenders frequently arrested, *are* illegal. This isn't right. It isn't just. It is, however, a fact.

As family, you have to help defendants break through this mental hang-up. Tell them this: "Stupid, thuggish, and annoying behaviors are violations of law. It doesn't matter that you didn't do anything violent or truly evil. You got busted, and here you are in jail. Ponder that!"

The fourth obsession, which is strong among petty offenders, is "It ain't fair." And it isn't. Police arrest poor people and those of modest means because they're low-hanging fruit. When cops stopped hundreds of cars and arrested casual drug users and petty offenders in a four-block area around my neighborhood, which is relatively poor, I was outraged but not surprised. If police were to stop and search vehicles in wealthy neighborhoods, or around colleges, universities, and expensive private schools, they also would make many arrests. But they don't. If you scream and rage at your wife in an apartment with thin walls, you'll get busted. If you do the same in a private home with thick walls in a gated community, you won't. If you have loud, rowdy parties on the street, the popo will come. If you get wild and crazy in private clubs and exclusive homes, they won't.

You have to impress on defendants the following lesson: the world is as it is. Just because cops don't arrest the rich, the privileged, and the merely lucky, they can, will, and already have arrested *you!* Here's what you say: "*You* are in jail. *You* have an arrest record. *You* are on the radar screen. Forget about the rich frat boy and rich sassy girl on the other side of town! *You* are busted, and your wild-and-crazy privileges have been cancelled."

When defendants get over these mental hang-ups, they hit bottom—hard. Where they land is as hard as concrete and as cold as ice. As they plummet, defendants will shout at you, insult you, scam you, and scream at you. Illusions are warm and comforting. The bottom is lonely. There's no one else there in the darkness, and the road up into the light seems impossibly long. To get there, defendants can't be themselves any longer. They have to become someone different, someone alien, someone other. They have to become citizens.

And that hurts.

How can you tell if your defendant has hit that cold, dank psychological floor? You can tell by the language. You will hear statements like these:

"I can't stand this! I'll do anything to get out of here and *never come back!*"

"This place makes me crazy! Tell me what to do to get out *and stay out.*"

What you're listening for is the second part of these statements, the part emphasized in italics. These show that inmates are thinking about their future, about cleaning up their act, about getting out of the hoodlum lifestyle and about staying far, far away from bad boys, drugs, and cops. This is music to your ears.

And if you are truly fortunate, and if your stars are aligned, you might hear this:

"Momma, I'm ready. Call the Marine Corps recruiter."

13

WHY GUNG HO IS GOOD
The Character Factories

IF YOUR DEFENDANT EXPRESSES an honest interest in military service, this is indeed auspicious. In fact, this option is so desirable that it warrants its own chapter. The armed services are character factories that socialize people *fast*. No government agency, probation system, church, or social service agency even begins to approach the military's ability to completely transform muddled men and women into citizens *in one year or less*.

Of course, the services have advantages. They draw upon the unlimited resources of the United States Treasury. They have more than two centuries of practice molding recalcitrant human clay into civility and citizenship. They do not concern themselves with recruits' past lives. When they enlist, what they were and what they did are unimportant. Right here, right now, they're soldiers, sailors, airmen, and marines, and that's all that matters.

(First, some disclosure. I did not serve in the military. In the seventies I had a high Selective Service lottery number and did not get drafted. I have often regretted this. Had I survived being killed by the Viet Cong or the North Vietnamese Army, I might have emerged a better person, even from the drug-plagued, demoralized, conscript forces of that era. I do, however, live in a military town and have come to admire the sailors, soldiers, airmen, and marines I have met over the years.)

To consider whether your defendant qualifies for military service, see the U.S. Army Qualification Standards for Enlistment on www.wesdenham.net. The requirements for other services are similar. But standards change, so consult local military recruiters for details. Here are important points to discuss with defendants:

1. Defendants must be willing to enlist. No one can be forced to serve in our elite, all-volunteer services.

2. Defendants must be serious about the effort required. Contrary to occasional news reports, the armed services do not have difficulty filling their enlistment quotas; they are *not* interested in becoming babysitters, jailers, and disciplinarians to delinquents. Hollywood movies like *The Dirty Dozen*, about hard-core felons who become heroic soldiers, are fantasy. Recruits who are not dedicated will wash out of basic training.

3. Arrests and criminal convictions necessitate special permissions from senior officers. With rare exceptions, the services will not enlist anyone who has a felony conviction. This means that if your defendant is so charged, you and defense counsel must do everything legally possible to reduce felonies to misdemeanors.

4. The military will want to know about all transgressions, down to and including traffic tickets. They want to know about every single arrest, no matter how the case was resolved. They will ignore niceties such as whether the case was nol-prossed, sentenced to probation, or diverted out of the legal system into treatment. They will consider each potential recruit's criminal record in terms of *moral qualities*. They want to know whether defendants can become soldiers, sailors, airmen, or marines and not unacceptable disciplinary and security risks.

5. Defendants must be completely and absolutely finished with the criminal justice system. They must have completed all sentences, including probation and parole, and paid all fines, court costs, and restitution. Military recruiters want to see whether defendants have the fortitude to finish their sentences without screwing up. Defendants must also be free of illegal drugs. The services make potential enlistees pee in a cup almost before they get through the door.

6. Honesty is a supreme military virtue and an absolute necessity for recruitment. One lie about any arrest or conviction, no matter how insignificant, can disqualify applicants. Defendants should study their criminal and traffic records and memorize the details. This will be time well spent.

7. Defendants who are flabby, malnourished, and weak need to get fit. Unlike prisons, most jails do not have weight-lifting equipment. Defendants who are serious about enlistment, however, can hit the deck and do push-ups, sit-ups, and crunches. Being weak in jail is inadvisable in any case.

8. In military service, getting killed in combat or accidents is always a possibility, but consider the alternatives. In my city, 112 men and women were murdered in 2008. Defendants are far more likely to get shot by the drug dealer on the next block than by al Qaeda or the Taliban.

The point of talking about military service while defendants are still in jail is that, should they make a sincere decision to enlist, it may convince a judge to reduce charges, divert the defendant to treatment, or sentence the defendant directly to probation. WARNING: Judges are immune to lip service and lies. A remark along the lines of "Yeah,

Your Honor, I'll enlist" will not convince. Defendants must show detailed knowledge of the service they want to join, its requirements, and whether their criminal history can be waived.

WHAT MILITARY SERVICE MEANS FOR FAMILIES

Military service changes families as much as enlistees. If you are a woman who is married to or living with a service member, you may have to relocate as your service member is deployed. You will spend long periods alone without your man. You will have to raise children alone, with no help for hard chores, and with no one to talk to, and no one to comfort you. You must live with the fear that your man could be injured or killed. During separations, you may be tempted to have love affairs that leave you guilty, torn, and confused. You may become envious that your husband is part of important things in faraway, exotic places while you work a humdrum job back at home.

If you are a man, you may feel challenged that your wife's military career comes first and that you have to play second banana to her. You will worry that during deployments she is surrounded by other men and may engage in affairs. You will be burdened with raising your own children without their mother.

When partners in a military family are separated, each partner can be dismayed to discover how well the other partner manages alone. These are some of the downsides.

There are many upsides. If you are married to a service member, you too are whirled away from mean, crime-ridden neighborhoods. Military housing is far from deluxe, but it's clean and safe. If there is no on-base housing available, the services will subsidize a private apartment. If you have children, you will discover, to your delight, that on-base schools are among the top-rated public schools in the nation, and perhaps the only public schools that have no—that's right, no—disciplinary problems. Parental involvement with education is 100 percent. Service members who do not participate in their children's education are simply ordered to do so by the base commander—end of story. You and your children will have health care and dental care provided by the military.

If you have children with a service member but are not married, the military will deduct child care payments from the service member's paycheck and send them directly to you.

After so many years of service, the military will pay for your service member's college education. While in service, your loved one can get training in trades that pay well in civilian life. Aircraft and diesel engine mechanics, for example, are highly sought. Once released from the military, the no-down-payment benefit of VA loans means that you and your veteran can almost immediately buy a house in a decent neighborhood.

When you're married to an active duty service member, or are listed as a cosigner on loans or as an authorized user of credit cards, you have rights under the Servicemembers

Civil Relief Act. Under this law, financial institutions are required to lower their interest rates on loans, mortgages, and credit cards. Some credit card companies will lower the APR even more than is required—to zero! This will save you a fortune. To take advantage of these benefits, make sure you have copies of your service member's enlistment papers and current duty orders. Get yourself named as an authorized user of credit cards. For loans and mortgages, file a power of attorney with the lending institutions so they can transact business with you. Make sure you know all user IDs and passwords for financial institution Web sites.

A warning is now in order. Many service members do not fully understand that while off base they are subject to civilian law enforcement. If arrested, they are on their own. The judge advocate general's office will not intervene, nor will it provide legal counsel. A conviction can cause immediate separation from service with a less-than-honorable discharge. All the benefits vanish.

On base, you and your children are subject to special federal laws that you might not be aware of. Speeding on base, for example, is a *federal* offense subject to huge penalties. Many wild-driving teenagers come to grief at the hands of military police and shore patrols and have to spend months of drudgery in low-paying jobs to repay fines that can be in the thousands of dollars. As a general rule, while on military bases or Indian reservations, including casinos, you should drive at a crawl and make long, slow stops at intersections and lights. Military personnel and their families should take extra care that their vehicles are street legal, squeaky clean, and drug free and that all documents are immediately ready to present to law enforcement during traffic stops. Take special care that any military-issued weapons are properly carried when transported off base.

Advise your service member to give some serious thought to police avoidance during the traditional boozy celebrations held after returns from deployments. These should be fun but kept low-key. They should be held in private homes, *not* in hotels and public areas subject to police surveillance. Music needs to be low, so as not to generate police calls by annoyed neighbors. Designated drivers are a must.

After the party, and the hangovers, discuss with your service member how to get those cool souvenir weapons snatched from prisoners of war legally permitted. If the weapons are to be mounted and displayed, check state laws, which may require that firing mechanisms be disabled by a gunsmith. Possession of machine guns and full-auto weapons without difficult-to-get permits is a violation of federal law and subject to harsh penalties. And for heaven's sake, get the explosives and detonators removed from artillery shells and those damn grenades!

Military personnel and their families have more to lose from arrests and convictions than civilians do. Don't risk all the hard work and valuable benefits with careless and illegal behavior. See my book *Arrest-Proof Yourself* for details on avoiding unnecessary interactions with law enforcement.

HOW MILITARY SOCIALIZATION WORKS

During basic training, the services pluck recruits from their hometowns and send them hundreds of miles away, where they are isolated among other military personnel, all of whom are volunteers, all of whom are disciplined, all of whom are citizens. Trainers and instructors boil off recruits' fat, drugs, and booze with exercise; buzz off unruly facial and cranial hair; and issue clean and tidy uniforms. For unsocialized young men and women, the military provides a simplified hierarchical social structure. Everybody knows his and her place in the hierarchy because status is conveniently indicated by stripes, stars, eagles, and anchors sewn on the blouse. Generals and admirals fly flags on their cars and ships to aid in long-distance recognition. Everybody gets great hats. Everyone has to memorize rules about what clothes to wear in what situations. For latrine digging, there's one uniform; for dinner at the White House, another. This is socialization simplified, and it works.

The military extinguishes the trapped-in-the-present, chaotic personality with relentless emphasis on the future. Periodically everyone in the military, from admiral to swabby, from general to grunt, has to appear before career boards, stand at attention, and announce what he or she plans to do *in the future*. What is your next step? Your next service school? Your next promotion? What are you doing right now in order to be a better person, to get that next stripe, that next star?

The military teaches people how to subordinate themselves, and how to behave without losing control when annoyed or frustrated. It demands that its personnel live not only for themselves but for a higher purpose: the defense of their country. This is citizenship mass produced.

The military imparts to its personnel another social skill essential in our era: dealing with bureaucracy. The military is itself a giant bureaucracy. Everyone has heard the joke that to do anything, there's the right way, the wrong way, and the army way. Nonetheless, all service members know how to fill out paperwork, print their name in block letters in the scanable spaces provided, and return forms in a timely manner. They bear with patience and fortitude every sort of bureaucratic absurdity.

It's weird, but it's effective. The all-volunteer force that has been developed since the dog days of the Vietnam War is the finest military force in history. Its members are proud of who they are and what they do. The reenlistment bonuses, zero-down-payment VA mortgages, health care benefits, and pensions aren't bad either.

For men and women prone to violence, the military provides a useful outlet. In the military, violence and aggression are thoroughly understood. They also are valued. More importantly, these tendencies are trained, disciplined, and channeled into useful activity, which is, bluntly, threatening or killing the enemies of the United States.

In the services, enlistees meet *real* tough guys. Pound for pound, the special forces such as the Navy SEALs are the most deadly human beings who have ever existed. You can recognize SEALs instantly by their huge shoulders and massive chests developed from endless hours of swimming in the open ocean. They look like gorillas that have swallowed an oil drum. Their capacity for violence, however, is coolly and logically applied, under strict command, for a higher purpose. That said, the puniest SEAL can coldcock a street brawler with one hand while picking his teeth with the other.

The military is a great place for women, especially those who are tough, aggressive, and mechanically inclined. In civilian life, such women are often derided for being mannish and unfeminine. In the military, they are valued. Although officially banned from combat, women now fly all combat aircraft. Hotshot female aviators attend the world famous Navy Fighter Weapons School known as Top Gun. Many military women become skilled mechanics. During the second U.S. war with Iraq, many Muslims were horrified while visiting American air bases to encounter female sergeants brandishing socket wrenches, repairing helicopters and jets, and bellowing orders at men!

No matter how menial their employment, all marines, including women, are trained to be riflemen. They are expected to be marines first, and clerks, cooks, mechanics, truck drivers, and office personnel second. When attacked, female marines and army soldiers are expected to shoulder their weapons and open fire. If they are the ranking officer or enlisted, they are required to command their unit as a combat team and to attack, or to escape and evade, the enemy.

I recall watching news reports about a female army helicopter pilot who was shot down during the first Gulf War then raped, tortured, and imprisoned. When she was released, she returned to the United States wearing the class-A uniform of a full colonel with a chest full of purple hearts and decorations for valor in combat. She and thousands like her have permanently changed public perceptions about women. The military has proven that with the possible exception of lifting heavy weights and digging trenches for hours on end, women can do anything and everything men can do.

When it comes to rapid, thorough socialization, the all-time champ among the services is the U.S Marine Corps. The marines do not merely ignore recruits' former personalities and lives—they obliterate them. Marine basic training is so intense that recruits emerge, months later, completely changed. The marines essentially erase individual personalities and install a marine standard-issue unit in its place. This is like having electrodes attached to your temples, getting hooked up to the household current, until—*bzzt*—you're gone. What saves this from being inhumane is that the marine standard-issue personality is quite serviceable.

I have personal experience with this. A woman I dated for years had a teenaged son who was headed for trouble. He was doing drugs, smashing cars into trees, dropping out of school, and heading for suicide or jail. He came to live with me in Miami, pale, weak, drugged, and depressed. Once he hit bottom, I took him to a barbershop, then delivered him to a marine recruiter. Two years later, when he returned on leave, I couldn't recognize him. He had become a veritable Hercules, tanned, muscular, and proud, and he was showing off some Soviet automatic pistols he had removed from Iraqi prisoners of war. His family, which had written him off as a loser, was stunned and amazed. Today he is a law enforcement officer with the Florida Fish and Wildlife Conservation Commission and is giving drug dealers hell in the rivers and marshes around Cape Canaveral.

The marine standard-issue personality lasts for life. You can always spot retired marines. Even in their 70s and 80s, they keep their gray hair cut high, tight, and regulation. When they buy a house, the first thing they do is dig a hole, pour concrete, and plant a flagpole. Every day, rain or shine, they fly Old Glory and beneath it the blood-red battle standard of the United States Marine Corps. Nobody gives them any grief, however, because everybody knows they're packing. Even with their cataracts and contact lenses, some of these old coots can shoot the eyes out of a gnat at 20 yards. When the red flags start appearing in a neighborhood, it's a good sign. It means that values, both moral and financial, are going up.

Retired navy chiefs are similar to marines. The way I tell them apart is that the chiefs usually have ships and anchors tattooed on their forearms instead of daggers and rifles. As for the army, consider this: My dad has a friend who is a retired army colonel of the artillery. He's got the same flattop he had at 18, and even today, in his 70s, he stands or sits *at attention*—even when drunk.

Sometimes I ride my bicycle along a trail that leaves the city of Jacksonville and goes out into the piney woods where people still keep cows, horses, and chickens in their backyards and a hound dog on the porch. Occasionally I see the grandsons of these military retirees, running, in military boots, with heavy backpacks, in 98-degree heat, in order to toughen themselves for army or marine basic training. I see them only on the trail; I never see these young men in jail. Military service is not a guarantee against future delinquency, but the numbers of veterans in jails and prisons is low.

Society has always valued most highly those virtues of courage and self-sacrifice that lead a person to prize certain things above life itself. Military personnel experience courage and self-sacrifice not extraordinarily, but routinely. In combat they know the real thing, not the phony version on movie or television screens or the pale imitation of the sports fields.

Character and virtue reveal themselves only in action and at the moment of decision. For the chaotic mindset, they're antimatter. For the lack of socialization, they're the antidote. The highest degrees of courage and self-sacrifice, when witnessed and attested, are awarded the Medal of Honor. Most people have never read a Medal of Honor citation. Take a moment to read this one for navy lieutenant and SEAL Michael P. Murphy.

> While leading a mission to locate a high-level anti-coalition militia leader, Lieutenant Murphy demonstrated extraordinary heroism in the face of grave

danger in the vicinity of Asadabad, Konar Province, Afghanistan. On 28 June 2005, operating in an extremely rugged, enemy-controlled area, Lieutenant Murphy's team was discovered by anti-coalition militia sympathizers who revealed their position to Taliban fighters. As a result, between 30 and 40 enemy fighters besieged his four-member team.

Demonstrating exceptional resolve, Lieutenant Murphy valiantly led his men in engaging the large enemy force. The ensuing fierce firefight resulted in numerous enemy casualties, as well as the wounding of all four members of his team. Ignoring his own wounds and demonstrating exceptional composure, Lieutenant Murphy continued to lead and encourage his men. When the primary communicator fell mortally wounded, Lieutenant Murphy repeatedly attempted to call for assistance for his beleaguered teammates. Realizing the impossibility of communicating in the extreme terrain and in the face of almost certain death, he fought his way into an open terrain to gain a better position to transmit a call. This deliberate heroic act deprived him of cover, exposing him to direct enemy fire. Finally achieving contact with his headquarters, Lieutenant Murphy maintained his exposed position while he provided his location and requested immediate support for his team.

In his final act of bravery, he continued to engage the enemy until he was mortally wounded, gallantly giving his life for his country and for the cause of freedom. By his selfless leadership, courageous actions, and extraordinary devotion to duty, Lieutenant Murphy reflected great credit upon himself and upheld the highest traditions of the United States Naval Service.

At the moment of decision, character will out. Courageous people do not ponder or hesitate. Their thinking is long done and their character formed. When they have to act, they do. Tragically, every Medal of Honor awarded since the Vietnam War has been posthumous. Why does society bother to bestow awards in such circumstances? The awards don't matter to the recipients. They're dead. They matter, however, to the living. They make us humble. They also make us proud to be members of the human race.

Enlistment is a tough decision for defendants. They sense that military life, regulated, ordered, duty-bound, with individual desires subordinated to the needs of the services, is alien to the very core of their being. If defendants do make the decision to join, however, it will change their lives, and yours, for the better. Wouldn't you like to see your defendant exchange mean streets and hoodlum companions for the company of men and women dedicated to honor, duty and country?

They live in a different, and better, world.

Stick 'Em Up!

CHECKLIST FOR MILITARY ENLISTMENT

☐ Get service information from recruiters. (For U.S. Army enlistment standards, see my website, www.wesdenham.net.) Mail this information to the defendant.

☐ Ask recruiters about their current recruiting needs and willingness to enlist men and women with criminal records.

☐ Discuss military service during jail visits. Emphasize that military service is a life-changing decision. Your defendant has to work to make this possible.

☐ Get detailed criminal records. Mail copies to your defendant for study. Test your defendant during visits to see if he or she has learned the criminal history.

☐ Obtain the defendant's traffic violation records from the Department of Motor Vehicles. Many states let you download these from the Internet. You will need the defendant's driver's license number. If the license is locked up in the jail's property room, ask jail staff whether it's possible for you and the defendant to get a photocopy of the license or the number written on paper. If they refuse, defense counsel should seek a court order to force production.

☐ Inform defense counsel of the defendant's desire to enlist following completion of sentence. Smart attorneys will use this to bargain with prosecutors.

☐ Defendants must study and learn everything they can about the service they intend to join. This is serious homework. Judges may quiz them at hearings. They want to hear detailed knowledge and a sincere desire to serve, not meaningless blah-blah.

☐ Some prayers would be in order. When you see your former defendant in the boot camp graduation photo, standing in front of the American flag and wearing the Class-A uniform of the United States Army or the dress blues of the Navy, Air Force, and Marines, you'll think you've died and gone to heaven.

14

TO HELP OR NOT TO HELP?
Rating Defendants

WHAT ARE THE CHANCES that your defendant will go straight and stay free? No one has calculated the arrest rate for all people charged with crimes, but according the Department of Justice, about one in three people who serve a criminal sentence will avoid future arrest. About half will avoid future conviction. Here are the statistics from a 2002 study:

> Of the 272,111 persons released from prisons in 15 States in 1994, an estimated 67.5% were rearrested for a felony or serious misdemeanor within 3 years, 46.9% were reconvicted, and 25.4% re-sentenced to prison for a new crime.*

Your personal odds are better because your defendant has family who care enough to help. Many defendants are not so lucky. Outside jail and prison, there's no one for them—no one responsible, that is. But you can better the odds by evaluating your defendant.

If you have qualms about judging another person, get over it. *Of course* you're judging the defendant. What right have you, especially if you're not the defendant's parent or spouse? This right—you're the *payer*. The defendant is asking for your time and your treasure.

The checklists and guidelines in this chapter will help you determine whether your loved one meets the three conditions that make your support a worthwhile investment:

1. Defendant is capable of living peacefully and lawfully and of internalizing morals and laws.

2. Defendant is willing to assist attorneys with his or her criminal defense.

3. Defendant will begin planning to resume education, child care, jobs, and/or a military career and to meet his or her financial obligations.

There is no absolute number of positive or negative factors that will guarantee your defendant will meet these conditions. It's a judgment call on your part. As you work through the following exercises, you'll know soon enough whether to help. Trust me on that.

You'll know.

---

* U.S. Department of Justice, Bureau of Justice Statistics, "Criminal Offenders Statistics," 2002, www.ojp.usdoj.gov/bjs/crimoff.htm.

THREE DEGREES OF INNOCENCE

Everyone is familiar with the system that classifies crime by degrees—first-degree murder, second-degree murder, etc. Many states also classify felonies and misdemeanors similarly—felony one, felony two, and so forth. For purposes of your evaluating defendants, I'm going to propose three degrees of innocence.

Please note that these degrees of innocence do not exist in the criminal justice system. In law, innocence is absolute. Defendants are either innocent or guilty. If you use this terminology with attorneys, they'll think you've taken leave of your senses.

In evaluating defendants, however, you are considering not only the immediate legal situation but also the larger picture—the likelihood that your defendant can live in freedom. This requires a more nuanced evaluation. In this sort of evaluation, degrees of innocence are appropriate:

► **Innocence in the first degree.** This is innocence pure as driven snow. Your defendant *did not do the crime.* The police have the wrong person. When this happens, defend to the max.

► **Innocence in the second degree.** Your defendant did not do this particular crime but lives the thug and drug life either as an active criminal or as a hoodlum wannabe. Your defendant was swept up by police, who because of the defendant's lifestyle or priors, are not too concerned about the niceties of justice.

► **Innocence in the third degree.** Your defendant did the crime but was overcharged or charged on the basis of flimsy evidence.

You can see that in each of these instances, a stout defense could certainly improve your defendant's outcome. Whether you want to devote time and treasure to this defense, however, is the question the rest of this chapter will help you to answer.

THE DEFENDANT EVALUATION

The Defendant Evaluation Stick 'Em Up on the next page has check-off boxes for positive and negative factors that affect a defendant's likelihood of becoming a citizen. Working through the list, you will gain insight into whether your defendant can become socialized. You may want to make a copy, mail it to the defendant, and compare your version with his or hers. It's useful to see how defendants rate themselves.

If your defendant holds a job and has a high school or college education, that's a positive factor. If your defendant takes advice, that's even better. If the rap sheet is not too long or felony-filled, and if the pending charges are for nonviolent crimes, there's

Stick 'Em Up!

POSITIVE FACTORS

- ☐ First offense
- ☐ Truthful
- ☐ Job
- ☐ Religion
- ☐ High school or college degree
- ☐ Volunteers for the community
- ☐ Keeps appointments
- ☐ Reads mail
- ☐ Completes paperwork
- ☐ Keeps files
- ☐ Decent friends
- ☐ Nice girlfriends/boyfriends
- ☐ Married
- ☐ Good manners
- ☐ Good hygiene
- ☐ Conservative dresser
- ☐ "Little policeman" inside
- ☐ Likes family and relatives
- ☐ Car street legal, license and tag valid, insurance current
- ☐ Has goals
- ☐ Deals with bureaucracy
- ☐ Will move to good neighborhood
- ☐ Takes advice
- ☐ Cares for other people
- ☐ Does not use drugs
- ☐ Controls temper
- ☐ Drinks only in moderation
- ☐ Speaks politely

NEGATIVE FACTORS

- ☐ Prior offenses
- ☐ Lies
- ☐ No job
- ☐ No religion
- ☐ No education
- ☐ Never volunteers
- ☐ Misses appointments
- ☐ Ignores mail
- ☐ Loses paperwork
- ☐ Cannot keep files
- ☐ Thug friends
- ☐ Scumbag girlfriends/boyfriends
- ☐ Not married
- ☐ No manners
- ☐ Bad hygiene
- ☐ Dresses sloppy or "thug chic"
- ☐ No conscience
- ☐ Dislikes family and relatives
- ☐ Car not legal, bad license and tag, no insurance
- ☐ Never thinks about the future
- ☐ Goes nuts around authority figures
- ☐ Won't move; likes bad neighborhood
- ☐ Won't take advice
- ☐ Self-centered; uses people
- ☐ Uses drugs
- ☐ Can't control temper
- ☐ Heavy drinker
- ☐ Curses constantly

Stick 'Em Up!

POSITIVE FACTORS, continued

- ☐ Avoids clubs and high crime areas
- ☐ No or few tattoos. No piercings
- ☐ Willing to change
- ☐ Reads general interest magazines
- ☐ Watches movies on DVD
- ☐ Pays child support
- ☐ Good parent
- ☐ Accepts responsibility for crimes

NEGATIVE FACTORS, continued

- ☐ Likes clubs and high crime areas
- ☐ Heavy tattoos and piercings
- ☐ Unwilling to change
- ☐ Reads *High Times* and dope magazines
- ☐ Watches DVDs on how to fool cops
- ☐ Deadbeat dad or mom
- ☐ Ignores or mistreats children
- ☐ Claims victimhood

GREEN FLAGS

- ☐ Innocent in the first degree
- ☐ Innocent in the second degree
- ☐ Police brutality
- ☐ Overcharged with gratuitous add-ons
- ☐ Holds state professional or occupational license
- ☐ Provides child care
- ☐ Has high-paying job and can pay most or all defense costs

RED FLAGS

- ☐ Long rap sheet
- ☐ Gang member
- ☐ Gun crime
- ☐ Jumped bail
- ☐ Violated probation
- ☐ Failed to appear in court
- ☐ Allergic to middle-class culture
- ☐ Child molester
- ☐ Rationalizes crimes
- ☐ Runs scams in jail
- ☐ Classified as violent inmate
- ☐ Drug addict
- ☐ Gambler
- ☐ Cannot express remorse
- ☐ Children seized by Child Services

HALLELUJAH!

- ☐ Will enlist in the armed forces of the United States of America hope. If you hear the defendant say, "I can't stand this place. I'll do anything to be free!"—be of good cheer. This is the sound of a defendant hitting bottom and preparing to change.

You'll note that in the checklist, driving a street-legal car is an important factor. Vehicles that are not street legal attract constant police attention. Defendants on supervised release must avoid encounters with police at all costs. Defendants who cannot understand why it is necessary to drive street legal are too ignorant to be free.

The evaluation also includes a list of red flags. These are factors that indicate your defendant may not be salvageable. Defendants who have multiple arrests and long rap sheets are unlikely to change. Jail doesn't scare them. They're a long way from hitting bottom. Defendants charged with gun crimes will, in most states, get long sentences no matter what you do. Drug addicts who maintain their addictions are poor risks. Defendants who rationalize crimes and who cannot express remorse do not have the social development to be free. Inmates who fight and gamble in jail and who confront corrections officers are too chaotic for freedom. Defendants who are being prosecuted under three-strikes laws or in repeat offender courts are going to get hammered, so save your money unless the defendant is innocent in the first degree. Gang members? Let the gang take care of them and foot the bills. (Fat chance!)

Note also a series of green flags, which indicate the defendant is highly likely to benefit from your help. If your defendant is innocent in the first degree, give all the help you can. Likewise, consider helping a defendant who is innocent in the second degree. Some jail time may help get his or her mind right. It's advisable to help defendants who have been grossly overcharged and hammered with gratuitous add-ons. These police and prosecutor shenanigans are shameful. A stout defense may get these tossed.

If your defendant was brutalized by police, your help is needed. Don't be surprised, however, if the brutality by itself is not sufficient grounds to free your defendant. The courts do not consider police brutality the same way you do. They will examine specific rules, police procedures, and case-law definitions of brutality that vary state to state. In general, getting bruised and scuffed up during an arrest is not considered brutality, just tough luck. Ditto getting chewed on by police dogs. In my city, I am sad to say, the K-9 squad specializes in letting the dogs bite suspects longer than necessary, enough to "put a hurtin' on" but just shy of the legal definition of brutality. Basically, to back a brutality charge, your defendant will need to have been beaten badly enough to require admission to a hospital. You'll need photos and video of the wounds, and don't forget to take the bandages off and get close-ups of the stitches. The same goes for the bloody clothes. Seek advice from defense counsel. If you're lucky, a dash cam or bystander video camera caught the action. Work quickly to get the evidence before it vanishes into the memory hole. Juries have a visceral hatred of police brutality, and prosecutors often will drop charges rather than face a humiliating defeat from the people themselves.

Defendants who hold state professional and occupational licenses are almost always capable of reform. They had to plan, study, and spend time and money to get those licenses. They have much at stake. If convicted of felonies, they will lose their licenses and be plunged into poverty.

If your defendant is a decent parent and provides crucial child care, and staying in jail may mean seizure of the children by state child services, help all you can. Children do not thrive in government custody. Children are truly innocent and don't deserve to live in foster care.

At the end of the evaluation, you'll see a box entitled "Hallelujah!" This refers to a defendant's decision to enlist in the military. As discussed in the previous chapter, if your defendant makes a sincere decision to enlist, and the charges can be reduced to misdemeanors, do everything you can. Not only is success likely, but you will also get your money back, because the military insists that its personnel honor financial obligations.

CHARACTER ASSESSMENT

Character is something that nobody can define, but everybody can recognize. Character is the essence of socialized humanity, and in every way it is the opposite of the chaotic, premoral state of mind. It is one of the few human qualities that improves with age.

Since the dawn of civilization, thinkers have pondered character and the ways in which humanity can improve itself. The struggle to become better human beings—more moral, more productive, more deserving of peace, prosperity, and divine mercy—has lasted for millennia. During the United States' first 200 years of existence, developing character was an objective, even an obsession, of people both ordinary and extraordinary. Books of sermons, allegories such as *Pilgrim's Progress*, and homilies of every sort were widely printed and eagerly read.

It is ironic and unsettling that this struggle to understand and achieve moral character has been debased, in my lifetime, into the self-help movement. It is as if this search for moral character, a brilliant light emanating from antiquity and passing undimmed through the centuries, has been diverted through a strange prism and refracted into a thousand bright, and meretricious, colors. We now seek not to be better citizens but to be thinner, more physically fit, with whiter teeth and thicker hair, better time-managed, more multitasking, entirely free of additives and insecticides, and with the carbon footprint of a turtle.

Fortunately, the criminal courts are not places of fad and fashion. Their modest task is to stop people from killing, maiming, robbing, burgling, drinking, drugging, smashing cars, destroying property, disturbing the peace, and in general being pains in society's collective posterior. The courts reward evidence of true character with leniency; they punish its absence with incarceration and death.

Character is what distinguishes civilized man from *Homo chaoticus*. The components of character are virtues.* In the Character Assessment Stick 'Em Up worksheet on p. 111, you'll see a list of virtues. It is neither comprehensive nor definitive, but it will do. Think about your defendant. Consider which virtues he or she has or may develop. Count them. The more virtues a defendant has, the more likely he or she is to be self-governing and to no longer need the heavy-handed supervision of cops, courts, and jailers.

Note the qualities that are not on the list: self-esteem; beauty; being fashionable, cool, or hip; being rich; having a perfectly organized closet; managing five different calendars on an iPhone that synchs with computers on four continents; and having 500 Facebook friends.

Virtues! Urge your defendant to get some today. It's never too late.

INMATE CHARACTER TESTS

Both character and its opposite are revealed in decision and action. Rely on deeds, not words, when judging whether defendants are worthy of support. To distinguish lip service from useful action, look for information gathered and steps taken by the defendants toward a useful objective. In talking with defendants, ask for specifics. For example, when you ask defendants whether they intend to finish their education, they *always* say yes. This is useless. Ask, instead, *how* they intend to do it. Defendants who are serious will know such things as:

1. When the next term begins

2. What papers have to be signed

3. What education costs

4. Where the school is located and whether classes are given during the day or at night

5. How much time is needed to get a degree

Serious defendants who are incarcerated will ask *you* to call schools, round up paperwork, and get course information. When they ask, get busy. This is what family are for. Asking for specific help is an excellent indicator of a desire to change.

The Stick 'Em Up worksheet on p. 112 is a list of the tasks you should ask defendants to perform in jail as a test of their character. They may appear to be simple, obvious actions, but whether inmates are willing to do them will quickly reveal whether they have made a decision to change.

---

* Social scientists would be horrified at such simplistic language. Fortunately the word "virtue" has, in Aristotle's famous formulation, "just so much exactness as the subject admits of."

For instance, you should ask inmates to get a haircut. Inmates who agree demonstrate that they realize they have to appear more middle class because, like it or not, the criminal justice system is middle class. If they're convicted and sent to prison, that mop is coming off anyway. Better to buzz it off now and work for a better outcome in court. You'd think that a haircut would be no biggie. You'd be wrong. An astonishing number of inmates just don't get it about the hair, the long pimp fingernails,* or the "Fuck You" tatts.

Another inmate character test, working on legal defense, is complex enough that it's discussed in detail in chapter 21. Other tests, such as using the jail phone responsibly, toughening up, obeying rules, and avoiding jail shenanigans, are common sense. Attending any classes, job training, or religious services offered and getting copies of religious texts also are important. Boredom is the main problem. In jail, the simplest things, such as rounding up pencils and paper, envelopes, and stamps, take a long time and require effort. These simple tasks will keep inmates well and profitably occupied and reveal to you whether they are serious about changing themselves.

NEVER UNDERESTIMATE YOUR INFLUENCE

Everyone who works in criminal defense has success stories. Most involve families who never gave up on their defendants, who worked and sacrificed to get the best outcome legally, then worked to socialize defendants for a successful reentry into society. Here is an example from my own experiences. Four years ago, a friend of mine called in desperation about a young man who worked as a pharmacist's technician in a large South Florida hospital. He had been arrested and charged with stealing and distributing Dilaudid and fentanyl, synthetic opioids more powerful than heroin and worth their weight in gold on the streets. Another defendant had ratted him out in return for leniency. The case was airtight.

Once convicted of a felony, the offender was barred for life from working in health care. His college degree and pharmacy certifications were worthless. Nonetheless, this guy had grit. He also had luck. He was assigned to a Florida prison that offered training and certification in skilled trades. He studied heating, ventilating, and air conditioning and earned his certification. He is free now, owns his own business, and makes more than he ever earned as a pharmacy technician. He has repaid his family's trust and their money and made them proud.

On the Crime City blog on my Web site (www.wesdenham.net), you can hear the stories of two young men who worked full-time jobs in order to put themselves through college. Following arguments and loud parties, both were arrested and faced ridiculous, jacked-up charges. With the help of their families, they avoided felony records and con-

---

* Pimps often wear long fingernails to advertise the fact that they don't do manual labor. That's why they have to pimp-slap their whores with an open hand, since if they use a closed fist, they slice their own palms.

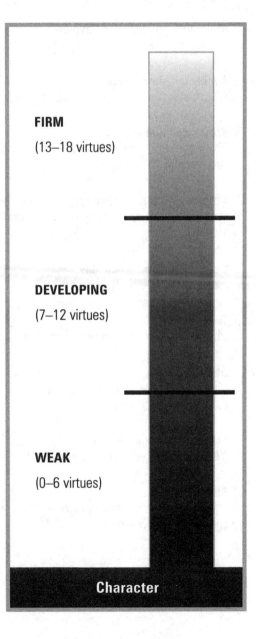

CHARACTER ASSESSMENT

VIRTUES

- ☐ Courage
- ☐ Honor
- ☐ Loyalty
- ☐ Self-sacrifice
- ☐ Honesty
- ☐ Prudence
- ☐ Wisdom
- ☐ Compassion
- ☐ Ambition
- ☐ Self-discipline
- ☐ Self-reliance
- ☐ Moderation
- ☐ Justice
- ☐ Industriousness
- ☐ Reason
- ☐ Temperance
- ☐ Piety
- ☐ Generosity

Total _____

FIRM

(13–18 virtues)

DEVELOPING

(7–12 virtues)

WEAK

(0–6 virtues)

Character

Stick `Em Up!

INMATE CHARACTER TESTS

☐ **Maintains grooming and hygiene**
(Cuts hair, trims nails, takes regular showers, and wears fresh uniforms)

☐ **Avoids jail shenanigans**
(Shuns fights, jail tatts, show outs, gambling, drugs, sex, and rules violations)

☐ **Works on legal defense**
(Develops story with defense counsel, advises on witnesses, gives accurate background information)

☐ **Attends classes, workshops, religious services**
(Attends GED classes, Bible, Koran, or Torah study, work details, reentry programs, 12-step meetings)

☐ **Uses jail phone responsibly**
(Stays within your budget limits)

☐ **Toughens up**
(Avoids whining, complaining, suicide threats, and useless drama)

☐ **Obeys jail rules**
(Avoids write-ups; makes complaints, seeks health care, and requests location changes using established jail procedures)

☐ **Plans life changes**
*(Has **detailed** plans for changes when freed; avoids lip service)*

☐ **Shows remorse**
(Shows genuine regret for crimes, victims, and the expense and heartbreak caused to you and other loved ones)

tinued their college and professional careers. Without family assistance, both might have served jail or prison time for exceedingly minor offenses.

IF YOU DECIDE TO SAY NO

Saying yes is easy. The remainder of this book will show you how to spend your money so as to maximize the benefit to the defendant and your family. Even if you can't raise enough money for a bail bond and private defense counsel, you can formulate a family management plan and ask the public defender to present it. Saying no is tougher. If you decide not to defend, then saying no has to have reasons.

First, bail bond and a private defense may be useless. If the defendant is being tried in repeat offender courts, or if the charges are serious and the state's case is tight, with eyewitness accounts, wire recordings, video surveillance, forensic evidence, confidential informants, or a codefendant who flipped, your money would be wasted.

And what if your money gets results? What if you hire the best attorneys and private investigators and they find some police sloppiness or deceit and poke enough holes in the prosecutors' case to get a violent, habitual criminal acquitted? All you're likely to get for your effort and expense is a wet, sloppy kiss and the Big Razzoo.

Which brings us to our second reason to say no: defendants may not want to change. Despite some lip service, they like the thug and drug life and don't plan to quit. They're impulsive, forever in crisis, and outside jail they stay busy committing crimes, using drugs, and creating unwanted, unsupported children. Do you really want to finance this? Is there a sign posted at your house that says Hoodlum Bank and Trust?

Nonetheless, saying no is never easy. Saying no can cause horrific arguments within the family. Relatives may break with you and never speak to you again. You may be consumed with self-doubt. Had you paid for a defense, would it have made a difference? No one will ever know, but when you think about it, you'll feel cold.

Like the ashes of love.

☠ ARE YOU A MOMMA'S BOY'S MOMMA?

Jails and prisons are full of momma's boys, all of them waiting. They're waiting for Mom to show up and to shout, threaten, wheedle, and plead. They're waiting for Mom to bring on the cash, the credit cards, the lawyers, and the therapists and to do, or promise, anything that will fix the problems and clean up the messes, just as she always has.

Is a momma's boy waiting for you?

Many of the most violent and incorrigible criminals I have interviewed are momma's boys. With Momma behind them, they think they're invulnerable. No matter what they do, they think Momma will always be there to make it right. In this chapter, you evaluated defendants. Now, for a small subset of readers, it's time for you to evaluate yourselves. Here's how you know if you're a momma's boy's momma:

1. Your son became, shortly after birth, the apple of your eye. Quickly, he became the center of your existence.

2. You were divorced or never married, so there has never been another man in your life. Your son's father contributed nothing to his upbringing.

3. Little by little, you not only loved your son but also fell in love with him.

4. You were secretly thrilled, beginning in grade school, to see how tough he was.

5. You were excited to learn how tough *you* were and how easily you could cow schoolteachers, social service workers, and even cops by yelling, making threats, and filing complaints and lawsuits.

6. You have always been willing to spend whatever it took to keep him out of trouble because his affection, trust, and need for your assistance were the most important things in your life.

7. You think that the entire world opposes you and your son and keeps you from happiness. It's you and your son against the world. Other than him, you have no friends.

8. You consider other women, especially those his age, rivals and enemies. You are relieved when your son beats, abuses, and betrays his girlfriends.

If most of the above are true for you, you're a momma's boy's momma. As long as this toxic relationship lasts, your son's crimes will only escalate. What he needs most is freedom from you. He may be able to find this only inside a prison.

For most families, I advise that you help as much as you can. For momma's boy's mommas, however, the advice is the opposite. Do your son, yourself, and society a favor. Give him up. Do it now.

It only gets worse.

☠ VAMPIRE DEFENDANTS

Vampires are repeat offenders who convince friends and family members to pay bail bonds, attorney fees, court costs, fines, and restitution, not once, not twice, but over and over again until their families are bled white financially. Most are sociopaths and master manipulators. Their ploys usually go like this:

1. It's *your* fault they're in jail. You're the one who divorced daddy, did a bad job in child rearing, didn't insist on high school graduation, ignored early drug use, didn't warn them about this or that floozy or thug, picked a lousy attorney the first time, etc.

2. *Somebody else* made them do it. The wife/husband/girlfriend/boyfriend made them go crazy, the cop forced them to flee and elude, associates tricked them into committing a crime, eyewitnesses were lying, the fingerprints and DNA evidence are faked, those drugs weren't theirs, etc.

3. They won't do it again! This time is different. You'll see! They're turning over a new leaf, this time for sure. By the way, please deliver a cashier's check to . . .

Some families never get it. They're enablers, and they will go on subsidizing criminal behavior, making up excuses, and pouring their assets into the criminal justice black hole until they're flat broke.

What the families never see is the way these guys act in jail. They strut and pimp-roll up and down the corridors, giving everyone the high-hat and bragging about how they have their mommy/grandma/girlfriend/sister under control.

They can play these bims like a piano, they declare. The old gals are like rigged slot machines. Pull the lever and they spit out money.

I recall one defendant in particular. He was the handsomest inmate I've ever seen—blond, blue-eyed, and buffed, with a Hollywood smile and the sort of razor haircut that you get in salons where you have to bust a C-note just for the tip. He was 30 going on 18, and for 10 years he had been hustling cocaine to the "in" crowd at the beach and tapping various women for condos, cars, and cash (between stays in the local jail, of course). Mommy, he informed me, was still ravishing in middle age, and stepdad was a pussycat loaded with money. One phone call, he told me confidently, and bail would be made, a fire-breathing attorney would appear like a genie from a bottle, and he'd be out cruising before sunrise.

When I talked to Mom, the story was different. She told me that over the years she had spent $75,000 in bail bonds and attorney fees, and her husband had finally read her the riot act. Not one penny more or he'd divorce her. The criminal justice system is not staffed by chumps either, and this time around, Mr. Hollywood got routed into habitual offender court and sentenced to hard time—enough to grow a third set of teeth.

I felt bad for him. Pretty boys do not do well in state custody. After a decade or so of prison proctology, he'll probably emerge wearing diapers—for life.

15

THE TICKLE OF THE TROCAR
Bail and Bail Bonds

WHEN I PASS BAIL bond offices late at night, I imagine vultures circling under a waning moon. I imagine a cheesy horror movie where you wake up paralyzed on an embalming table. You feel the tickle of the trocar along your thigh, then a stab as the hollow needle is thrust into the femoral artery to drain your blood while, in the second leg, another needle floods your veins with formaldehyde.

Aiee!

On the streets around every jail in the United States, the neon signs of bail bond offices, red as a whore's lips, wink a promise of freedom to men and women clutching credit cards, checkbooks, titles, and deeds and sitting in rusty metal chairs on linoleum that looked cheap even when originally installed circa World War II. All night, every night, it's midnight madness in the bail bond netherworld of the criminal justice system.

Bail and bail bonds are a necessary evil, but because loved ones don't understand the rules of the game, they are frequently fleeced by transactions, some of which are merely unethical, some of which are illegal. This chapter is about when and how to make the decision to post bond—and when and how not to.

First, some definitions. Bail is property, usually cash, deposited or pledged to a court in order to guarantee that a defendant will return for hearings and trial. If the defendant fails to do so, the bail amount is forfeited. If the defendant does report as ordered, in most cases bail money will be returned after sentencing. The amount of bail varies, depending on the defendant's risk of flight and the danger he or she poses to the community. Bail usually has conditions. Here are the most common:

1. Defendants must seek employment or continue to work.

2. Defendants must matriculate or continue education.

3. Defendants must abstain from illegal drugs and be drug tested.

4. Defendants must live with a responsible person and not alone.

5. Defendants, while free on bail, must not commit new crimes or contact victims or witnesses.

Other conditions may include mandatory check-in calls to the police, surrender of passports and firearms, home detention, electronic monitoring, alcohol counseling, and avoidance of known felons.

If you hire private attorneys, insist that they negotiate bail conditions in order to get the *least restrictive terms possible*. Remember, you're on the hook financially if your defendant screws up, violates the conditions, and gets tossed back into jail. If your defendant cannot be trusted to comply with the release terms, face that fact and consider leaving the defendant in jail.

The most common problem is drug use. When out on bond, your defendant will be randomly tested for drugs. It is essentially impossible for regular drug users to beat these tests. Best to leave druggies in stir so they can go cold turkey and cold sober and give some long, hard thought to the price of freedom. I've interviewed dozens of inmates pouring sweat on the floor and jumping like jitterbugs as they fight the monkey. For them, jail is free drug treatment. Bailing out such addicts would be a financial disaster.

Bail can take several forms.

1. A detainee *released on recognizance* (ROR) signs a promise to appear. No cash or bond is required.

2. Release may require a *surety*. This is a third party who guarantees bail payment if the defendant flees or violates bail conditions. The third party is typically a bail bondsman, and the guarantees he or she presents to the court is known as a *bond*.

3. Sometimes judges will order bail to be paid in *cash only*.

The United States is unusual in using commercial companies to act as bail sureties. In most countries bail is paid directly to the court. Illinois, Kentucky, Oregon, and Wisconsin have banned commercial bail entirely. In most other states, bail bondsmen are required to charge 10 percent of the bail amount for a bond. Thus a bail bond for $10,000 will cost $1,000, plus in most states *collateral* for the remaining $9,000. Note the emphasis on collateral. If you post a bond and the defendant skips or violates, bondsmen can execute on your collateral, which means you can kiss that house, car, or insurance cash value good-bye. The repo man will arrive shortly with the hook, and the deputy will show up all too soon at your door with the locksmith.

THE BAIL REDUCTION HEARING

Most defendants and their families have no idea that most state constitutions guarantee defendants a bail reduction hearing. They think that the original arraignment, a brief hearing that takes a formal plea then sets bail, is the only hearing to which defendants are entitled.

But in a bail reduction hearing, defense counsel can show cause why bail should be reduced. These hearings, which may be requested at any time prior to sentencing, give defendants, their counsel, and their loves ones time to gather relevant documents, develop arguments, and file motions. One of the main uses of the family management plan discussed in chapter 26 is to make a case for bail reduction. When defendants prevail in a bail reduction hearing, the cost of bail or bonds can be eliminated or substantially lowered. In such hearings, the court will not consider guilt or innocence, merely whether the defendant is a flight risk or a danger to the community and whether there exist circumstances that require the defendant to be free.

WHEN TO POST AND WHEN NOT TO POST BOND

I've emphasized several times that you *should not* race off into the night with a car full of hysterical friends and relatives and post bond just because your defendant was squealing on the jail phone. Defendants are reasonably safe in custody. They need to butch up, and you need to cool down. Consider your options:

First, your defendant may be released because charges are dropped or nol-prossed. As I've mentioned, in my city this occurs in 30 percent of all criminal cases. If you post bond and charges are later dropped, you're out the money.

Second, bail bonds consume funds that in many cases could be better used to pay private defense counsel or to pay the long-term costs of probation and parole. Prosecution doesn't go away just because the defendant is out of jail.

Third, too many families rush out to post bond before a bail reduction hearing and don't realize that bail might have been reduced or eliminated. If bail is lowered enough, you won't need a bond. You can pay cash bail to the court and *get your money back* after the hearings and trial are done.

Fourth and most importantly, because defendants have to hit bottom before they decide to change, you need to give jail time to work its magic. Here's an example from my family. One of my relatives has a nephew who was raised in Southern California. He attended college at Georgia Southern University in Statesboro, a small town about 100 miles northwest of Savannah, Georgia, where nothing much has happened since Blind Willie McTell wrote "Statesboro Blues" in 1928. To this California kid, the place was a million miles from nowhere. Twangy music, a slice of watermelon, and a bowl of hot goobers during the Peanut Boil Appreciation Festival were no compensation.

One day while riding through the fields of cotton, peanuts, and tobacco, he noticed some white things growing in the cow pastures. He stopped, walked about, and immediately recognized, shooting up from the cowpats, the gray stems and delicate yellow caps of *Psilocybe zapotecorum*, a.k.a. the "magic mushroom." The psilocybin and psilocin contained in these famous fungi are nature's own form of LSD and have sent shamans on mental thrill rides for millennia. Soon this kid is peddling 'shrooms to bored undergraduates. Business is brisk, and before long he is paying farmers not to spread manure or spray fungicide on their pastures. Within months he'd accomplished an alchemical miracle—the transformation of cow shit into gold.

In all the excitement, he forgot to keep his license and tag current, which occasioned a visit from a sheriff's deputy. Like a fool, he let a law enforcement officer enter his house without a warrant. The deputy saw a pile of 'shrooms on the dining room table and promptly made an arrest. While the Bulloch County Courthouse and City Hall are elegant buildings of red brick made from fine Georgia clay, the jail, sadly, is a hellhole. This kid got on the phone and pleaded for bail. My relative listened to all this, then said one word.

"No."

The result is instructive. The deputy, in making an arrest without a search warrant, violated constitutional search and seizure protections, so the charges were tossed in due course. A week in the clutches of the Bulloch County sheriff, however, scared this kid out of his wits. He went straight with a vengeance. He finished college and moved back to California. He now works hard, invests in real estate, and is on the way to his first million.

Sometimes "no" is a good thing. So is a little jail.

Of course, bail is beneficial in many circumstances. If your defendant is innocent in the first degree, if the cops truly have the wrong guy, the defendant deserves freedom. If bail is high, petition for a reduction hearing. A good attorney can use the flimsiness of the state's case to get bail lowered or persuade prosecutors to drop charges.

In complex cases, securing a defendant's release on bail can be useful as a legal tactic. It slows the prosecution, and as time passes, witnesses vanish, prosecutors' caseloads swell, evidence gets lost or mishandled, and defense counsel has time to poke holes in the prosecution's case.

If the defendant has a high-paying job, post bond and ask for your money back. Bail is also important when the defendant is the sole caregiver for children who, without their parent, would be seized by state family services.

Lastly, it is much easier for a defendant to formulate a family management plan when out on bail. The plan requires running around to gather information about schools, churches, jobs, and military services and to obtain records and character references. Out on bail the defendant, not you, can do the running.

THE TOUGH COOKIES CROWD

Bail bonding is a rough business run by hard-nosed men and women. They deal with crooks all day and night, and when a defendant skips and forfeits bond, they will foreclose on granny's house without shedding a tear. Bail bonding is subject to numerous scams and abuses. These are lightly regulated and punished because many judges, sheriffs, police chiefs, and prosecutors are elected officials, and bondsmen are bountiful contributors who can be counted on to donate year after year.

When defendants flee, bondsmen whistle up bounty hunters. These guys are authorized to make arrests but are far less regulated and disciplined than cops. Don't expect bounty hunters in your city to be as colorful as Duane Chapman, the famous television star of *Dog the Bounty Hunter*. Dog always makes a gentle arrest, prays over the miscreant, then suggests that while cooling off in jail, the suspect give his life to Jesus. Most bounty hunters are hard boys who can get really, really, pissed off about chasing fugitives up and down the state. They sometimes administer rough justice, such as a pistol-whipping in handcuffs, to fugitives in custody. They have no qualms about trashing houses and cars in which fugitives are hiding. If your defendant flees and gets beaten to a pulp by bounty hunters, redress will be difficult. The state has nothing but contempt for defendants who flee, commit crimes while on bail, or fail to show up for hearings and trials.

BAIL BOND MISFORTUNES AND SCAMS

Below is a list of the problems—and the scams—encountered by families seeking bond for an incarcerated family member.

Bond and Dismiss

You run out and post bond. Shortly thereafter, charges are dismissed. You lose. Because of the high percentage of dismissed cases, it's wise to wait a few days before posting bonds or paying private attorneys.

Bond and Bust

You post bond; then at the jailhouse door the defendant is rearrested on outstanding warrants or detainers from other states. Bye-bye bond bucks! Before you post bond, the defendant should petition a bond reduction hearing. You should use the time to research the defendant's rap sheet. It will take time to obtain criminal histories from other states and from the FBI. Most defendants are maddeningly vague about prior arrests and routinely lie about priors to family members and defense attorneys, so trust only information provided by law enforcement agencies. If the information is incorrect, it can be expunged or corrected by judicial order.

Bait and Switch

A bondsman tells you that bond is available under a special arrangement for only 5 percent! Once you get to the bonding office, you discover that this special deal actually is 5 percent cash now, then the rest in E-Z payments, with collateral, naturally, for the balance. In other words, the bond still is 10 percent cash and 90 percent collateral. This bait and switch is an unethical but not illegal practice in most states. Don't expect government to help you in these situations. Complaints to state licensing agencies usually result in a flurry of paperwork then a stern letter to bondsmen warning them never, ever, to do such a naughty thing again!

Bond "Sales"
Many cities are plagued by bondsmen who actually will write a bond in exchange for a payment of less than 10 percent of the bail amount. This practice is both illegal and unethical and can result in loss of licensing by the bonding agent. Mostly the offending bondsmen go unpunished. Courts compensate for this abuse by simply doubling the bail amount.

Bond Solicitation
Bondsmen are strictly prohibited from soliciting your business in person or by telephone. Many ignore this prohibition and hang around jail lobbies and entrances selling to all and sundry. If you complain, they'll simply deny it. It's your word against theirs. And by the way, how much did you contribute to local judges' and sheriffs' campaigns this year?

Bond Fraud
Scam artists will look up inmates' names on the Internet, then telephone relatives and purport to be bonding agents acting at the defendant's behest. To save you a trip, they'll be happy to bring the paperwork to your house and take your check or cash. When the phony bondsmen vanish, so does your money.

Never meet with someone claiming to be a bond agent outside a bail bond office or the offices provided for bondsmen in your local jail. If bond agents cold-call you on the phone, hang up. If they show up at your house, slam the door. These are illegal practices. If agents call at the behest of the defendant, which is legal, say you'll verify this with the defendant, then call back—maybe.

Bail Bond Disasters
Do not pledge your house and car as bail bond collateral. If your defendant flees, fails to appear, or violates a condition of parole, such as failing a drug test, you're toast. Do you want to risk your future on someone who by taking a single hit on a joint can wee-wee himself back into jail and you into poverty?

Do not harbor fugitives. If a fleeing defendant shows up at your house, try to persuade him or her to surrender. If the fugitive refuses, leave the house and call the police. Cops or bounty hunters will be coming soon anyway, since the homes of family members are the first places they search.

Harboring fugitives is a crime, and you may get busted if you do something so foolish. If your house gets trashed during a mad scuffle among cops, bounty hunters, and the fugitive, you'll have to clean up and pay for the damage yourself. If a fugitive brings guns, drugs, or contraband into your house, then later denies ownership when police make seizures, guess who's going to jail?

Don't take a stupid pill just because you love the defendant and can't bear to hear the complaints. If you lose everything because of bail forfeiture and harboring fugitives, you'll have nothing left for legal defense.

You may need a defense yourself.

16

HOW A WINO SAVED
THE SIXTH AMENDMENT
Public Defenders, Plea Bargains, and the Caseload Gorilla

> In all criminal prosecutions, the accused shall enjoy the right to a speedy and public trial, by an impartial jury of the State and district wherein the crime shall have been committed, which district shall have been previously ascertained by law, and to be informed of the nature and cause of the accusation; to be confronted with the witnesses against him; to have compulsory process for obtaining witnesses in his favor, *and to have the Assistance of Counsel for his defence.*

—Sixth Amendment, United States Constitution

PEOPLE ASSUME THAT PUBLIC defenders have been around forever. If they think about the subject at all, they probably imagine that there was a public defender aboard the *Mayflower* who scrambled up Plymouth Rock, spotted pilgrims being scalped by Indians, then began to shout objections.

Not so. I was a teenager before public defenders were common in state courts, which try the majority of criminal cases. Despite Sixth Amendment guarantees of legal representation, state legislatures in the past routinely defined the constitutional guarantee as limited to death penalty cases. All others, facing charges from second-degree murder on down to spitting on the pavement,* had to hire a private attorney or take their chances representing themselves.

Universal access to public defenders for noncapital crimes began, aptly enough, in Florida, in the landmark case of *Gideon v. Wainwright* (1963). The case began with a burglary at a cheesy pool hall in Panama City, along the famed "Redneck Riviera." A burglar or burglars trashed a cigarette machine and a jukebox and made off with coins, smokes, beer, and wine. A witness phoned the cops to say that Clarence Earl Gideon had been seen loitering around the pool hall earlier that morning. Gideon was apprehended with a bottle of wine and some change in his pocket, and on this flimsy evidence he was arrested and charged with breaking and entering. At trial, Gideon, a largely uneducated man, represented himself. He requested a court-appointed defense counsel but was

---

* Spitting on the pavement was a criminal offense for many years because it was thought to spread tuberculosis.

refused. He proclaimed his innocence and lectured the judge on the Sixth Amendment, which was pretty ballsy for a guy who ate wine for breakfast.

Newly sobered in one of Florida's fine prisons, Gideon scoured the law library for inspiration. Using a stub pencil* and writing on prison paper, Gideon filed suit against the Florida Department of Corrections, then appealed to the United States Supreme Court on the basis that his right to counsel under the Sixth Amendment, and his right to due process of law under the Fourteenth, had been violated. Astonishingly, the court accepted his case and appointed as his counsel one of the country's most famous lawyers, future Supreme Court justice Abe Fortas. Gideon won a resounding victory. In their decision, the justices affirmed that the right to counsel is fundamental and may not be denied in noncapital cases. Upon retrial, Gideon was acquitted. In the aftermath of the case, the states rapidly established the system of public defenders that we have today.

Nonetheless, defendants dislike public defenders. All of them want the best defense that money can buy, and all of them feel that the taxpayers aren't buying much for them. In small towns this may be true. In most large cities, however, this is a misconception. I have never met a defendant who understood public defenders. These hardworking attorneys provide a basic defense that reasonably protects the rights of the accused. They do not, however, hold hands, have heart-to-heart chats, and listen with teary eyes to complaints about crappy jail food. With thousands of cases to defend, public defenders cut short the bedside manner and the idle chatter. They will not spend much time with the defendant's loved ones, who are not, after all, their clients. They have to work fast. The cops arrest trainloads of new defendants all day, all night, and double that on weekends. Almost all of these will require a public defender.

The quality of public defenders, like that of private defense attorneys, varies. Here's a rough breakdown. The best public defenders are full-time government employees. They have their own offices and staff, including investigators and psychologists, and budgets to hire experts in forensics, document authentication, and other specialties. The worst are court-appointed private attorneys, who are paid low hourly fees, sometimes with a fee cap. When they reach the cap, their financial incentive is to dump the defendants as quickly as possible. Many court-appointed private attorneys are struggling young lawyers without experience or boozy old hacks who need a case to make rent. God help defendants who fall into their weak and greedy grasp!

PUBLIC DEFENDERS AND THE STANDARD DEAL

Defendants and their families are always distressed at how little time public defenders spend with their clients. Sometimes these attorneys just meet defendants at the courtroom door. Sometimes the interview is brief indeed:

---

* Prisoners are not allowed to possess full-length pencils and pens, which can be used as shivs.

"What's your name?"

"What's the rap?"

"Got any priors?"

"Let's go."

This makes defendants absolutely crazy. Not for nothing do they refer to public defenders as "dump trucks." Nonetheless, the reason public defenders can mount a reasonable defense and negotiate reasonable pleas with only a few minutes of conversation is that they know something that defendants don't—the Standard Deal. This is the sentence defendants can expect to receive given the magnitude of the charges and their criminal histories. The Standard Deal is the first plea offer, and almost every defendant gets one, even the most heinous murderers, rapists, and child molesters. In some states, and in the federal criminal system, the Standard Deal has been codified. Thus, for a certain offense, with so many priors, there is a fixed sentence—no variations and no judicial discretion allowed.

In most states, however, the Standard Deal is unspoken and unwritten. It is set, on the days when courts are in session, in an open market of crime and punishment. Many people find market operations bewildering, so I will briefly explain. A market occurs when buyers and sellers communicate freely among themselves to set prices for goods and services based on supply and demand. To see a market in action on a small scale, just visit a flea market early in the morning. At first, the same merchandise, such as used toasters, will have different prices. Soon, buyers and sellers will begin to talk with each other. "Great deal," says one buyer while looking at a toaster. Another, however, walks by and declares that the same used toaster is on sale for $5 less from a guy on the next aisle. Within minutes, prices will be adjusted. Similar toasters will have similar prices. Markets enable fast, subtle, and amazingly accurate matching of supply and demand via price. They perform the same price-setting function in criminal justice, in the form of sentences and pleas, just as they do in the economic market for goods and services.

In the criminal justice system, prosecutors sell sentences, which defense attorneys buy via plea bargains. The length of sentence is the price paid. Prices vary according to the demand on the system from the number of new arrests. This is matched to the supply of jail and prison space, the time available on court calendars, and the resistance to prosecution offered by defense counsel. The sellers and buyers communicate continuously by telephone, e-mail, and letter. They meet in offices and courtroom hallways. Courtrooms used for preliminary hearings resemble trading floors where the final deals are hammered out. Plea courts have much in common with exchanges for pork bellies, corn, wheat, and oil. The Standard Deal is dynamic. It varies constantly in response to the following:

1. Changes in supply and demand

2. Changes in laws and police procedures

3. Changes of judges, prosecutors and defenders, sheriffs and chiefs of police

As bewildering as this all may seem, the Standard Deal is remarkably accurate on any given day. It is, however, not pretty to watch pleas being negotiated:

PROSECUTOR: "I want four years for this perp."

DEFENSE: "What? Are you nuts? This kid has no priors."

PROSECUTOR: "I don't care. I'm up to here with corner boys."

DEFENSE: "You go hard-ass on me, and we go to trial. Judge so-and-so will ream you a big one. You're overreaching."

PROSECUTOR: "All right. Two years. Not a day less. Then two probation and back in the slam if this dimwit fucks up even one time."

DEFENSE: "Done."

The Demand Side: Caseload

Defendants and their families are understandably preoccupied with their own cases and may not perceive a force that obsesses attorneys, judges, and jailers. This is caseload, the never-ending avalanche of new criminal cases. In Los Angeles, for example, there are, on any given day, 20,000 people in jail and *more than* 20,000 cases pending.

¡Ay Chihuahua!

Even in my modest metropolis, police arrest a new defendant, on average, every six minutes. That's a new case, and a new case file, in the time it takes to boot up a computer. Jacksonville's jail and the outlying prison farm are bursting from 51,500 arrests every year. Inmates sleep atop one another in bunk beds, with some guys crammed into plastic and foam "boat beds" wedged into corridors and showers. The courtrooms for arraignments and bail hearings are built underneath the jail to allow inmates to be dropped down quickly by elevator. With attorneys and family members milling around and sometimes standing in lines around the buildings, these august forums look like, sound like—and alas, sometimes smell like—bus terminals.

Caseload is the demand side of the criminal justice economy. The demand is never ending because criminals, and police, are relentless. Caseload obsesses the players. Cops want to clear cases, judges want to clear calendars, jailers want to free up beds, and attorneys want to see fewer files piled on their desks. Caseload is the 900-pound gorilla of the system. Prosecutors and public defenders cut plea deals not out of the goodness of their hearts but because they are always thinking about the hundreds of other cases piled on their desks. Deadline clocks are always ticking. By a certain time, defendants must be tried or freed. The Sixth Amendment's guarantee of a speedy and impartial trial is a granite mountain against which the freight train of criminal justice is always hurtling.

The Supply Side: Jails, Courts, Prosecutors, and Defenders

Against the unceasing demand of new defendants stands the supply of jails, prisons, courts, prosecutors, defenders, staff, and budgets. The supply is never adequate. Because of the near religious belief in zero-tolerance policing, and the enthusiasm of elected officials who know that jamming jails wins votes, the system in most cities teeters on the verge of collapse.

The orderly processing of defendants into prisons is rudely interrupted by defense counsel. With their motions, discoveries, points of law, and occasional insistence on going to trial, they slow the process and thereby *increase the caseload*. When demand overwhelms supply, as it does occasionally, judges order prisoners freed en masse. When this happens, editors howl in righteous indignation. Preachers thunder in even more righteous indignation. Citizens shriek. Inevitably, the taxpayers get squeezed for more jails, courts, and cops, and the whole game ratchets up to a new level. This is criminal justice politics, American-style.

The Price Paid: Plea Bargains

Plea bargains keep the criminal justice system operating. The plea, which sets a length of sentence without going to trial, is the selling price that matches demand and supply. Without plea bargains, the criminal justice system would implode. A favorite topic of speculation among criminal attorneys during adult beverage hour is what would happen if all the inmates in a city jail simultaneously demanded their right to trial by jury. The justice system, which currently brings approximately 10 percent of defendants to trial, is already strained to the limit. If everybody demanded their day in court, the result would be chaos—mass trials held in football stadiums; mass release of cheering, hooting, inmates; mass publicity; mass hysteria.

Yikes!

Plea bargains are so necessary that defendants who insist on a trial by jury face the possibility, if convicted, of serving sentences that can be double to triple those offered in plea bargains. Plea bargains do get cases resolved reasonably quickly. Defendants, however, are shoved through the justice chute like cattle to the slaughter. Sloppy police work and flimsy prosecutions that would lose at trial never get challenged. More than a few innocent men and women go to prison. Defendants feel that they are getting hustled. They are. Market-driven, plea-bargain justice is fast, bewildering, and preemptory. It is roughly fair but not perfect. Not by a long shot.

THE ROLE OF THE FAMILY IN PLEA BARGAINS

Nine times out of 10, a negotiated plea will be the best—and only—deal that defendants can get. This will be true regardless of whether defendants are represented by private attorneys or public defenders. The alternative, going to trial, has huge risks. Every defense attorney has stories of defendants who turned down a deal of five years and got life in prison instead.

Defendants have unrealistic notions about trials. They have watched too much court and cop TV and think that mistakes made by police or prosecutors will result in acquittal or dismissal of charges. This was true occasionally in the confused 1970s, but not today. Unless mistakes are absolutely outrageous, they will, at most, gain defendants a new trial. The prosecution, having tried the case once already, will usually win conviction easily. Defendants also overestimate the sympathy of juries. Because jury duty requires time away from work, most jurors are retirees, government workers, or union members who are guaranteed pay when they take jury duty. Such people fear crime in their personal lives and do not take kindly to criminal defendants. In my city, which is conservative and religious, I'd sooner face the Inquisition than a jury.

One of the hardest things that you, the family, must do is discuss with defendants whether to take or refuse a plea. Is the plea offered the best deal available? You'll never know. It's the only deal on the table, right here, right now. Take it or leave it. When defendants take the deal, you will never know what might have happened had they chosen trial instead. At this point in the proceedings, defendants usually recoil from defense attorneys. They will turn to you for advice. You're their family. What do you think?

Here, you must rely on your knowledge of your defendant and the evaluation you undertook earlier. Seek advice from defense counsel. They will advise you on tactical situations, such as whether judges and juries in your jurisdiction may or may not be favorable. Think about the charges. If your defendant is innocent in the first degree, or if the charges are jacked up or absurd, defend to the max. Most situations are murkier. There is no right or wrong answer, merely choice A and choice B, clear cut and cold as ice. Once you give your opinion, you're done. Defendants must make the final decision alone.

HOW GOOD ARE PUBLIC DEFENDERS?

Because of the enormous number of cases they try, public defenders have wide and deep experience. They are in jail and in court at all hours. They know all the judges and prosecutors, who are, like themselves, government employees. How good are they? According the Department of Justice, pretty good. Here are the actual figures from the Bureau of Justice Statistics:

In both Federal and large State courts, conviction rates were the same for defendants represented by publicly financed and private attorneys. Approximately 9 in 10 Federal defendants and 3 in 4 State defendants in the 75 largest counties were found guilty, regardless of type of attorney. However, of those found guilty, higher percentages of defendants with publicly financed counsel were sentenced to incarceration. Of defendants found guilty in Federal district courts, 88% with publicly financed counsel and 77% with private counsel received jail or prison sentences; in large State courts 71% with public counsel and 54% with private attorneys were sentenced to incarceration.*

The short version is that defendants, whether represented by public defender or private counsel, face the same rate of conviction. From private counsel, however, they get a slightly better outcome with somewhat less incarceration. The differences in conviction and sentence are significant, but they are not large.

This is definitely *not* the impression left by TV crime shows, where defendants are represented by tough talking, swell-dressing private lawyers who file tricky motions and, during pointed cross-examinations, tie prosecution witnesses in knots. On TV, mobster/killer clients go free as their posses and *carnales* applaud and shout. Defendants in jail believe the TV version. Too many of them are convinced that private attorneys are magicians who, with political pull, a well-placed contribution to a vote-hungry judge, and some legal sleight of hand, can somehow get them off the hook no matter what they've done. Sometimes this is true. Mostly, however, it isn't. You do the crime, you do the time. The only question is how much.

Many defendants also don't like the fact that a large number of defenders are young women. Most female public defenders are plenty tough, whatever their age. In any case, everyone who works the jails and criminal courts gets hard boiled fast. If defendants knew anything about history, they'd thank their stars for those tired, harassed, and hurried women who drag files on rolling carts through U.S. jails and courtrooms. The alternative, which existed in my youth, was for defendants to face the apparatus of police, prosecutors, and judges legally naked and alone.

Public defenders, especially those in well-funded departments in large cities, do surprisingly well. Their activities set the Standard Deal, and that's what they can usually negotiate with prosecutors. In the most serious cases, for example, murder, armed robbery, capital rape, terrorism, and major drug smuggling, public defenders may be *better than* private attorneys. The reasons are practical and financial. Although they use them sparingly, given their enormous caseloads, public defenders in big-city departments have

---

* Caroline Wolf Harlow, *Defense Counsel in Criminal Cases*, U.S. Department of Justice, Bureau of Justice Statistics, November 2000, www.ojp.usdoj.gov/bjs/pub/pdf/dccc.pdf.

on-staff investigators and forensic experts. The most senior public defenders have years of trial experience with the toughest cases. They often appeal cases based on disputed points of law and on constitutional grounds. Although the best private attorneys can do all of these things, often with distinction, the problem is that few defendants can afford them.

Here is a telling example. Just recently, a Jacksonville defendant convicted of murder in a trial by jury won an appeal after a public defender successfully challenged jury instructions that did not empower the jury to consider the lesser charge of manslaughter. The defendant now will be granted a new trial, and he has a fighting chance to reduce his prison sentence by decades. Had private attorneys tried and appealed this case, the full ride of trial by jury, appeal, then a second trial by jury, with the costs of investigators and experts, could easily have risen into six figures. Few defendants and their families have this kind of money. For the most serious charges, public defenders are often the only option. Fortunately, they often excel at these challenges.

For the protections defendants receive today from public defenders, we can thank one middle-aged wino from the Florida Panhandle. For most of his life, he had too many wives, too many kids, too much alcohol, and not enough employment. But for several years, a man scarcely literate and rarely sober buried himself in dusty law books and won legal representation for millions of defendants. In so doing Clarence Earl Gideon became a great American and won a place in history and law books forever.

And what did Gideon do after he was freed? Did he write a book and appear on talk shows? Did he rake in bucks from plush speaking gigs at universities and high-minded bar associations? Alas, he did not. He got married again, hit the hooch, and avoided work whenever possible. For most defendants, even when victorious, the world is a hard place.

Fairy-tale endings are few.

17

THE PIN-STRIPED MAFIA

Fee Whores, Voodoo Doctors, Dodo Birds, and Other Legal Vermin

THE PRICE AND QUALITY of private defense attorneys vary wildly. If you decide to hire one, understanding the business of criminal law will help you make a better choice. So in this chapter I'll examine the weird world of law and how it operates differently from other businesses. Then I'll discuss horrible private attorneys, how to recognize them, and how to avoid them. In the next chapter I'll talk about the great private attorneys who can work wonders for your defendant, and explain how to find them.

THE FUZZY-WUZZY WORLD OF LAW

The practice of law is largely unregulated and unscrutinized. Most businesses are regulated by the iron hand of government. Attorneys are regulated by the feather-light touch of bar associations. When businesses violate government regulations, they get inspected, sanctioned, and fined. When attorneys violate bar association rules, they are theoretically subject to disbarment—which might actually happen if they are caught on videotape committing a felony or if they embezzle client "trust" accounts* too often and with too much blowback. But mostly, when they violate bar association rules, they receive a mildly annoying blizzard of paperwork.

In my state, the bar association enforces pettifogging rules, such as limiting the scope of advertising, instead of enacting tough regulations against unfair contracts, theft of client funds, and unethical business practices. This state of affairs is unsurprising. State legislators who write the laws are predominantly attorneys. Attorneys themselves are astonishingly unaware of their privileged status, because they rarely work outside law.

Competition operates differently in criminal law than in other businesses. Attorneys are, of course, subject to supply and demand. In most cities, there isn't enough demand for private defense attorneys. Zero-tolerance policing results in mass arrests of indigent

---

* Ironic quotations are used because attorney "trust" funds are not insured in the manner of bank accounts. Attorneys do not even have to post fidelity bonds in most states. When you close a business transaction and deposit funds into an attorney bank account, you just have to "trust" that you can withdraw them later!

defendants who can't afford private representation. Police arrest few professional and white-collar criminals who can afford a maximum private defense including trial by jury. So while public defenders are overwhelmed with cases, private counsel have too few. As a result, it can take years for private attorneys to acquire enough trial and appellate experience to sharpen their skills. Most defense attorneys do not have a full-time criminal practice and also work in family and real estate law to earn a living.

The limited supply of paying clients does not, however, serve to lower attorney fees or make them uniform, because the market for private criminal defense services is inefficient. It lacks one vital factor—buyer information. Efficient markets, in which prices for comparable services and products vary only slightly, require that buyers have sufficient knowledge to make informed purchasing decisions.

To give you an example of how efficient competition works, let's use a simple consumer product. When you buy cotton swabs at the store, you know exactly what they are. There's a cotton ball on the end of a stick. You twirl one in your ear, and you get wax. What else is there to know? All that matters is price and packaging and the choice of a wooden stick or plastic. When you buy, you have near perfect information.

Now let's consider a market where consumers have somewhat less perfect information, nonlegal professional services. You know less about the skills required, but in most instances, you understand the work. Dentists clean, drill, cap, implant, and whiten. Accountants prepare taxes, audit books, and draft financial reports. You may not know *how* professionals work, but you know *what* they're doing. You can distinguish good work from bad and meaningfully compare prices.

Criminal defense, by contrast, is the most opaque of professions. It is unlikely that you understand criminal law. You don't know how much work attorneys should be doing to earn their fees, so you have to make a purchasing decision based solely on reputation. You judge by the size of the ad in the Yellow Pages, the glossiness of the color brochures and newsletters, or even the thickness of the Persian carpets in the office. The most common way you hear about defense attorneys is through word-of-mouth advertising. Unfortunately, this word of mouth comes from inmates who repeat what they've heard through the jail grapevine:

> INMATE: Mom, I heard that so-and-so is a great lawyer. He got a guy freed over in the next dorm, and that guy was guilty as hell.
>
> MOTHER: Well, son, I'll go see him.

Think about this for a minute. The number-one source of purchasing information for legal defense services is jail gossip! Inmates are notoriously unable to compare attorneys and cases because they don't know details.

Attorneys compete on price and reputation but *not* on service and performance. Most cases plead out, so when families hire private counsel, they usually are buying a plea bargain. But how much should a plea bargain cost? How much work does it require? How do you distinguish a good bargain from a bad one? This is not easy. Most people know only the TV version:

> PROSECUTOR: We've got fingerprints, an eyewitness, and the gun. We're going for murder one with the death penalty.
>
> DEFENSE: My client will name the person who hired the hit. It's an important name.
>
> PROSECUTOR: He'll testify in open court?
>
> DEFENSE: Only if he gets man one and 10 years tops.
>
> PROSECUTOR: He's got to allocute, with every grisly detail.
>
> DEFENSE: He'll chatter like a trained parrot.
>
> PROSECUTOR: Done deal.

In real life, of course, things aren't so easy and the dialogue isn't so snappy. Nonetheless, many plea bargains require only brief conversations followed up by standard, fill-in-the-blank documents. Defendants appear in a short court hearing, agree to the terms, and a judge blesses the deals.

Every family wants to know the answer to the following questions: Was the plea bargain they purchased from a private attorney better than the Standard Deal the defendant would have received *for free* from the public defender? Are a few minutes of conversation, a document, and a five-minute court appearance worth thousands of dollars? Are private attorneys that much better than public defenders who handle many times more cases? Families may never know. The people who do, other attorneys and judges, will never tell. They, too, are members of the pin-striped mafia.

WHY DEFENDANTS AND THEIR FAMILIES TAKE SUCKER BAIT

Most defendants believe, with nearly religious passion, that the criminal justice system is crooked. They see it as an instrument of the state that is racist and is dedicated primarily to putting black and brown people in prison. They consider public defenders to be in cahoots with The Man—fuddy-duddy functionaries who usher defendants from jail to prison. By contrast, they think private attorneys are fixers who can miraculously get them off by pulling strings, whispering in the judge's ear, or paying somebody off. How many defendants have I interviewed who said, "I want a smart, Jew-boy lawyer"?

Numberless!

Both these beliefs are exaggerated and largely incorrect. If the system were corrupt, and an acquittal cost nothing more than a payoff to a judge, some defendants, at least, would get better results. The problem for defendants is that the system is, with occasional lapses,* honest. It is also hardworking and tough. Cops are better trained than ever and less likely to make gross mistakes that get charges dropped. Laws and court opinions have made it more difficult to obtain acquittals based on police and prosecutorial mistakes. But the belief persists that private attorneys are fixers, which makes defendants and their families suckers for the sales pitches of unscrupulous lawyers who hint, with a wink, a nod, and a roll of the eyes, that miracles can be accomplished with a well-placed phone call.

The reality is more mundane. As you read in the Department of Justice study in the last chapter, private attorneys get results that are somewhat better than those obtained by public defenders, but not extraordinarily so. Good attorneys, whether public or private, get results with hard, tedious work. Bad attorneys do little work, no work, or awful work, and get defendants sent down the river for years more than is necessary. They also sock families with big fees that have no relation to the value of the work done. Some of these characters are colorful and amusing, in the way carnival barkers and three-card monte operators are amusing.

Mostly they make you want to puke.

THE ROGUES' GALLERY

Fee Whores
Like their street-walking sisters, fee whores specialize in seducing clients to pay the maximum possible fee for the minimum amount of work. Essentially they charge big bucks for the Standard Deal, which the defendant could have received for free from a competent public defender. The inability of families and defendants to evaluate an attorney's performance creates enormous financial incentives for attorneys to do a quick phone plea and then take the money and run. This practice is unethical, but not illegal.

Contractors
These are the most execrable of fee whores. They deserve a place in the lowest circles of hell where the sinners boil in molten tar up to their eyeballs. Contractors take a case, charge a large fee, then subcontract all the actual work to another attorney, usually the lowest bidder. The contractor keeps the lion's share of the fee and does no work.

First, some explanations are in order. It is common for different attorneys within a single law firm to work on a criminal case. This is not subcontracting. Most criminal

---

* A recent corruption case in Mississippi indicates that the price of a fix today is somewhere north of $50,000.

firms have multiple hearings and trials occurring simultaneously, so they use several attorneys to make appearances, especially at preliminary hearings. In big-ticket defenses, where six- and seven-figure fees are being charged, a firm may hire outside attorneys who are specialists in particular areas, such as cross-examination, DNA, juror challenges, and so forth. This is not subcontracting either, since the lead firm still does most of the work. The abuse I write about is subcontracting that adds no value to the defense and is merely a tactic to take advantage of gullible defendants, grab the money, and subcontract the work to some poor gork who needs a case.

I've witnessed the effects of such abuse firsthand. I worked as a Spanish translator on a federal case in which the FBI arrested and charged two Mexican nationals with hauling 60 kilos (132 pounds) of methamphetamine from Texas to Florida. Both of these mopes were Otomí Indians whose native language was a dialect of Nahuatl. Prior to their arrests, one had been a watermelon picker in the Rio Grande Valley. The other had been raking and baling pine straw for the nursery trade. One of the brothers was guilty; the other was a hanger-on whose involvement was limited to talking big drug talk and dreaming of the day when he, too, could traffic dope, earn the big bucks, and drive a Mercedes, instead of a donkey, back to his native village. Despite headlines ginned up by government flacks ("Major Drug Ring Smashed!"), the G-men had actually rounded up a humble drug mule and his wannabe kid brother. The big drug dealers, as usual, had stayed snug south of the border, where mansions are large, police are tame, and incomes are tax free.

A lawyer hired by the family charged an upfront fee of $50,000. The lawyer pocketed $45,000, then jobbed out the case to one of those lawyers who think that Wheaties and bourbon are the true breakfast of champions. After a few bungled hearings, the family realized they'd been handed off to a lush. They then hired another attorney, who, for a substantially lower fee, got one brother freed and the second sentenced to 10 years.*

Another shameless form of subcontracting is hiring disbarred attorneys as paralegals. In most states, this dubious practice is permitted. The objective is for the supervising attorney to get lawyer-quality work at secretarial prices, all while charging full fees and enjoying a fat mark-up on cheap, disgraced labor.

When you hear that an attorney you're considering is contemplating contracting out the actual defense or hiring a disbarred attorney to do the work, leave the office at once. Try not to scream until you're in the elevator. Of course, attorneys planning to contract out the work won't put things so baldly. They'll say that while another attorney outside the firm will be handling the case, they will, of course, be supervising things and adding their wit and wisdom, like secret sauce, to the proceedings.

---

* Ten years sounds harsh, but this defendant had been caught on wiretaps and ratted out by a confidential informant. Consider also that 60 keys of tweak is enough to send a medium-sized city to the psycho ward.

Unfortunately, in law as in restaurants, secret sauce is expensive and used primarily to season junk food.

Voodoo Doctors

These are attorneys whose true forte is not law but salesmanship. They make their living taking advantage of defendants and their families who are looking for a fix rather than a defense. Here's how it works. After a hearty handshake and a warm smile—maybe even a hug—voodoo doctors will sit you down in their beautiful offices and tell you some interesting stories:

1. They'll tell you they know the judge and the prosecutor very, very well. They've worked with them for years. They play golf with these guys and swat around the tennis ball. Heck, just last week, they attended a birthday party for the judge's kid. This sounds great, but it's meaningless. All defense attorneys know judges and prosecutors. In any case, most judges avoid socializing with attorneys who appear before them, to avoid having to recuse themselves.

2. They'll hint that judges and prosecutors owe them favors. They'll hint that strings got pulled for some unruly relative of His or Her Honor or that some political contributions got paid during the last election. With a wink or a nod, voodoo doctors will imply that the criminal justice system is unfair—we're all adults here and can acknowledge these things!—and that what matters most is not what the defendant did but who the defense attorney is pals with.

3. Lastly, voodoo doctors will do what salesmen call "painting a picture." The picture is always some monstrous absurdity in the law or quirk in the justice system that can be rectified only by a foxy and worldly wise attorney. Those poor schlubs in the public defender's office, voodoo doctors declare, haven't a clue about this stuff. Besides, public defenders are mostly girls, for crying out loud. Do you want to leave your defendant's fate to some frail who spends most of her time dreaming about her boyfriend and worrying about her lipstick shade?

A friend of mine was victimized recently by a voodoo doctor extraordinaire. My buddy was arrested in Valdosta, Georgia, about two hours northwest of Jacksonville. At a drunken party some expletives were exchanged; some shoving may have occurred. When it was over, all involved were as angry as hornets in a jostled nest, but no one was hurt. Several of the partygoers, however, called the police and pressed charges, and my buddy was busted for felony assault and battery. He got tossed into the Lowndes

County Jail, fed a bowl of mush, and assigned a six-foot length of damp concrete to sleep on.

The next day, he called his family, who bailed him out. The family then went in search of a good attorney. The lawyer they chose had a grand office. He sat everyone down and told them an astounding story. This involved a traffic accident where one driver, going straight ahead and obeying all laws, was T-boned by another. Because of a quirk in the law, driver number one, blameless though he might be in the eyes of God, was going to get hammered. Fortunately, this lawyer was hired, and with some tricky motions and some goodwill from his buddies on the judicial bench, the whole mess was soon put right. Justice triumphed against madness!

My friend's case, alas, was all too similar, said the good voodoo doctor. A silly argument could result in a long sentence in a Georgia prison. As for my buddy's plan to attend law school, he could kiss that good-bye. Instead of poring over the law books, my friend could look forward to years of sewing blue jeans for some chump prison labor contractor.

So sad! Of course, if a really top-notch attorney were to get involved . . .

My friend and his family took the bait and forked over a $20,000 fee. In return, the lawyer got the felony reduced to a misdemeanor. My buddy was sentenced to probation.

What's wrong with this picture? Ethics and economics! The defendant and his family had no idea that the arrest was a bullshit bust with the typically gross overcharges that occur with zero-tolerance policing. It's the kind of felony case that a public defender can bust down to misdemeanor over the phone between bites on a doughnut. My friend and his family paid, in essence, for the Standard Deal. A better attorney, of the type who files motions of discovery and bills of particulars, deposes complainants, questions police officers, and challenges the validity of charges point by point, might have forced the prosecutor to drop the case. And consider the price: in my city, which is much larger than Valdosta, $20,000 will buy you a better-than-average defense for murder one.

The defendant and family were victimized because they had no way of knowing the value of criminal defense services. They made a buying decision with no information about what such services should cost and what distinguishes an excellent defense from a poor one. They had no idea how much work would be involved in negotiating a plea, or even what the work would be. Voodoo doctors always imply that work is irrelevant. What you're really paying for, they tell you, is magic.

Fee Mills

These are criminal defense law firms that rope in clients with low, low fees. When families comparison shop, the fee mill is always the low bidder. Fee mill attorneys tell clients and their families that the low fees are possible because they specialize in negotiating plea bargains and never go to trial. They allude to a large caseload, to economies of scale, to an automated office, to years of experience. What they actually specialize in is a line of chatter so bright it would leave the wiliest grifter stunned and amazed.

This sales pitch is hokum. Public defenders handle larger caseloads and negotiate more pleas than any private attorney. More importantly, the threat of going to trial is the defense attorney's most powerful weapon. Trials require enormous amounts of time, labor, and money. They increase, by orders of magnitude, the caseload pressure on the prosecution and induce the state to make a better-than-average plea offer in order to avoid the ordeal.

Sucker Fish

These are attorneys who charge by the hour and conduct endless hearings, depositions, and motion filings in order to run up the fee. Like lamprey eels, they attach their tiny teeth to clients and families, secrete toxins that impede common sense, then suck up financial blood and tissue. When clients and their families are dry husks, they plead out the defendants, generally to the same offer that could have been negotiated at no charge by the public defender.

Dodo Birds

Some states, lamentably, allow attorneys who flunk the bar exam to practice law under the supervision of another attorney. Always ask for a bar association number when interviewing attorneys. Avoid dodos at all times and in all cases. Like the creatures for which they are named, dodo birds are clueless and flightless, but in the practice of law, they're not yet extinct.

Disbarred Attorneys

Disbarred and suspended attorneys hang around the legal system like vultures around a carcass, snatching the odd job or fee. An astonishing number of them continue to practice by filing documents under phony names and bar numbers or by filing under the name and number of a gullible, usually junior, attorney.

All disbarred attorneys have one thing in common—they're crooks. Given the extraordinary privileges attorneys have voted themselves over the years in state legislatures, about the only causes for disbarment are felony convictions and egregious theft of clients' money. In fact, attorneys disbarred because of felony convictions often can be *reinstated* to the bar and allowed to practice. They are the only felons permitted to work in licensed professions without having their civil rights restored.

How do you discover if an attorney you are interviewing is disbarred or suspended? Simply check online or phone your state bar association, which is usually located in the state capital. Ask to check an attorney's disciplinary status. If the attorney is, or has been, suspended or disbarred, or has received multiple bar sanctions or letters of admonition, avoid this person like the plague. There are honest, hardworking attorneys who will be happy to represent your defendant.

Crooks

The U.S. criminal justice system is remarkably free of corruption, but the level of honesty is not 100 percent. I lived in Miami in the 1980s, when the FBI investigated massive corruption in state courts. During a sting called Operation Court Broom, the feds arrested and ultimately convicted numerous judges, lawyers, and businesspeople. The FBI gave the judges the full monty—a perp walk in front of the cameras and microphones from which to proclaim their innocence and "welcome" their day in court. Later, on the evening news, surveillance videos showed these same judges stuffing their coat pockets with cash.

Unless you have serious money, it is unlikely that you or your defendant will be asked for a bribe. Should this happen, however, regard it as a golden opportunity—not for the bad guys but for your defendant. If this occurs, I recommend the following:

1. Call the FBI office in your city and ask to be transferred to the public corruption unit.

2. If the FBI is interested, hire an honest attorney to negotiate a deal with the feds. This should include leniency, and lots of it, in return for cooperation in prosecuting corrupt attorneys and judges.

The FBI and United States Attorneys handle almost all public corruption cases. These cases spatter political mud everywhere, and local prosecutors are reluctant, if not incompetent, to prosecute them. In fact, when corruption cases occur, the local establishment may find it convenient to attend lengthy legal conferences, preferably on the other side of the planet.

Unprepared Attorneys

Attorneys unprepared for hearings and trials are the bane of the judicial system. In no other business is lack of preparation so tolerated. At most, clueless attorneys get a scolding from judges. Defendants represented by these sloths get years of added prison time to lament their poor choice of counsel.

The only way to control this shameful behavior is to pay private attorneys in installments. As strange as this may seem, this is, in the business of criminal law, a radical notion. It will be explained at length in chapter 20.

THE PLEA BARGAIN AS A FREE GOOD

To protect yourself from many of the unscrupulous practices outlined above, it's important to understand that, in economic terms, a plea to the Standard Deal is a *free good*. This is a technical concept, so let me elaborate: A free good is not valueless or unimportant. The classical example of a free good is air. We all need air to survive, but because it surrounds us and does not require manufacture, it costs nothing. To get it, we merely inhale.

The Standard Deal is likewise a free good because with few exceptions it is available free of charge from the taxpayers via a public defender or appointed attorney. Therefore, *the actual plea negotiation has no economic value*. In a case that will plead, the only legal services for which you should pay are the preliminary work—hearings, motions, challenges, and investigations. This leads to one of the most important precepts of this book:

Do not pay attorneys merely to negotiate a plea. Pay for motions, challenges, and investigations that *improve* a defendant's bargaining position and result in a plea agreement that is better than the Standard Deal.

You will be asking attorneys, before you give them your money, to tell you what work they intend to do in return.

The following chapters will show you how.

18

CRACKERJACK PRIVATE ATTORNEYS
How to Find the Prize in the Box

WHAT IS IT THAT *GOOD* private attorneys do that public defenders can't? The answer is W-O-R-K. The best private attorneys get better deals because they do more preliminary work *before plea negotiations even begin.* In this chapter you'll learn what kind of preliminary work you should expect from an attorney you hire and how to interview the candidates to make sure they will provide it.

By reading this far in the book, you already are much better informed than most defendants' families. By the end of the next chapter, and with the Attorney Evaluation and Quotation Stick 'Em Ups in hand, you will be *substantially* better informed. You will amaze, and probably annoy, the attorneys you interview. You will avoid the denizens of the rogues' gallery, and in the end, get better representation for your defendant and better value for your money.

BETTER PLEA BARGAINS ARE WORK, NOT ART

Think of plea negotiation as a game of five-card draw. The defendant's freedom is on the table, a high ante indeed. Unless the police have screwed up the case in an obvious way, the initial situation is unfavorable. It's like picking up a hand and seeing nothing but a high card. At this point, to begin betting, or in the legal analogy, to begin negotiating the plea, is madness. The defendant, facing the prosecuting power of the state, has a hand full of nothing. To improve the odds, the defendant needs to draw more cards.

The best attorneys draw more cards for their clients by filing motions, scheduling hearings, and challenging the arrest, the evidence, lineups, confessions, interrogations, and the application of law. They investigate witness statements, evidence, and police personnel records. They may visit the crime scene. Attorneys may even give defendants a polygraph exam to corroborate their version of events and assess their truthfulness. Under challenge, all sorts of things turn up: bad searches and seizures, wiretaps with bad paperwork, absurd applications of law, even outright bluffs.

There is always one card in every defendant's hand, and it can, if smartly handled by a great attorney, be a trump card: caseload. Great attorneys, like judo masters, turn the force of the state against itself by taking advantage of the overwhelming demand of the caseload. Even if the defense's motions, discoveries, challenges, and hearings do not uncover prosecutorial or factual error, they force the prosecution to show up, reply in writing, and explain itself, all of which takes time. Every day and every hour that prosecutors spend in hearings and trials, new defendants stack up in the jails. If prosecutors spend too much time in court, that 900-pound caseload gorilla will climb up their backs and jump on their heads.

Hardworking defense attorneys throw sand in the gears of the prosecution and slow it down as its caseload inexorably rises. Often prosecutors offer them better deals just to make them go away. Private attorneys can do this because, unlike public defenders, they have a smaller, more manageable caseload.

Many in the criminal justice system abhor such tactics. I do not. The police and prosecutorial powers of the state are overwhelming. Some grit in the gears and some smoke over the proceedings are useful preservatives of our rights. Regardless of what defendants did or didn't do, they have an absolute right to defend themselves as vigorously as possible. Too many defendants despair. They sit passively in jail and wait for the sentence. When defendants do go down, they should go down fighting and go down hard.

DESIRABLE OUTCOMES

Here are the desirable outcomes you and defense counsel should work for:

► **Dismissal of charges.** This occurs when judges dismiss charges. This is freedom. Prosecutors can press charges again, with new evidence, in a new court. Generally, they don't.

► *Nolle prosequi/*"nol-pross." In this scenario, the prosecutor simply declines to prosecute the case. Perhaps the evidence was flimsy or the charges inflated. Perhaps the prosecutor had an overwhelming caseload. Perhaps the fish were biting. Regardless, this is freedom.

► **Acquittal.** This occurs after trial, when a judge or a jury finds the defendant not guilty. The state is constitutionally barred from prosecuting the defendant again on the same charges. This is absolute freedom.

► **Bond reduction or recognizance.** This releases defendants from jail. It is easier to mount a legal defense and refine a family management plan when defendants are free. Lower bond or no bond preserves the families' assets and cash for attorney fees and the costs of probation and parole.

► **Diversion.** This is a superb outcome, because it is a diversion *out of* the criminal justice system and *into* drug treatment, therapy, and family management. During diversion, the court suspends criminal proceedings. Upon completion of diversion, the court expunges the charges so that defendants can truthfully say, and sign employment applications to the effect, "I have not been convicted of a crime." Diversion is so desirable that families should do everything possible, up to but not including flogging with a cat-o-nine-tails, to get diverted defendants to complete their treatment and therapy and comply with all terms and conditions. With diversion, the court is doing defendants a huge favor. Diversion is generally on the table only for first-time defendants and those facing less serious charges.

▶ **Direct sentence to probation.** This desirable outcome is a sentence directly into the probation system and avoidance of further jail and prison time. It works for defendants who have the character and motivation to abandon crime and drugs, pay everything they owe, and complete all terms of probation right down to the last bit of paperwork.

▶ **Reduction of charges.** This is reduction of the severity of charges and a corresponding reduction of the sentence. Reduction of felony charges to misdemeanors means that time will be served in county jails, not in state and federal prisons, which are stuffed with hard-core criminals. Defendants who avoid felony convictions maintain their civil rights and remain eligible for military service.

How do you know whether a lawyer will do the hard work necessary to facilitate one of these outcomes? You interview attorneys. They will be glad to see you. They need your business.

PREPARING INFORMATION FOR ATTORNEY INTERVIEWS

The first step is to gather and organize the relevant information. Review chapter 3, "You, the Gumshoe," for details. On the next page is a brief checklist of what to present to attorneys during the initial interview. You probably won't get everything on the list, but don't fret—get as much as you can. Make notes and write out a short version of the case as you understand it at this point. Writing down the key points helps you organize things mentally.

The Fog of Lies

You will need to rely on your defendant for some of this information, but it will not be easy to get even the most basic version of the truth. With rare exceptions, defendants lie to family members and defense attorneys about what happened. While in jail they ponder endlessly how to concoct the least damaging version of events. They want to sell this story to you and have you pay a defense attorney to sell it to the prosecutor, judge, and jury. This is unwise. Once a lie is debunked, defendants have no fallback position.

ATTORNEY INFORMATION CHECKLIST

Get as much of this information as you can before you interview attorneys. Make copies for each attorney interviewed.

- ☐ Charge sheet
- ☐ Arrest report (*crucial!*)
- ☐ Prior arrests and convictions
- ☐ List of witnesses other than law enforcement officers
- ☐ Alibis (if any)
- ☐ Jail number and jail location
- ☐ Case number from the court
- ☐ Name of public defender currently assigned
- ☐ Current bond
- ☐ Arraignment plea (usually a pro forma "not guilty")
- ☐ Has defendant confessed or signed statements?
- ☐ Has defendant been interrogated by law enforcement officers?
- ☐ Will there be a lineup?
- ☐ What physical evidence does the prosecution possess?
- ☐ Were weapons, drugs, or contraband recovered during the arrest?
- ☐ Is there forensic evidence such as blood or fingerprints?
- ☐ Is there a victim who will testify against the defendant?
- ☐ Are there wiretaps or surveillance video?
- ☐ Names of codefendants
- ☐ Concise statement of what happened during the arrest

Stick 'Em Up!

ATTORNEY EVALUATION

1. Which attorneys will appear at hearings, do research, and prepare motions?

   _____ Bar No. _____ ☐ Partner ☐ Associate

   _____ Bar No. _____ ☐ Partner ☐ Associate

2. What are their backgrounds? _____

   _____

3. Will non-firm attorneys work on subcontract?   ☐ yes   ☐ no
4. Are there bar association complaints pending against the firm?   ☐ yes   ☐ no
5. Will you mail defendant copies of motions, filings, and discovery?   ☐ yes   ☐ no
6. Will you interview the defendant in jail prior to hearings?   ☐ yes   ☐ no
7. How many times in the last 12 months has your firm gone to trial? _____
8. Do you defend federal cases?   ☐ yes   ☐ no
9. Do you have an appellate practice?   ☐ yes   ☐ no
10. Do partners appear before the state supreme court?   ☐ yes   ☐ no
11. Have you successfully suppressed wiretap evidence?   ☐ yes   ☐ no
12. Have you ever suppressed evidence from a K-9 alert?   ☐ yes   ☐ no
13. Have you successfully excluded informant testimony?   ☐ yes   ☐ no
14. Liquor on breath? (Yes, you have to check this!)   ☐ yes   ☐ no
15. Have you served as a law enforcement officer?   ☐ yes   ☐ no
16. Do you have a firearms permit?   ☐ yes   ☐ no
17. Who is your on-call private detective? _____
18. Who is your on-call polygraph operator? _____
19. Who are your on-call expert witnesses for:

    Breathalyzer challenges _____

    Radar and laser speed gun challenges _____

    Forensic evidence challenges _____

20. Do you offer payment plans?   ☐ yes   ☐ no

I have interviewed defendants who insisted for weeks that kilos of cocaine found in their vehicle just appeared—suddenly. Maybe some dealer had excess inventory and wanted to dump some product to keep prices up! Maybe the Cocaine Elf put them there! Guns also appear as if by magic, not to mention stolen merchandise and the occasional corpse. Have no patience with such fairy tales. Urge your defendant to tell the truth to the defense attorney. The truth is defensible. Lies are not.

It is best to get information from defendants during visits. Never ask defendants to discuss their cases on recorded jail calls. If it is impossible to have a secure conversation with your defendant, ask that he or she mail a statement of what happened to an attorney with the words "Privileged Attorney Communication" printed plainly on the envelope and the statement. Make sure you give your inmate the attorney's address. Make a commissary payment to fund envelopes, stamps, and paper. You'll find a Jail Mail form for this purpose in chapter 21.

Why Brief Information Is Enough

A parlor trick in which I occasionally indulge is to have people relate a criminal legal problem. After they finish the first sentence, I announce exactly what happened, without any prior knowledge. People find this amazing. It isn't. Every cop, prosecutor, defense lawyer, bailiff, corrections officer, probation officer, and private detective can do the same thing. The reason is that most crimes are routine. The unusual ones are those you read about in the newspaper or see on TV. Most others follow patterns. For this reason, with basic information, a good attorney should be able to estimate what preliminary hearings, motions, challenges, and investigations should be undertaken prior to negotiating a plea, and what all of this will cost.

THE INITIAL INTERVIEW

Before you interview a particular attorney, ascertain whether there is a fee for the initial consultation, a practice that is common in civil law. In criminal defense, the initial consult generally is free, but top-notch attorneys, who have their pick of paying clients, may charge. This is not a prohibited or unethical practice. So check it out beforehand by calling the attorney's office. If the fee is modest, and you really want to talk to this attorney, pay it. Otherwise, let your fingers do the walking through the Yellow Pages and call someone else.

In each interview, be courteous and businesslike. You're the buyer. Don't get emotional and fall apart. Don't be ashamed. Defense attorneys are familiar with crime and violence. They will not be shocked by anything you say. Especially do not get crazy with defense attorneys and start shouting. A calm and methodical demeanor is what gets results for your defendant.*

---

* Never assault or threaten an attorney. Many defense attorneys install bulletproof glass in windows and doors. More than a few pack heat. If you or your defendant attacks an attorney, you will be arrested. You may be shot.

Cut out the Attorney Evaluation Stick 'Em Up on p. 146 and the Quotation Stick 'Em Ups in chapter 19, pp. 157 and 165, and make copies. Use separate copies for each attorney you interview.

Here are brief explanations of the items on the attorney evaluation:

▶ **Partner or associate.** In law firms, partners are owners. Associates are salaried employees. Partners are usually older and have more experience.

▶ **Bar number.** An attorney without a bar number is a dodo bird who flunked the bar exam and is to be avoided—strenuously. Bar numbers allow you to check with the bar association for pending complaints from other clients. Almost all criminal attorneys have complaints from time to time. Many of these are frivolous and are filed by bored and angry convicts. Nonetheless, you should check.

▶ **Backgrounds.** The law schools from which attorneys graduated are less important than their practical experience. The best attorneys usually spend several years working as public defenders or prosecutors. It is not unusual for former prosecutors to take up criminal defense. Don't let this put you off. It is extremely useful experience.

▶ **Non-firm attorneys.** Unless you are a millionaire and paying for a seven-figure Dream Team Defense, with specialist attorneys hired for each stage of hearings, motions, and trials, you should not tolerate subcontracting the defense to attorneys outside the firm. This is an outrage.

▶ **Mailing motions.** Some attorneys do not mail clients copies of motions and legal documents. Such behavior is disgraceful. Defendants need to see what work is being done on their behalf. Often, when defendants read motions, they can make useful suggestions. You, the family, as financiers of the defense, should also receive copies of all documents. This will require a written waiver from the defendant. The purpose of your receiving documents is not to second-guess the defense, but to make sure you are getting the work you paid for.

▶ **Jail visitations.** Any private defense attorney who does not visit a client in jail is a fee whore. Avoid.

▶ **Going to trial.** This is important because the threat of going to trial is the defense attorney's main weapon for extracting a better-than-average plea deal. When attorneys tell you they never go to trial because they're specialists at plea bargaining, they're fee mill hacks. Avoid!

▶ **Federal cases.** The federal system is different from state criminal justice. The conviction rate is higher. Prosecutions are tougher because they are brought by federal law enforcement agencies like the FBI, DEA, and the Bureau of Alcohol, Tobacco, Firearms and Explosives. Unlike local police, federal agents are promoted based on the quality, not the quantity, of arrests. The feds strenuously avoid zero-tolerance policing and the vacuuming up of petty criminals that clog local jails and state courts. Only good private attorneys take on the FBI and the federal government. Only the best win.

▶ **Appellate and supreme court practice.** Only the best attorneys appear before appeals courts, which try points of law, not facts. State supreme courts, and the United States Supreme Court, require attorneys that appear before them to have special qualifications.

▶ **Wiretap suppression.** Wiretaps, bugs, and surveillance cameras all require warrants and must be deployed pursuant to strict guidelines. Astoundingly, wiretaps and videos often do not show what they purport to. The defendant may appear in them, but may not be shown committing, or planning to commit, a crime! Because most cases plead out quickly, such evidence is rarely challenged. Cops and prosecutors get sloppy with this stuff. Good attorneys challenge this evidence and sometimes get it excluded. Bad attorneys roll over like whipped puppies.

▶ **K-9 alert suppression.** Dog alerts give police cause to make searches of vehicles, buildings, and persons. Few attorneys know that dog alerts can be prompted by handlers who whisper, "Get it, get it," or something similar during a search. The dog will alert, usually by scratching with one paw, just to please the handler. This is a dirty cop trick. Getting a cop to fess up requires tough questioning, under oath, by a smart attorney. Evidence obtained by a faked K-9 alert can be excluded, thus causing all or part of the prosecution's case to collapse.

▶ **Exclusion of confidential informant testimony.** Ask if the attorney has successfully excluded CI testimony. Many informants are slimeballs. I had personal experience with one called "Little Nicky," who ran a cocaine bazaar in his apartment. He tossed the cops a few names now and then, and now and then the cops tossed him a few dollars, emphasis on few. Nicky was a hopeless, garbage-head addict who, when buzzed, had a disturbing habit of walking headfirst into trees. Mopes like this wilt under questioning. If you're lucky, they will show up wasted for statements, depositions, and trial, which, naturally, a sharp attorney will point out to His or Her Honor.

▶ **Booze.** A few attorneys, regrettably, still show up at the office and in court sloshed to the gills. Check for liquor breath when you interview attorneys. A large, well-stocked bar in the office is a clue that this is an attorney to avoid with the same alacrity with which you might avoid onrushing trains, improvised explosive devices, and plutonium dust.

▶ **Law enforcement experience.** This is extremely useful. Most defense attorneys lack detailed knowledge of police procedure. Many have never read their local police department's standing orders! Former cops who become defense attorneys can more easily spot dirty cop tricks, many of which are legal but unethical, and all of which enrage juries. They also can spot deficient police procedure, which can become the basis for exclusionary hearings to toss evidence.

▶ **Firearms permit.** Guns are used in the most serious crimes and are often recovered from crime scenes and defendants. When attorneys have a firearms permit, you know that they understand how weapons work, and how they're used, both legally and illegally. Here's an example. Imagine that a witness testifies that he saw your defendant "jack a round into the chamber," which describes the operation of an automatic pistol. The weapon recovered, however, is a revolver. An attorney who understands firearms would spot the inconsistency immediately, since revolvers do not have firing chambers.

▶ **On-call detectives and polygraph operators.** When you ask these questions, a top-notch attorney will respond immediately with names. The best attorneys have people on call whom they trust and have worked with in the past. A phony will say something like, "We call them in when we need them." Private detectives, especially former cops and FBI agents, are useful for questioning witnesses and reviewing crime scenes. Lie detector results, although not admissible in court, are excellent bargaining tools for pleas.

▶ **Expert witnesses.** Crackerjack attorneys can immediately name experts they use in psychology, forensics, breathalyzer analysis, and traffic radar and laser technology. Phonies and rookies will bumble and mumble.

▶ **Payment plans.** Since most defendants are guilty, many will be disappointed and angry that they were convicted. After sentencing, they, and their families, become reluctant to pay. For this reason, private attorneys demand all or most of their fees up front. Some will offer a payment plan, so always ask this question. Payment options will be discussed in detail in the following chapters.

The attorney evaluation will help you make sure you're hiring a crackerjack and not a rip-off artist. Unfortunately, even excellent attorneys can be maddeningly vague about the actual work contemplated in exchange for your money. Like banks, they rejoice in extra fees and charges. So during the interview it's also crucial to request a quote for specific services.

If, for example, the firm charges for photocopies and postage, ask to have documents and correspondence sent via e-mail. If the attorney plans to hire investigators, polygraph operators, expert witnesses, and outside forensic examiners, make sure you get cost estimates up front. The next chapter will provide the Stick 'Em Ups and the details.

19

SHOW ME THE WORK,
I'LL SHOW YOU THE MONEY
Getting a Quotation for Legal Services and Fees

WHY WOULD ATTORNEYS BE reluctant to tell you what work they will do for the fees they charge, especially when you have provided them with case information and an arrest report? Heck, you expect a quotation from the guys who change your oil. In criminal law, however, quoting work as well as fees is—*gasp!*—a radical notion. There are reasons.

First, attorneys regard themselves not merely as professionals but as high priests of the mysteries. Only they understand the devious inner workings of jails and courts. Only they can divine the intentions of judges, prosecutors, and juries and make offerings to appease these furies. Like humble devotees of terrible gods, clients and their families are supposed to leave offerings in the form of fees then tiptoe away. The priests will then close the curtain, face the idol of justice, and begin the magic!

Until recently, physicians occupied a similar pedestal. They have been brought back to earth by malpractice lawsuits and by the Internet, which gives patients accurate medical information in an easy-to-understand format. It is routine now for patients to check the Internet for information about their illnesses and prescription drugs. With this information, patients challenge physicians, get second opinions, and suggest alternative treatments. If ordinary people reading medical Web sites and health information books can absorb enough anatomical, medical, pharmaceutical, and surgical knowledge to usefully participate in their health care, how much more easily should people be able to understand the processes of criminal defense, which are only laws, rules, arguments, and documents? Criminal defense is complex, but brain science it isn't. The level of knowledge you need is only enough to make an intelligent purchasing decision. Clients, like doctors' patients, should begin to act less like supplicants and more like customers. Private criminal defense is, after all, a business. Clients should ask questions, evaluate work, and seek value for money. What could be more American?

The second reason why attorneys have difficulty providing a detailed quotation is because, unlike business people, they compete only on reputation, which is nebulous, and price, which is whatever the market will bear. They almost never compete head-to-head on work, service, and quality. And most defendants and their families don't know what work to request or how to evaluate its quality.

Third, attorneys themselves are usually not accustomed to breaking down the costs of specific services. Typically, they quote prices off the top of their heads. They'll say, "I charge $2,000 [or $5,000, or whatever] for preliminary hearings and a negotiated plea." Do not let this deter you when seeking the most work for your money. Do not accept lame excuses like "I haven't looked into the case yet," or "Motions are a matter of professional discretion." That's baloney. Any attorney worth hiring knows how much time *on average* it takes to file motions and attend hearings. They know, *on average*, what motions are useful in particular cases. Unlike manufacturers, attorneys have only labor and overhead to calculate. Their materials and other unit costs are insignificant.*

PERVERSE INCENTIVES

This aversion to specificity is evident in the payment system lawyers currently prefer: a lump-sum fee, paid up front, that is unrelated to the amount of work performed. Such a system does not serve defendants and their families, because it creates perverse economic incentives. In this payment scheme, attorneys' economic interests are served by *minimizing the work done*. The temptation is to sleepwalk through preliminary hearings and plead out the defendant to the Standard Deal with a phone call or a hallway chat. Currently there is little risk of blowback, because defendants and their families are so unfamiliar with the legal system.

But for clients who know what to ask for, the realities of the criminal justice system provide ample opportunity to negotiate more favorable payment terms. Private attorneys don't have enough paying clients. Zero-tolerance policing has stuffed the jails with indigent defendants. To give them the minimum, constitutionally guaranteed defense, public defender offices have grown exponentially. The avalanche of poor defendants and free defense has resulted in slim pickings for private attorneys. Professional hoodlums and white-collar frauds, who make full-time incomes from criminal enterprise, are largely untouched by local and state law enforcement. This is a pity, because pro crooks have the money to afford big-time legal defenses, which in turn would nourish a larger, more vigorous cadre of private attorneys. If law enforcement were different, more professional crooks would be arrested, and stoutly defended by private counsel. More of these crooks would also be in prison, which would improve things for the rest of us.

Life is not without irony.

---

* I spent years estimating jobs in the commercial printing industry, where quotations take into account labor, machine time, paper, chemicals, dies, die-cutting, finishing, building overhead, utilities, taxes, and delivery. Quoting this stuff sounds complicated, but once unit costs are determined, quoting a job is mostly plugging numbers into a spreadsheet and hitting the buttons for "add" and "print."

In addition, criminal defense is an interesting and fulfilling field of law. So there is a surplus of attorneys, many of them former public defenders and prosecutors who want to get into private practice. This means that families with funds for private defense can force attorneys to compete for their business and to agree to specific work in order to earn their fees. For most families, money saved in attorney fees will be sorely needed for probation and parole.

When you interview attorneys, use the Stick 'Em Up forms on pp. 157 and 165 to request quotations not only of price but also of specific work. Doing so aligns the lawyers' economic interests with the legal needs of your defendant. To earn your money, attorneys will have to agree to perform particular tasks on the defendant's behalf. In other words, they will have to act, economically speaking, like the rest of the world.

HOW TO USE THE QUOTATION STICK 'EM UPS

The Quotation Stick 'Em Ups list the names of the major motions, challenges, and appearances made by defense attorneys, and the rest of the chapter provides a brief explanation of each one so you can make an informed buying decision. Remember that plea negotiation, as important as it is, has no economic value, since the Standard Deal is available at no charge from public defenders. If you seek a negotiated plea, what you're looking for is a commitment to the *preliminary* motions, challenges, appearances, and hearings that improve your defendant's bargaining position. For trials, you're looking for the trial preparations and challenges of witnesses and evidence that can give your defendant a better outcome. Attorneys may ask to visit the inmate or to look into more details of the arrest and charges prior to making a quotation. This is reasonable.

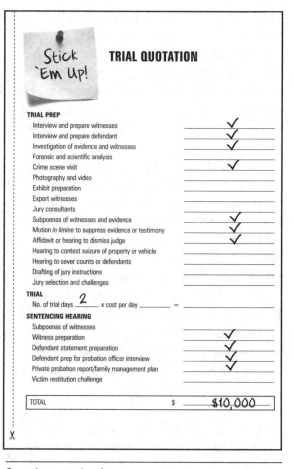

Sample quotation form.

In any event, it is unlikely that attorneys will give you a detailed quotation with prices for each work item. They're never asked to do so and in any case are completely unused to families who understand the business side of criminal defense. Most likely you will fill in the quotation yourself, simply placing a check mark by each task the attorney agrees to perform.

Use the Stick 'Em Ups as prompts for your attorney interviews. They should generate questions like these:

- ▶ "When will you petition a bond reduction hearing?"
- ▶ "What are the least restrictive terms you can negotiate for release under bond?"
- ▶ "What motions and hearings will you petition?"
- ▶ "How do you handle lineups and police interrogations?"
- ▶ "How do you counter negative information in a probation report?"
- ▶ "How do you negotiate better terms for probation and parole?"
- ▶ "When do you plan to review disclosure with the defendant?"
- ▶ "What outside experts and professionals will you hire?"
- ▶ "Do you charge extra for postage, copies, and office supplies?"
- ▶ "Will you mail copies of motions to the defendant?"
- ▶ "Will you visit the crime scene?"

I've been present at many fee negotiations with attorneys, and I have never encountered a family that knew thing one about criminal defense. Already, by reading this book, you know more about the business end of criminal law than 99.9 percent of the public! Use your knowledge to get better representation for your defendant and better value for your hard-earned money.

OCEANS OF MOTIONS: THE REAL LEGAL WORK

Motions are the meat of criminal defense. *These are what you're paying for.* Motions have to be written, filed with the court, and then served on the prosecution. They require the prosecution to appear in court and oppose them. They are W-O-R-K. They're also food for the caseload gorilla. Crackerjack attorneys file motions and work the prosecution hard before sitting down to deal. Here are the most common:

Notice of Appearance

This is a letter filed with the court and served on the prosecution that announces that a private attorney will represent the defendant. The notice also triggers your payment liability. An amusing situation that occurs with some frequency is the dropping of charges *before* a private attorney files the notice to appear and does any work. If this occurs, a reputable attorney will return your fee.

Voodoo doctors will keep your money and give you a snow job about how their miraculous behind-the-scenes maneuvers resulted in the dismissal. When this occurs, you can sue, often in small claims court, and get your money back. Judges are not amused by this scam. A friend of mine was recently sued for $500 by some attorneys with whom he talked briefly on the telephone but who did no actual work. I served as an expert in the case and was overjoyed when the judge tossed out the lawsuit like last week's garbage.

Motion to Reduce Bond

This motion petitions a hearing to reduce bail and bonds. It is an excellent forum to present a family management plan. Such hearings create work for the prosecution and force them to reveal part of their case as grounds for denying the reduction. In most states, defendants have a right to this hearing. Generally you should not post bond until after a reduction hearing, as this can save you a considerable amount of money.

Motion to Dismiss

This is the big one. It forces the prosecution to explain its case. If the defense has discovered weaknesses in the charges, the evidence, or the police work, defendants sometimes can be freed. Even if dismissal is denied, this hearing can persuade the prosecution to accept better plea terms.

Motion for Speedy Trial

Defendants have a constitutional right to speedy trial. This motion is useful when the prosecution has jumped the gun and pressed charges before evidence has been recovered or tested or when prosecution witnesses are flaky or nowhere to be found. If the speedy trial clock runs out before the prosecution has its act together, your defendant will be freed. This is a delicate call. Defendants should rely on their attorneys' judgment.

Subpoenas

The defense can subpoena witnesses, documents, and evidence. It's useful to put some heat on eyewitnesses, who often will babble, contradict, and perjure themselves when questioned. Sometimes they vanish!

MOTIONS, FILINGS, AND HEARINGS

Notice of appearance _____

Motion to reduce bond _____

Motion to dismiss _____

Motion for speedy trial _____

Subpoenas of witnesses and evidence _____

Motion to suppress evidence _____

Motion to strike counts _____

Motion for a bill of particulars _____

Motion to contest seizure of property or vehicle _____

Motion to provide exculpatory evidence _____

Motion to sever counts or defendants _____

Motion to compel discovery _____

Proffer of cooperation with police and prosecution _____

Motion to strike priors _____

Motion to suppress identification by a witness _____

Motion to preserve evidence _____

Motion to disclose identity of government informant _____

Motion to examine police officer personnel file _____

Probation terms and conditions _____

HEARINGS AND PROCEDURES

Lineups _____

Police interrogations _____

Witness questioning/deposition _____

Plea negotiation _____

Other _____ _____

Stick `Em Up!

PLEA BARGAIN QUOTATION,
Page 2

PROFESSIONAL SERVICES

Private detective _____

Polygraph operator _____

Document authenticator _____

Forensic analysis _____

Scientific expert _____

Breathalyzer/speed gun expert _____

Translator _____

OTHER COSTS

Copying _____

Postage _____

Court costs _____

Jail phone calls _____

Video and wiretap analysis _____

Review of discovery _____

Probation terms and conditions _____

Other _____ _____

| TOTAL | $ _____ |

Motion to Suppress Evidence

This is a big cannon for the defense. If eyewitness testimony, confidential informant testimony, or wiretaps can be excluded, the prosecution's case will wither. Don't forget to suggest a challenge to that K-9 alert that triggered search and seizure.

Motion to Strike Counts

This is a request to the judge to toss out the routinely grotesque overcharges tacked on by arresting officers and prosecutors. This motion whittles down the charges to a point that a better plea deal can be made. Doing this with a motion and hearing, rather than with a chat in the corridors, adds to prosecutorial workload, which is a good thing.

Motion for a Bill of Particulars

This is a demand for a written explanation, in detail, of the prosecution's charges. Crackerjack attorneys will use a bill of particulars to pick apart the prosecution by asking them to justify, and define, their charges. This is especially useful for "all purpose" charges like disorderly conduct, which are frequently used as add-ons. State statutes define such conduct as "tumultuousness," or "hurly-burly." These are not words that most police officers use with any frequency, especially if they don't read Shakespeare. Such a motion can put the prosecution in the ridiculous position of defining such vagaries.

Motion to Contest Seizure of Property or Vehicle

Many laws allow vehicle and property seizures, especially in drug cases. Prosecutors have a nasty habit of seizing cash, vehicles, and valuables that defendants might otherwise use to fund a defense! This motion can free seized property. This will be an urgent necessity when the defendant was driving your car when arrested and the cops have pimped your ride straight into the impound lot.

Motion to Provide Exculpatory Evidence

The state has a constitutional requirement to divulge all its evidence in a case to defense counsel, including exculpatory evidence that would tend to exonerate the defendant. Withholding exculpatory evidence is grossly unethical yet common. That's because most prosecutions end in pleas and prosecutors are insufficiently challenged.

In the notorious rape case against members of the Duke University lacrosse team, the prosecutor, Michael Nifong, was found guilty of lying to a judge and withholding exculpatory evidence. He was disbarred and later indicted and convicted. Sadly, the judge sentenced him only to a single day in jail. A decade would have been more appropriate. If the defense can discover such detestable behavior on the part of the prosecution, the case will collapse. In some cases, the state and city will become liable for civil damages, which after a few years of legal wrangling, will give a defendant a soft landing indeed.

Motion to Sever Counts or Defendants

This is a motion used in complex cases with multiple defendants and tangled evidence. If successful, it can improve your defendant's outcome. The decision to file is difficult. Defendants must trust their attorneys to make the right call.

Motion to Compel Discovery

"Discovery" is legal jargon for the prosecution's evidence and testimony. Discovery can consist of documents, recordings, photographs, forensic evidence, and witness statements. Defendants have a constitutional right to examine this material. In practice, delivery of the discovery is often delayed because of bureaucratic inertia. This motion forces the prosecution to cough up.

Fee whores sashay into court without even looking at the discovery. This is an outrage. Not only the defense counsel but also the defendant should peruse all discovery materials carefully. Defendants should demand video and sound players to examine recorded evidence. Cops and prosecutors often will use surveillance videos to scare defendants into a confession. They say things like "We've got your sorry ass on tape!" When examined, tapes often show nothing of the sort. They may reveal that the culprit was, in fact, that notorious bad guy, Man Wearing a Hat.

Proffer of Cooperation

Cooperating with the prosecution is a delicate—and often dangerous—decision for both the defendant and the family. A proffer is a written, signed document in which the prosecution agrees to leniency for the defendant in return for cooperation. Proffers are detailed and specify exactly what "cooperation" means. When defendants decide to cooperate, they should always do so with a written proffer drafted *in the presence of, and with the assistance of*, defense counsel.

Constantly remind your defendant never, ever, to talk to cops or prosecutors without the assistance of counsel. The oldest sucker play in the book is a promise by cops to "put in a good word with the judge and the prosecutor" if the defendant will confess and sign a little statement! This promise is absurd because it is unenforceable.

For defendants charged with serious offenses and faced with a strong prosecution, a proffer may be the best, and only, deal available. For more information, see chapter 24.

Motion to Strike Priors

This is a motion to correct errors in the defendant's rap sheet. This can be extremely important if the defendant is in jeopardy of being tried as a habitual offender.

Motion to Suppress Identification by a Witness

It is interesting how many witnesses claim to see things clearly on dark nights, from great distances, while drunk or stoned, without their glasses or contacts, or from a place where no view of the crime scene is possible. Some confidently report conversations in languages they don't understand! This motion can get their testimony tossed. Eyewitnesses are notoriously unreliable. It is not unusual for witnesses to lie in order to settle scores or for multiple witnesses to contradict themselves. Investigating eyewitnesses and stressing them with questioning are useful.

I once spent an hour interviewing a red-headed, blue-eyed Lithuanian who was locked up for an armed robbery committed, so said five eyewitnesses, by a black male with dreadlocks. Nonetheless, a sixth witness fingered the Lithuanian and whispered that he looked black because he was a master of disguise! This defendant should have been released immediately. Unfortunately, he had an additional problem—he was a class-A knucklehead. Every time a private or public defender tried to help him, he'd start bellowing in Lithuanian and English and tell that lawyer to stuff his learned puss up where the sun don't shine.* After six months or so, a judge popped him loose.

Motion to Preserve Evidence

This is useful in cases in which a time-consuming analysis of the evidence, such as DNA identification, might later serve to exonerate the defendant. Strange things happen as time passes. Cash, jewelry, firearms, and narcotics sometimes tiptoe out of the evidence locker. Now and then a Rolex gets replaced with a fake. A motion to preserve, coupled with an audit, can discover such skullduggery. The prosecution might cut your defendant some slack in order to avoid the arrest and prosecution of police officers, not to mention a media roast of the police chief!

Motion to Disclose the Identity of Government Informant

If your defendant is among the small fry swept up in a larger ongoing prosecution, the state may offer leniency or dismiss charges rather than identify an informant in open court. Informants can become corpses in a hurry, so the state may offer a tasty deal rather than blow a cover.

Motion to Examine Police Officer Personnel File

This is useful when defendants are used as a punching bag by cops or turned into cube steak by police dogs. If the arresting officer has a "hot jacket," a smart attorney can in essence put the police on trial, or threaten to do so, in order to get a better plea deal.

---

* When I talked to him, I understood the part about stuffing my f#*@ing head up my . . . The rest was in Lithuanian, at some length.

Probation Terms and Conditions

Don't forget to include negotiating the terms of probation in your quotation for private criminal defense. Probation and parole last a long, long time. They are full of pitfalls that can precipitate your defendant back into jail or prison. Prisons are stuffed with inmates charged with probation violations.

Make sure your attorney negotiates the least restrictive terms possible and explains to your defendant how easy it is to get hammered for what appear to be petty violations. See chapter 23 for details.

HEARINGS AND PROCEDURES

When you pay private attorneys, expect them to appear at all crucial proceedings when your defendant's liberty is at stake.

Lineups

Attorney representation at lineups is critical. Because they are infrequently challenged, police can get careless. They may use body language, hand gestures, or whispers to prompt a witness to identify your defendant instead of another person. Police prompting is a prohibited practice that can result in the witness identification being excluded. Smart attorneys often take a staff member to the lineup so there will be two witnesses to refute police denials. Where permitted, attorneys may video record the lineup.

Police Interrogations

Attorneys should *always* be present at interrogations. Cops will sometimes go to great lengths, and push the law to the breaking point, to persuade defendants to talk without a lawyer.

Another advantage to having attorneys present at interrogations is that, as officers of the courts, they have extraordinary privileges in communicating with police and prosecutors. As long as their clients remain silent and let the attorney talk for them—not for nothing are lawyers called "mouthpieces"—attorneys later can withdraw statements. They can claim to have made a mistake or not to have heard the defendant clearly! A civilian who tries to change a statement gets busted for perjury and lying to a law enforcement officer. Lawyers, like politicians, are permitted to "clarify" their remarks.

Lawyers can also speak hypothetically to police and prosecutors. For example, an attorney can say, "If my client *were to admit* that he indeed stole the cash, would you consider a lower sentence?" "If my client *were to name* so-and-so as the trigger man and testify in open court, would you lower or dismiss charges against him?" Lawyers have the privilege of sparring, probing, speculating, and bargaining with prosecutors and police without committing the defendant to anything. This is an amazing privilege, and defendants should make full use of it.

QUOTATION FOR TRIAL

As with quotations for pleas, the most important elements of a trial quotation are the preparatory work. A good attorney does heavy prep to develop the case and to reduce the possibility of surprises at trial. Bad attorneys "wing it." They do not interview witnesses, prepare the defendant, or investigate evidence, crime scenes, and witnesses. They don't even research applicable case law to support motions. They just show up and ad lib their way through the process. This is a serious waste of your money and your defendant's life.

Interview and Prepare Witnesses

All defense witnesses need preparation prior to appearing at trial. They need to understand the question-and-answer format of testimony. Many witnesses are not articulate. They will need cautions against going crazy on the witness stand. An attorney also needs to question witnesses carefully to make sure they do not harbor grudges against the defendant and do not plan to pop a surprise at trial.

Hostile prosecution witnesses also need prep. A few states, but not the federal system, allow hostile witnesses to be formally deposed by defense counsel prior to trial. An attorney may choose not to do this, since a formal deposition, with transcript, is expensive and allows the prosecution to preview the defense's intentions and tactics. Where allowed, a crafty defense attorney may interview hostile witnesses informally on the telephone. This can give the attorney a sense of the witness's credibility without tipping off the prosecutor.

Interview and Prepare Defendant

Defendants lose track of their own defense, especially when they're locked up in jail. They have to be briefed on trial procedures and on any testimony they may be asked to give.

Investigation of Evidence and Witnesses

Although attorneys will receive discovery information prior to trial, it behooves them to check things out. Attorneys themselves, or private investigators they hire, may want to visit the crime scene (see below), investigate the backgrounds and criminal histories of witnesses, and challenge police statements and evidence. Things will turn up.

Forensic and Scientific Analysis

An attorney may want to check, and challenge, forensic evidence. Keep in mind that unlike on TV, most crime scene technicians are not highly trained scientists (much less drop-dead-gorgeous Hollywood starlets and studs). Mostly they are civil servants dropping things in baggies. They can, and do, goof up.

Crime Scene Visit

Attorney eyeballs on the scene of the crime can be useful. An attorney willing to get out of the office and burn some shoe leather is likely to be a crackerjack.

Photography and Video

These are useful when attorneys need to show a judge or jury something about the crime scene or the evidence. Most attorneys use specialized firms for this work, because their photographers and videographers are skilled at giving testimony.

Exhibit Preparation

Attorneys use professional firms that specialize in preparing large charts, graphs, and photographic enlargements and mounting them for presentation.

Expert Witnesses

Attorneys may employ experts in forensics, psychology, ballistics, and other fields to analyze evidence or testimony and to testify on behalf of your defendant.

Jury Consultants

These are experts who make recommendations on juror challenges and assist in the selection of a jury that may be favorable to your defendant.

Subpoenas of Witnesses and Evidence

Under subpoena, counsel may demand production of documents, evidence, or witness testimony.

Motion *In Limine* to Suppress Evidence or Testimony

This is one of the most important motions of the defense. Motions *in limine*, Latin for "within the boundary," are motions made to suppress evidence or testimony, usually at the beginning of the trial or in a separate hearing. They are always made in the absence of the jury. If granted, they can collapse the prosecution's case. If denied, they may form the basis for appeal.

Affidavit or Hearing to Dismiss Judge

Judges vary in how they decide cases. In some states, the defense has the right to dismiss one judge, with or without cause, merely by filing an affidavit. In other states, dismissal requires a special hearing and requires evidence of gross, and difficult-to-prove, bias.

Stick 'Em Up!

TRIAL QUOTATION

TRIAL PREP

Interview and prepare witnesses   _____

Interview and prepare defendant   _____

Investigation of evidence and witnesses   _____

Forensic and scientific analysis   _____

Crime scene visit   _____

Photography and video   _____

Exhibit preparation   _____

Expert witnesses   _____

Jury consultants   _____

Subpoenas of witnesses and evidence   _____

Motion *in limine* to suppress evidence or testimony   _____

Affidavit or hearing to dismiss judge   _____

Hearing to contest seizure of property or vehicle   _____

Hearing to sever counts or defendants   _____

Drafting of jury instructions   _____

Jury selection and challenges   _____

TRIAL

No. of trial days _____ x cost per day _____ = _____

SENTENCING HEARING

Subpoenas of witnesses   _____

Witness preparation   _____

Defendant statement preparation   _____

Defendant prep for probation officer interview   _____

Private probation report/family management plan   _____

Victim restitution challenge   _____

| TOTAL | $ _____ |

Hearing to Contest Seizure of Vehicle or Property

When the government grabs valuable assets, it undermines the defendant's ability to fund a stout defense. This motion can be made at trial as well as at pretrial hearings.

Hearing to Sever Counts or Defendants

This is another pretrial motion that is sometimes brought at trial. When there are codefendants who may testify against one another, your attorney may want to have your defendant tried separately.

Drafting of Jury Instructions

Most judges have boilerplate instructions that they give to juries. The defense, however, has the right to draft its own instructions and submit them to the judge. Crackerjack attorneys rarely overlook the opportunity to draft specific instructions that may benefit the defendant during jury deliberations.

Jury Selection and Challenges

The defense has the right to challenge and strike jurors who may be prejudiced against the defendant. These hearings, called voir dire,* are supremely important if your defendant has chosen, one hopes on advice of counsel, to have a jury trial.

Trial

This is the big show. Actual trials are considerably more muddled, and less dramatic, than the television versions. You and the defendant, of course, will find them riveting.

Witnesses at Sentencing

The attorney should meet briefly with witnesses who will give character references. In some cases, these witnesses may have to be subpoenaed.

Defendant Statement Preparation

The attorney should meet with the defendant to review any statement the defendant may make in support of a lenient sentence.

Probation Meeting Prep

Prior to sentencing, many judges order probation officers to prepare reports on defendants' criminal history, character, behavior in jail, and potential threat to society. Attor-

---

* This term, which means "to give an oath to speak the truth," isn't Latin. It isn't even French. It's Anglo-Norman, for crying out loud. Trust lawyers, who mostly can't read Latin, to come up with a term in proto-French! *Sacre bleu!*

neys should prepare defendants, and prepare notes, so defendants can include positive information about themselves, with details, during their interviews. Such positive information should include work history, education, military service, any volunteer activities, religious observance, and support of children and family. These reports are unimportant when pleas have been negotiated, but after a conviction at trial, they can influence a judge's sentencing decision. Countering probation reports is an important service in the efforts to reduce the severity of the sentence.

Private Probation Report/Family Management Plan
It is possible to commission private probation reports to emphasize defendants' positive qualities. Another possibility is the homemade version of the private probation report, the family management plan, which will be explained in chapter 26.

Victim Restitution Challenge
Many states award compensation to victims to be paid by convicted defendants. Although most states disallow charges for unquantifiable losses, such as pain and suffering, victims do have an incentive to pad the numbers. Attorneys should challenge unreasonable claims.

DECISION TIME

When you're done interviewing attorneys, you should have two or three attorney evaluations, and two or three quotation forms with different prices and services. Take time to think and compare. You may not want to take the lowest bid, which is usually from a fee mill. Quality counts, and a good attorney can reduce not only the jail and prison time but also the cost of fines and the length of probation.

Interviewing will take several days, but don't hurry this big decision. Don't throw your money at the first defense attorney who wows you with a sales presentation. If whining jail calls make you crazy, stop accepting calls for a few days. Your inmate will calm down soon enough. Everyone gets used to jail.

That's what's so sad about it.

IF YOU CAN'T AFFORD A PRIVATE ATTORNEY

Remember that your defendant can get the same hearings and motions discussed in this chapter from public defenders. They may not agree to the extra work, but the defendant should always ask. In many states, defendants have a right under the state constitution to certain hearings, like bond reduction. Defendants, however, have to *request* the hearing to exercise this right. Always educate defendants on the motions and hearings that may be applicable so they can request them.

WHEN DEFENDANTS CHANNEL THEIR INNER IDIOT

Some knuckleheads insist on representing themselves in court and refuse the assistance of counsel. They do this for a variety of reasons. Some believe they can figure out the criminal justice system by reading a few dusty tomes in the jail law library. Some think they're smarter than the attorneys or that the judge is a nincompoop. Some want to turn the trial into a circus for a moment of celebrity or promotion of a political agenda. Some are just bored and want some fun before a long stretch in prison. Strongly discourage this notion. Self-representation invariably leads to disaster.

20

NEGOTIATING A CONTRACT FOR LEGAL DEFENSE
Getting the Bang for Your Bucks

ONCE YOU'VE CHOSEN a private attorney, you should get a contract for specific legal services. In this endeavor you'll be on your own. There are few restrictions on unfair business practices and no restrictions on unfair contractual language. In fact, criminal defense contracts are rarely negotiated at all. This chapter will help you redress that imbalance.

Mostly attorneys fill in the blanks, shove a contract over, and say, "Sign here." Before you do, remember what your and the defendant's goals are:

1. For a negotiated plea, to get specific motions, hearings, and challenges agreed to

2. For trial, to get specific preparatory work agreed to

To ensure that the written agreement reflects these goals, just use the quotation form you have already filled in. Since the attorney has previously agreed to do the work specified, just *attach the quote form to the contract and initial it*. The attorney also must initial it. This is rough-and-ready, without the fancy dress of contract language, but it will do.

STRUCTURED PAYMENTS

Criminal attorneys have a tough time getting paid. Most defendants are guilty and will serve a sentence. They and their families may become reluctant to pay after sentence is pronounced. So most attorneys will ask for 100 percent payment up front. This is entirely understandable; nonetheless, you should refuse to pay up front and instead make a counteroffer of payment in installments as work is performed. You, of course, should understand that if you fail to meet your payment obligations, attorneys will petition to withdraw from the case.

That said, here's what you do. If you have funds for the entire legal fee, divide payments into three installments. Pay the first up front. Pay the second after the performance of agreed-to services. Pay the third after negotiation of a plea or sentencing at trial. If you have funds only to pay half the fee, with the rest in monthly payments, divide the first half into two installments. Pay the first up front. Pay the second after performance of agreed-to services. The balance you will pay monthly. Keep things simple by using the quote form again, jotting down your payments as in the sample.

Don't allow yourself to get buffaloed by fast-talking attorneys. Where money is concerned, be calm and businesslike but firm. Remember, you are probably baffling the attorneys! By reading this book and handling your money in a businesslike fashion, you are confronting them with something they have never encountered in their legal careers—an informed buyer.

Once all the terms are agreed upon, make sure you get a copy of the signed contract—with the quote form attached. At home, make a file for all documents and receipts from your dealings with the attorney. If

Sample payment agreement.

later you have to litigate the contract or dispute a charge to your credit card, the attached quote form page will be crucial.

I have been involved with several lawsuits over the grosser excesses of attorney billing. So far I have found that judges favor families. They are not sympathetic to crude fee grabs for little or no work.

PLAN B: INCENTIVE PAY

To some readers, filling out Stick 'Em Up forms and negotiating installment payments may appear bewildering. For them I suggest a simplified alternative, which is an offer to pay additional fees for better outcomes.

The key to this strategy is to remember that a plea bargain for the Standard Deal is a free good, and the only reason to hire a private attorney is to get something *better* *than* the first plea offer. So while negotiating with an attorney, you might want to say something like this: "The first offer is already on the table.* It's a plea of X years in prison in exchange for a guilty plea. How much will you charge to get something better than that?"

Let me herewith define "better." Getting an offer of five years in prison reduced to four years and 11 months is trivial. "Better" means *lots* better—fewer years, lesser charges, diversion into drug or psychological treatment, or a sentence directly to probation. So offer a minimal fee, say, $2,000, if the attorney can obtain nothing better than the first offer. Offer higher, incentive pay for better outcomes, whether through negotiated pleas or at trial.

BACKSEAT DRIVING

Once you hire private counsel, you may be tempted to second-guess attorneys. Forget this. Most peoples' knowledge of criminal law is gleaned from television and is wildly inapplicable to ordinary cases. You hired the defense attorneys because you and the defendant trust their judgment. So stand back and let them work. In any case, the defendant, not you, is the client and must make all legal decisions regarding the defense.

It's showtime now. The heat is on. Stay busy, stay focused, and stay calm. Do not— repeat, *do not*—appoint yourself amateur detective and blunder about confronting witnesses and police officers. This can wreck the defense. It can get *you* arrested. Do not bug attorneys for daily updates. If you've structured the contract correctly, you'll receive notices and motions, so you'll know work is progressing. Follow the attorneys' suggestions about attending hearings and trials.

That's best for your defendant.

---

* How do you find out what the first offer is? Just ask your defendant. Since most defendants are represented in initial hearings by a public defender, they will already know the Standard Deal.

21

HOW TO HELP THE DEFENSE
Getting Busy In Jail and Out

To GET THE BEST outcome from public defenders and your money's worth from private attorneys, you should demand that your defendant assist in his or her own defense. This appears obvious to you. It isn't obvious to inmates. In jail, defendants get passive; they get goofy; they get distracted; they get crazy. They get busy doing everything except what they ought to be doing, which is working on their legal defense.

But what, you ask, can defendants possibly do? Most of the time, they're still in jail! The answer is they can do plenty. Regardless of how much they lie about the circumstances of their arrest, defendants know what happened. They can put this knowledge to use by reviewing witness lists and, most importantly, the evidence contained in the discovery package. They can review the arrest report and inform attorneys of errors and omissions. They can name witnesses to the crime and discuss those witnesses' veracity, if any. They can name character witnesses. They can report education and work status, all of which are important in hearings, pleas, and probation negotiations. They can report prior arrests and convictions, and warrants and detainers in other states. They can report their willingness to cooperate with police and accept a proffer. They can bring their story together and get over their initial evasions.

This is a lot.

Of course it's difficult! Many inmates don't read or write well. Most are unused to telling the truth. It will take time. But time is all defendants have in jail. And if they're not working on their defense, what else can they be doing? Getting jail tatts? Drinking jail wine? Smoking/shooting/snorting jail dope? Playing cards and dice? Having jail sex? Fighting, scuffling, arguing, and showing out? Learning how to be a better criminal?

The attorneys will tell you what's important in this case, what needs to be done first, and what need not be done at all. Your work on the outside was detailed in earlier chapters. This chapter concerns the work that defendants can do, in jail or out. Since most defendants remain incarcerated until sentencing, I present the information here as a series of Jail Mails. Just tear them out, make copies, stamp, and send. Make sure to write the name and address of the defense attorney, whether public or private, on the forms. To speed things up, include a stamped return envelope addressed *to the attorney*, not to you.

Whether defendants use these forms or write on pads or scratch paper, it's important, at the top of each page and on all envelopes, to write "ATTORNEY-CLIENT COMMU-NICATION." This keeps nosy jail censors at bay.

You will need to do some legwork yourself on the outside to fill in all the information, especially about witnesses. This is a group effort!

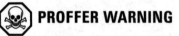 **PROFFER WARNING**

When defendants want to proffer information and cooperate with police and prosecutors, warn them *not to write anything on paper*. This can get them killed. They should simply request a meeting, urgently, with defense counsel. Pass the word to counsel if defendants tell you they want to proffer.

Jail Mail

Attorney-Client Communication

WHAT HAPPENED

Attorney _____

Address _____

_____

This is what I believe happened to cause my arrest:

_____
_____
_____
_____
_____
_____
_____
_____
_____
_____
_____
_____
_____
_____
_____
_____
_____
_____
_____
_____

Client Name _____   Jail number _____

Jail Mail

Attorney-Client Communication

DISCOVERY REVIEW

Attorney _____

Address _____

_____

I have reviewed the discovery package that contains the evidence against me. Here are the things that I think are incorrect or need to be brought to your attention:

_____

_____

_____

_____

_____

_____

_____

Here are some things that might improve my case or show me to be innocent:

_____

_____

_____

_____

Here are things that are missing:

_____

_____

_____

_____

Client Name _____   Jail number _____

Attorney-Client Communication

WITNESSES

Attorney _____

Address _____

_____

(Send multiple copies to defendant)

Here are the names, addresses, telephone numbers, and identifying details of witnesses who can help my defense:

Witness _____

Address _____

City _____ State _____ Zip _____ E-mail _____

Home telephone _____ Work telephone _____ Cell phone _____

Other names, including aliases, women's names before they married, and "street" names:

_____

Witness acquaintances _____

Home telephone _____ Work telephone _____ Cell phone _____

Race: ☐ Black ☐ White ☐ Hispanic ☐ American Indian ☐ Asian

Height _____ ft ___ in Weight _____ Eye color _____ Complexion _____

Tattoos _____ Body piercings _____

Scars, marks _____

Vehicle _____

How to find this witness _____

_____

What the witness can say _____

_____

_____

Client Name _____ Jail number _____

Jail Mail

Attorney-Client Communication

CHARACTER WITNESSES

Attorney _____

Address _____

_____

(Send multiple copies to defendant)

Witness _____

Address _____

City _____ State _____ Zip _____ E-mail _____

Home telephone _____ Work telephone _____ Cell phone _____

The good things the witness can say about me _____

_____

_____

_____

_____

Witness _____

Address _____

City _____ State _____ Zip _____ E-mail _____

Home telephone _____ Work telephone _____ Cell phone _____

The good things the witness can say about me _____

_____

_____

_____

_____

Client Name _____ Jail number _____

22

MONEY! MONEY! MONEY!
The Budget

ALMOST NOBODY BUDGETS FOR criminal defense. Here's what happens most of the time.

First, everyone goes nuts. "Omigod! He's in jail!" Then everybody runs to the bondsman, cash in hand, to spring the poor soul. This is followed by a visit to that picturesque junkyard known as the impound lot, there to pass a few more C-notes through the slot in the bulletproof glass to liberate a vehicle that got towed.

Or if the inmate remains in jail, it's "Omigod! He's got nothing to eat, and no stationery, and no soap!" Then it's off to the jail to plug some cash into the commissary account. Next, it's "Omigod! The attorney wants $5,000! What are we gonna do?" More running around for credit cards, bank loans, and cash.

Right about this time, the phone bill rolls in with those jail phone calls at extortionate rates. Then there's another "Omigod! They're gonna cut off the phone if we don't pay this bill!"

Expenses appear as a continuous series of surprises. Decisions are made willy-nilly, topsy-turvy, and on the fly. The one thing that is always flying away is your money.

When a loved one is arrested, people come at you from every direction asking for money. Budgeting and prioritizing will save you money, reduce the craziness, and help your defendant get a better outcome.

You have, by now, resisted the siren promises of freedom from the sellers of bail bonds and politely deflected the first sales pitches of oleaginous attorneys. It's time to make choices and allocate funds.

PREPARING THE BUDGET

To get to the bottom line, an estimate of the multiyear cost of criminal defense and inmate rehabilitation, use the Budget Stick 'Em Up on the next page. First, make copies. The budget will be a work in progress, subject to frequent change. It takes time to discover many of the costs. You'll be doing a lot of checking by phone and personal visit, especially for the tail-end costs of probation and parole. Neatness doesn't count. You don't have to be accurate to the last dollar, either. The budget is a worksheet to aid decision making, not a tax return. Expect to cover it with cross-outs, arrows, and scribbles and to fold, spindle, and mutilate it regularly.

Involve defendants in budgeting and decision making. They are ultimately responsible for legal decisions, and they need to be aware of the financial consequences. They need to recognize what their families have to do to assist them in regaining freedom. There is another, more important reason: Budgeting is a quintessential middle-class activity. It will be unfamiliar to most inmates but will encourage them to embrace those middle-class values that will help keep them out of jails and prisons in the years to come:

1. Budgeting causes inmates to think about and plan for the future.

2. Budgeting makes inmates think about others instead of sailing obliviously through life and letting everyone else clean up the messes.

3. Budgeting alongside the family teaches inmates to work in groups rather than to act alone.

4. Budgeting includes child support. States are unlikely to consider leniency for inmates who do not demonstrate responsibility for supporting their children.

5. Budgeting is active. Too many defendants become passive in jail and wait for others to make decisions for them.

6. Defendants need to pay for at least a part of their defense and rehabilitation. The earlier they start thinking about this, the better.

To make the budget realistic, you will need to work with defense counsel. Ask for a meeting to review the budget. If counsel thinks, for example, that a sentence of a year in jail plus two years' probation is negotiable, formulate the budget for that. Therefore, calculate 12 months of jail or prison costs plus 24 months of probation costs.

Stick `Em Up!

BUDGET, Page 1

Item	Monthly/ Unit Cost	x	Months	=	Total
JAIL					
Jail phone	_____		_____		_____
Jail commissary	_____		_____		_____
Jail fees	_____		_____		_____
Health care co-pays	_____		_____		_____
Other	_____		_____		_____
DEFENSE					
Private attorney/plea	n/a		n/a		_____
Private attorney/trial	n/a		n/a		_____
Private attorney/appeal	n/a		n/a		_____
Public defender reimbursement	n/a		n/a		_____
Bail or bail bond	n/a		n/a		_____
Other	_____		_____		_____
Other	_____		_____		_____
PROBATION/PAROLE					
Fines	_____		_____		_____
Restitution	_____		_____		_____
Vehicle impoundment	_____		_____		_____
Traffic tickets	n/a		n/a		_____
Driver's license reinstatement	n/a		n/a		_____
Probation service fees	_____		_____		_____
Drug tests	_____		_____		_____
Classes (parenting, anger mgt.)	_____		_____		_____
Drug treatment	_____		_____		_____

Stick 'Em Up!

BUDGET, Page 2

Item	Monthly/ Unit Cost	x	Months	=	Total
PROBATION/PAROLE, continued					
Counseling	_____		_____		_____
Child support	_____		_____		_____
Classes	_____		_____		_____
Other	_____		_____		_____
DEFENDANT OBLIGATIONS					
Rent/mortgage	_____		_____		_____
Child support/alimony	_____		_____		_____
Utilities	_____		_____		_____
Bank loans/credit cards	_____		_____		_____
Installment loans (furniture, etc.)	_____		_____		_____
POST-PROBATION/PAROLE					
Expungement	n/a		n/a		_____
Sealing of conviction	n/a		n/a		_____
Restoration of civil rights	n/a		n/a		_____
Pardon	n/a		n/a		_____

GRAND TOTAL	$ _____

WHO PAYS?

Defendant	$ _____
_____	$ _____
_____	$ _____
_____	$ _____

Defense counsel should also present the completed budget to the court. Make sure defense counsel *uses* the budget to demonstrate that the defendant has family backing and merits leniency.

GETTING MONEY

Cash

Checking and savings accounts are the first resort, but stocks, bonds, life insurance, and securities also can be converted to cash. Make sure you receive a receipt for all payments you make to jails, prisons, bondsmen, and attorneys.

Bank Loans

You and other family members can apply for standard bank loans. Make sure you borrow from federal or state banks, savings banks, and credit unions. These are institutions regulated by government. Avoid sucker loans at usurious interest, such as the ones described in "Toxic Loans" on p. 186.

Social Security

Defendants' social security, disability, and other checks from the United States government should be signed over to you, *not* to private defense counsel, to fund legal defense, jail fees, and the costs of probation and parole. Once defendants are convicted and sentenced to prison, they will become ineligible for benefits because their maintenance is at the taxpayers' expense. Prior to conviction, those checks will be handy indeed.

Credit Cards

Most private attorneys and bondsmen accept credit cards. Most courts and jails do not. For attorneys' fees, credit cards make installment payments easy. Always get a receipt and note on it that the payment is for "installment 1," etc. If the attorney makes unauthorized charges to your credit card, for example, to get the entire fee instead of the installment amount without your authorization, you can dispute the charges pursuant to rights granted to credit card users under the Fair Credit Billing Act. For details, please consult appendix B, "How to Dispute Attorney Credit Card Charges" (p. 243).

You can also borrow money from credit card accounts—but be careful how you do this. *Cash advances* are high-interest loans with fees of 3 to 5 percent on top of interest rates of 19 percent or higher. The interest on cash advances is too high to use them for anything other than emergency loans in small amounts.

A better option is a form of credit card loan called a *balance transfer*. Balance transfers have low interest rates, usually in single digits. The best are "life of the loan" offers, by which the low interest rate does not expire after a period of time. **Important:** When you use balance transfers, you lose your right to dispute improper charges.

Most credit cards go into default when you bounce a check, go over the credit line, or make a payment late. When defaults occur, interest rates can rise to 29 percent or higher and late fees are assessed on the statement following the default. Allow plenty of time for your payments to be credited: 3 to 5 days for electronic payments* and 7 to 10 days for mailed payments. Pay *microscopic* attention to your statements and look for interest rate changes and fee assessments. Always register your credit card on the bank's Web site so you can print out statement copies, make payments, and set up e-mail alerts to warn you of upcoming due dates. Credit card balance transfers are wonderful sources of cheap loans, but they require vigilant management to avoid default.

Credit card issuers are beginning to offer what is called a "loan on your card." Here's how it works. Suppose you have a card with a $10,000 credit limit. With a loan on your card, you may be able to borrow part of this credit line in the form of an unsecured installment loan with a fixed term, usually 12 to 48 months. So, in this example, you might be able to borrow $8,000 of your credit line in the form of a standard loan, leaving $2,000 for credit purchases.

Virtual Account Numbers

If your credit card is issued by one of the larger banks, such as Citibank or J. P. Morgan/ Chase, you can prevent unauthorized charges to your card by using a virtual account number. Banks designed this service to combat the deluge of unauthorized charges to credit cards by Internet, radio, catalog, and TV infomercial merchants who charge cards for unordered and unwanted merchandise and who have deluged banks with disputes, headaches, and losses in recent years. You create virtual account numbers on your bank's Web site and use them in place of your regular credit card number. Unlike your normal number, they have specific dollar limits that *you* specify.

So, for example, if you need to pay an attorney in three installments of $1,000 each, you generate three virtual account numbers, each with a $1,000 payment limit.

---

* Electronic payments may be instantaneous, but banks drag their heels releasing and crediting such funds. Attempting to pay credit cards on the actual due date is the financial equivalent of Russian roulette. Many people are under the illusion that clicking a button on a bank's Web site actually executes a payment. Wrong! All this does is queue up a request for payment to be made *in due course*. Big difference.

To pay the initial fee, give the attorney, on paper, the first virtual account number, then the special expiration date and 3-digit security code associated with the virtual account. (These will be different from the expiration date and security code on your actual, plastic card.) The attorney can then use the number to bill your credit card for $1,000—but no more. You *do not* hand over your credit card or give out the actual credit card account number.

For details and assistance regarding virtual account numbers, call your credit card–issuing bank's customer service line. The phone number is generally written on the back of the card.

Ignore protestations that attorney staff do not know how to use virtual account numbers. All credit card merchants, including attorneys, know how to get money from cards. All have access to MasterCard, Visa, and Discover customer service reps to assist them in using virtual account numbers and to get authorizations that guarantee their payment. Getting paid by the credit card banks is the attorney's problem, not yours.

I also strongly recommend using virtual account numbers for Internet payments to services like JPay and to all prepaid calling services for jail phone charges.

Letters of Credit

For large fees, you may wish to use letters of credit issued by your local bank. A letter of credit is an IOU. It says that the bank holds money or collateral from one party and will pay a second party a specified amount of money—*when goods and services are delivered*. Letters of credit are routine in international trade. No one in his right mind would send money to a foreign country and then wait, and wait, and wait, to have goods delivered. Instead, buyers post letters of credit so that shippers can ship with confidence that they will be paid. If you can get a letter of credit for all or part of your payment, the other party will know that the money is, quite literally, in the bank.

Equity Loans

You may be able to get an equity loan, draw from an equity credit line, or refinance a mortgage on your house. These options can be useful for paying legal fees, but you should avoid them if they cause your monthly payment to rise to a level where you risk default. Remember that when housing prices are falling, as they are currently, lenders can call the loan, that is, demand immediate payment in full, when your equity decreases.

☠ TOXIC LOANS

There are several types of loans that you should avoid entirely.

1. **Bail bond mortgages.** When you mortgage your house as collateral for a bail bond, you're securing the *entire bail amount*, not the 10 percent fee to the bondsman. For a $100,000 bond, you're on the hook for 100 large, not 10. Do you want to risk your house on the good behavior of somebody in jail? Two answers: no and hell no.

2. **Payday loans.** Don't be tempted by this grift when your defendant is whining for more commissary goodies or a probation payment. Interest rates are sky-high. Fees are higher. When these loans roll over, you'll be in hock for life to some weasel who runs a check-cashing joint.

3. **Car title loans.** Don't get me started on these horrors. The interest and fees are monstrous. Some of these goons actually grab your car and lock it up behind the pit bulls and the barbed wire until you pay up. Others install a GPS locator so the repo man can get a quick read on the vehicle's location when it's time to set the hook.

4. **The sharks.** Need I remind you not to borrow money from guys who win arguments with baseball bats and soft, expanding bullets?

5. **Pawnbrokers.** How do you define pawnbroking? Champion collateral for chump change. When you hock the jewels, gold, TV, and power tools, you're lucky to get a dime on the dollar. Miss a payment and it's bye-bye buzz saw.

6. **Tax refund anticipation loans.** These are another trap for the credulous. Annual percentage rates can top 100 percent. Fees abound. Besides, the IRS now refunds money quickly, especially to taxpayers who file online and arrange for direct deposit. Wait two weeks for your refund—please!

Rule of thumb? Don't borrow money in buildings with neon signs. When you pledge your house and car for sucker loans, you could find yourself living in a rat apartment and riding the bus. And you know what?

That sucks.

DEFENDANT CONTRIBUTIONS AND POWER OF ATTORNEY

It's amazing how few family members ask defendants to make a contribution to their own defense costs. Since most defendants will be away from the world for a while, it makes sense for them to start making a contribution immediately. Defendants may need help to do so. If they are in jail, it will be fiendishly difficult to access funds and assets from the inside.

The solution is to have your defendant sign a document that grants you financial power of attorney. This gives you the right to make specified transactions on the defendant's behalf. A simplified power of attorney document for incarcerated inmates appears in appendix A (p. 236). Other reliable forms can be obtained at no charge at the Web site of the Internet Legal Research Group, www.ilrg.com. Customized forms are available for a fee at LegalZoom.com. Other standard documents come on business-forms CDs that you can purchase at office supply stores. Most inmates have few assets, so for them a standard form will do.

Whatever version you use, ensure that it grants you the right to act for the defendant in the following capacities:

- ► Execute or cancel leases and contracts

- ► Open or close bank accounts and sign checks

- ► Open, close, or draw money from credit cards and credit accounts

- ► Open a safe-deposit box

- ► Sell property and vehicles

- ► Purchase or maintain insurance

- ► Operate or sell the defendant's business

- ► File documents with, and request information from, government agencies

- ► Prepare and file tax returns

Ask the jail staff to arrange for the defendant to sign the power of attorney and have the signature notarized. If they make this difficult, a defense counsel's notary usually can get access. *Important:* Just calling credit card companies and banks and declaring, "I have a power of attorney!" accomplishes nothing. To exercise the power, you have to *file* it with financial institutions, which will then add your name to bank or credit card accounts. Ask each financial institution for their procedure. Many require original documents with handwritten signatures of both the inmate and the notary. Make sure to get multiple copies with manual signatures and seals.

CLEANING UP THE MESS

While your defendants are incarcerated, you may have to handle their personal affairs.

► **Clean out apartments.** You need to move quickly. Valuable electronics, such as computers, plasma screen TVs, and high-end stereos, fly out of unoccupied apartments as if on wings. Storage may cost more than most defendants' possessions are worth, so have a yard sale for any items you can't use or store economically. Cancel the lease if possible, or sublet.

► **Bank accounts.** Take over accounts that have automatic deposits of federal benefits. Close inactive accounts.

► **Defendant credit cards.** Keep the accounts open whenever possible, since your defendant will need credit when freed. Make small purchases from time to time, then pay them off in order to keep the card active. Change the card numbers and passwords so that other inmates cannot force your defendant to reveal the cards' numbers and expiration dates.

► **Utilities:** Cut them off quickly to avoid fees that are charged when the utility companies cut them off.

► **Loans.** Pay the monthlies if the defendant is in for a short time. You'll have to let them go into default if they are too large or if the defendant will be incarcerated for years.

► **Houses.** If the defendant cannot service the mortgage, arrange to sell or rent the house. In a down market, this can be tough, but you can generally rent the place for enough to cover the mortgage and taxes.

► **Pets.** Take them into your home or get them adopted.

► **Vehicles.** Sell them if the defendant needs funds for defense. If you store but do not regularly use the defendant's vehicle, you will need to drive it at least every two weeks to keep the battery charged. If not used or replaced, gasoline changes chemically within 90 days. Once it does, the car will not start and fuel system parts may become clogged or damaged. Consult a mechanic about how to store an unused vehicle for extended periods.

▶ **Tax returns.** Get them filed. Defendants don't need the IRS on their cases. They've got enough problems.

The above advice is for defendants who work legit jobs and have assets. Many others work in the underground economy, pay no taxes, are uninsured, and drive cars whose ownership is, to put it charitably, somewhat murky. They don't own much, so sorting through their stuff may be a waste of your time.

You've got more important things to do.

OUTDOOR JAIL
Probation and Parole

To MIDDLE-CLASS PEOPLE, probation and parole seem easy. You pee in the cup, attend your classes, scrub some graffiti, mow some parks, or serve a few Meals on Wheels. Now and then you show up at the probation office with a file of receipts and forms, all signed, dated, and tickety-boo. To socialized individuals, the experience appears to be mostly Mickey Mouse and always boring. For white-collar criminals and celebrity offenders, who have all the middle-class values except honesty, this is true. They breeze through probation and parole with nary a hitch. About the worst that happens is that photos of these formerly distinguished citizens weed whacking in the local park with other losers appear in the *Daily Fish Wrap*.

No biggie.

For other offenders,* who have spent their lives running and gunning on the streets, completing probation or parole is horrendously difficult. The reason is that probation and parole are cunningly—some would say fiendishly—devised to exploit the weaknesses of the chaotic mindset and to precipitate offenders back into jail and prison.

PROBATION

Probation is a *suspension* of jail or prison time. It is a criminal sentence handed down by a judge, and it can be revoked easily. Most offenders don't understand this. Once released, they think, "Hooray, I'm free!"—then rush out to schedule the usual drug- and booze-fueled whorefest with the usual unhappy results. Offenders need to understand that while on probation, *they're serving their sentence*. They're still in the grip of The Man. The only change is that The Man's claws have loosened—slightly. Life on probation is highly restricted.

Probation is, essentially, outdoor jail. It comes in three degrees:

1. **Active supervision.** This is the toughest form of probation. Under active supervision, probation officers will visit the offender, frequently and unannounced. They will search the offender's home, which could be

---

* Jailed inmates cease to be "detainees" or "defendants" at the moment of conviction. Post-conviction, they are referred to as "convicts" or "offenders." Most guys glom onto their change of status when they get the mandatory haircut. Adios mullets, rooster combs, dreads, and Mohawks!

your home if the offender is living with you. Any dope, guns, or stolen merchandise found will result in immediate return of the offender to jail or prison and may result in the arrest of others in the home, including, most unfortunately, you. Drug tests will be random and supervised. This means there will be no time to detox, and the offender will have to strip buck naked in front of technicians before peeing in the cup.* Probation officers may vary this routine by requiring hair and skin patch tests, which are extremely sensitive. Offenders have to make office visits to probation officers, and they may be confined to house arrest except for work and religious observance. GPS ankle bracelets can enforce compliance and track offenders' movements.

2. **Standard supervision.** This is a slightly less tough level of probation. Visits to probation offices are less frequent, perhaps quarterly, but expect the midnight knock on the door, followed by probation officers tossing the home.

3. **Unsupervised probation.** This is probation lite, and it does not require meetings with probation officers. Probationers show compliance with the terms of their release by mailing forms to their probation officers.

Probation is available primarily for offenders convicted of misdemeanors and low-level felonies. For violent criminals and habitual offenders, it's off the table. This is another reason to urge attorneys to work on reduction of the number and severity of charges. Getting charges busted down from felony one to felony two, or from felony to misdemeanor, makes probation possible.

PAROLE

Parole is derived from a French term that means "spoken word." It once referred to the release of captured knights in shining armor who gave their word of honor not to participate in future hostilities. In this cynical century, "word of honor" is enforced by parole officers, police, jails, and prisons. Whereas probation is a sentence in and of itself, parole is the reduction of a previously determined prison sentence. Parole occurs when

---

* Most people attempt to cheat on drug tests by hypersaturating themselves with water. This is largely ineffective with current, highly sensitive tests. They also substitute "clean" urine concealed in a baggie. One problem with this latter tactic, aside from its being illegal, is that many offenders don't know anybody with clean urine. Many a junkie has scored some cash by selling his foul brew to eager probationers. The more sophisticated alternative, self-catheterization and injection of clean urine into the bladder, is seen mostly in movies. I've never yet met an offender willing to shove a greasy catheter up the pipe. In any case, you won't find a Clean Wee-Wee Kit for sale at the pharmacy.

an offender serving time in prison is released early under supervision, with conditions similar to those of probation.

Parole does not exist in the federal system. With the feds, you do the crime, you do the time—period. In state criminal justice, parole takes two forms. Time off for good behavior, known in prisons as "good time," is an automatic reduction of sentence that occurs when a prisoner has few or no prison rules infractions. Each state defines "good time" differently and sets different criteria for awarding it. The second type of parole is reduction of sentence by a parole board. Parole boards make decisions using three criteria:

1. The danger the prisoner poses to the public if released

2. The likelihood that the prisoner will commit new crimes

3. The degree of overcrowding in the prison system

During parole hearings, prisoners will usually give a statement and ask for early release. They will be expected to show remorse, which for many is difficult. Victims and their families may appear and argue against parole. A family management plan, showing specific steps by which the parolee plans to become a citizen, is useful.

OTHER CONDITIONS OF PAROLE AND PROBATION

Regardless of the level of probation or the type of parole, release comes with many conditions and restrictions.

Curfew

Offenders must be home by a certain hour. Probation officers check by calling the landline number. Forget the cell phones. Probation officers know all about *72. They may insist that call forwarding be removed from telephone service. Many states prohibit offenders from having dial-up Internet access, which ties up phone lines. If the offender was convicted of sex crimes, Internet access may be prohibited entirely.

Geographical Restriction

Probationers and parolees are forbidden to leave the state without prior permission. They may be banned from liquor stores, bars, strip joints, and high crime areas of town. Their whereabouts may be checked by GPS trackers. Many of the new systems prepare maps of offenders' locations so probation officers can check movements periodically and order an arrest when an offender enters a "red zone." Many jurisdictions require driving logs and will bust probationers and parolees who lie on paper about their whereabouts. Computer mapping makes checking mileage a snap for The Man and his minions.

Rights Waivers

Probationers and parolees have to waive their right to extradition. If arrested out of state, they will be extradited without hearings.

Offenders must also sign away their constitutional protections against warrantless search and seizure. Their homes, vehicles, *and computers, cell phones, beepers, and PDAs* can be searched at any time for any reason. Hoodlum text messages and e-mails will merit return to jail and prison. *Important:* Text messages, e-mails, and phone numbers can be subpoenaed from telephone and Internet providers. Erasing them from cell phones and computers is not enough. And for heaven's sake, no porn!

People Avoidance

Merely being seen with known felons is enough to violate probation and parole. How do parole and probation officers know? Enemies, naturally, will rat out probationers and parolees who hang out with hoodlums, and in any case, cops know who's who in their patrol areas and can always check photos on their computers. Offenders on supervised release have to say bye-bye to their homies, *carnales*, and all their tong, yakuza, and mafia mates, preferably forever.

Offenders are almost always banned from contact with victims, witnesses, codefendants, ex-spouses, former lovers and, in the case of sex offenders, with children. Of course, victims, witnesses, and the various exes may lie to probation officers to get offenders busted back to prison. In these cases, that GPS locator can be a lifesaver when it corroborates an alibi.

Employment and Education

Employment status will be checked and verified. If a probationer is in school, perfect attendance is mandatory. Probation and parole officers will give a ting-a-ling to school administrators to check.

Classes and Community Service

For most probationers and parolees, socialization school is back in session. They may be required to attend classes on parenting and anger management. Attendance is mandatory, and attitude counts. Offenders should look happy and smile, even when they're bored stiff.

Judges are also serious about getting those parks mowed, graffiti washed, and school kids lectured. Participation is compulsory. It's checked.

Restitution, Fines, and Criminal Justice Fees

Victims must be paid as ordered. In addition, fines, court costs, and jail fees must all be paid in full in order to complete probation and parole.

Paperwork

The probation and parole systems, like courts, jails, and prisons, run on paperwork. Offenders must file forms notifying probation and parole officers about changes in their address or in their job or education enrollment status. They have to have written certification of attendance at classes, therapy, drug tests, work, and school. Always, they must have receipts showing payment of fees, fines, and restitution. Since family members are generally better organized than defendants, your help in maintaining files, with copies of all paperwork, will be essential.

No Funky Tools

Possession of lock picks, slim jims, and inflatable car-door openers is prohibited. Ditto for dope tools like syringes, bongs, and pipes. If your defendant is diabetic, make copies of the *prescription* for syringes. Have your offender keep one copy in the wallet and one at home. Offenders also will get busted for possession of ammonia and pseudoephedrine (Sudafed), which are used to cook street meth.

Ignition Interlocks

Offenders convicted of DUI may be sentenced to drive with an ignition interlock. This is a gadget that has an ethanol sensor. The driver has to blow into the tube in order to start the car. Periodically while driving, the driver has to blow into the tube to keep the vehicle running. This prevents friends from blowing into the tube to allow drunks to start cars.

Firearms Ban

For offenders under supervision, firearms are poison. Not only should parolees and probationers not carry weapons, but they should avoid being near them as well. Many states have "constructive possession" laws by which offenders are considered to be in possession of firearms when they are in the same building or vehicle as the weapon. Whether offenders bought the weapons or even know of their existence is irrelevant. Once weapons are discovered, probationers are busted. When offenders are arrested for firearms possession, expect judges to be merciless. What makes this so tough is that many offenders base their identity and self-worth on firearms. They define themselves as Man with a Gun. This leads sooner rather than later to a new self-definition—Prisoner Number So-and-So.

PROBATION REPORTS

Whether offenders are even offered probation or parole can depend on the content of their probation reports. In these documents, probation department employees (or, more rarely, private individuals) offer recommendations as to whether the offender deserves leniency. These reports are heavy on criminal history, drug use, and behavior while incarcerated. They are light on religion and other forms of socialization and extra light on the all-important subject of family support. Nonetheless, judges take the probation officer's recommendations seriously. Attorneys can and do challenge probation reports, but too often this comes across as meaningless quibbling.

Rather than arguing about a probation report, or accepting the report without challenge, it is better to present a family management plan as an alternative. The plan addresses the wider issues of offender socialization. It details family support, which is crucial in the real world but unmentioned by probation reports. It addresses the critical issues of finance and paperwork, which are unaddressed in official probation reports. By presenting such a plan instead of challenging the probation report, attorneys also avoid having to dispute in court with faceless, and usually absent, officials of the probation department.

WHY PAROLE AND PROBATION ARE SO TOUGH

Outdoor jail is tough for several reasons. First, merely *not committing new crimes* is insufficient to complete parole and probation successfully. Supervised release requires, in addition, specific middle-class behaviors. "Probation" comes from the Latin word for "testing." It tests specific middle-class skills such as keeping appointments, being on time, and planning for the future. For offenders who have never owned a calendar in their lives and don't wear watches, such feats are scarcely imaginable. Worse, probation and parole require documentation—receipts, forms, evaluations, notices, and on and on. Many offenders do not read well. Paper flies off them like dandruff.

And that's not all. Probation and parole create an entirely new class of administrative crimes that apply *only* to supervised offenders. Failing to file a change-of-address or change-of-employment form is, for them, a crime! Failing to show up on time for an appointment? Ditto. Getting snarky in class and not doing those little exercises? Crime city! Too frequently, offenders who violate parole and probation spend more time in prison for administrative violations than they would have if they had completed their original sentence without conditional release.

For citizens, not filing paperwork and not showing up on time have repercussions, but never the loss of freedom. Millions of mostly upstanding citizens use illegal drugs recreationally. If they're smart enough not to get crazy, to do their dope at home, and to avoid carrying drugs in their cars, they can go a lifetime without being arrested. For probationers and parolees, there's no slack. They're monitored and drug tested. One dirty squirt into the cup, and they're toast.

Even worse, parole and probation require frequent interaction with government employees and contractors and the social skills to deal effectively with bureaucracy. Since too many offenders simply express whatever emotion they feel at the moment, when a probation or parole officer, or therapist or teacher, annoys them, their response is likely to be "Fuck off!"

This is not wise.

Offenders will also discover that enforcement is arbitrary. They may miss an appointment, and nothing happens. They may forget to file paperwork, and still nothing happens. Suddenly, by failing to file, say, a single postcard, they trip a wire and they're busted.

Two years ago, I interviewed an inmate facing two years of hard time for failing to file a change-of-address postcard! On the surface, this appears outrageous. Here's the real story. The guy had an altercation with his girlfriend, which necessitated, naturally, a sudden change of residence. He moved to one of the trailer parks that infest the exurbs of my fair city but failed to notify his probation officer, even though he was on active supervision. The officer, duly tipped to the absconder's whereabouts, roared out to the boondocks for a raid.

Unfortunately, this probation officer had been watching too much cop TV. When he located the trailer indicated by the tipster, he decided to smash down the door and charge in for an arrest! Alas, the trailer was occupied not by the absconder, but by a good ol' boy who was reclining in his lounger and watching sports TV with a beer in one hand and a double-barreled shotgun in the other (a state of near-perfect happiness). When the door smashed down and the glass flew, he leveled the gun.

"Hands up, shitbird," he said. "Wrong trailer!"

Thus the probation officer found himself under citizen's arrest at gunpoint. In due course the police arrived and sorted out the matter. Naturally they went to the trailer next door and arrested the probationer. After that little drama, the guy was lucky to get *only* two years. Moral: pissing off probation officers is not recommended.

By contrast, the state of Hawaii has a commonsensical approach to probation that takes into account the offender mentality. It is called flash incarceration. In Hawaii, every probation violation, no matter how trivial, is immediately punished by a short return to jail. For the first offense, the return is one day. The jail term increases to a week or a month for subsequent offenses. Officials refer to this as "puppy training." The program is remarkably effective in persuading offenders to complete their probation successfully, because it matches punishments to the severity and frequency of violations. However, this approach requires that police, judges, and prosecutors cooperate for a common goal and coordinate, and fund, their activities to make flash incarceration possible. In most states, sadly, getting such worthies to cooperate is about as easy as teaching snakes to sing.

Knuckling under to authority figures, especially those who have the power to toss you into the sneezer, is absolutely necessary for completing probation and parole.

Most probation and parole officers, like everyone else in the criminal justice system, are hard working, long suffering, and lightly paid. Nonetheless, offenders should expect to encounter some petty tyrants and the occasional flaming asshole. For offenders on supervised release, there's only one strategy that works:

Be on time for meetings and classes, drug free, with paperwork and cashier's checks in hand.

Smile!

Be nice!

Stay focused on freedom—sweet, elusive freedom.

VIOLATION

In the criminal justice system, "violate" is a transitive verb, and offenders are its direct object. Probation and parole officers can "violate" offenders back into jail and prison. When offenders are arrested for a new crime, fail a drug test, or otherwise do not conform to the terms and conditions of parole, officers will file a notice of violation and seek an arrest warrant. In some states, probation and parole officers themselves are sworn law enforcement officers, with firearms and statewide arrest powers.

In any case, violators are soon back in jail. Public defenders are appointed, or private attorneys hired, hearings are held, and judges render a verdict. Punishments range from extension of parole and probation time to remand to prison. The number of probationers and parolees sent to prison is stunning. In many states this influx is straining budgets and causing crises in the prison systems. Relief, however, is not at hand. No politician ever got tossed out of office for being tough on crime. On the other hand, the political heat generated when a probationer or parolee commits a murder, rape, or armed robbery is unbearable. For elected officials, it is better that a thousand violators be imprisoned than a single offender generate an ugly headline!

WHAT FAMILY MEMBERS CAN DO

Because supervised release lasts for a long time and one slipup or one paperwork mix-up can get an offender violated, your assistance with probation and parole is essential. Family are the only people in this world that many offenders respect. They're the only people offenders will listen to. Here's how you can help.

Permanent Address

Even if the offender doesn't live with you, you may wish to have all official mail sent to you. In most cases, you are more organized than the offender and can read, manage, and explain the paperwork.

Calendaring and Scheduling

Offenders need help to wake up, dress up, and show up at required meetings, classes, and therapy. You may find it advisable to maintain the calendar and urge compliance. Nagging is also useful. Offenders won't like it, but they'll thank you later once they're completely free. So nag away!

Paperwork

You should assist the offender in maintaining files, making copies of paperwork, and getting forms filled, signed, and mailed in a timely fashion. Send the most important by certified mail, return receipt requested.

It is crucial that you assist the defendant in maintaining files of all court orders and probation and parole documents. Once defendants are free of the criminal justice system, they will have to produce these orders many times over the years as they seek employment, government benefits, education, and loans from financial institutions.

Budgeting and Payments

Most offenders want to be free so badly they never think about the financial aspects of parole and probation. You will need to make arrangements to get fees, fines, and restitution paid.

If defendants are paying alimony and child support, they may need to get payments lowered by a family court judge to reflect changed circumstances. Lowered child support and alimony allow defendants to complete probation and parole rather than getting busted back into the joint for nonpayment. This is tough on ex-spouses and children, but the alternative may be for them to receive nothing at all.

Check the Computer!

One of the most infuriating problems with the criminal justice system is incorrect information entered into law enforcement databases. For example, when defense attorneys succeed in reducing felonies to misdemeanors, defendants will have orders signed by a judge to this effect. However, if no one makes appropriate changes in databases, government computers may still show that defendants are convicted felons! They will be denied civil rights, jobs, and the right to bear arms, and they will get extra-thorough scrutiny from cops who run their license plates. Many don't even realize this is happening! They just assume they're being hassled, which they are.

Inside jail or prison, incorrect information doesn't matter. Outside, it does. When your offender is released, as first priority, have a clerk in the court system or the public defender's office run the offender's record to make sure that what appears on the computer corresponds with actual sentences and judicial orders. Defense attorneys are woefully unaware of this problem, since they usually are out the door before the ink dries on sentences and orders. This is a responsibility of defendants and their families. In assisting defendants with computer records checks, you are performing an invaluable service.

Living Arrangements

Most supervised offenders, of necessity, take low-paying jobs. Most cannot afford the costs of supervised release and child support while living alone and paying rent, utilities, and insurance. When offenders cannot afford to live alone, give help with alternatives, such as living with roommates or living with relatives. This will not be easy, especially if the offender has to move in with you. It's tough emotionally to take an adult offender into your home.

There is another downside. You are at risk of arrest if the offender brings drugs, guns, and thugs into your home and porn into your computer. When offenders refuse to give up the thug-and-drug lifestyle, *you have to throw them out*. They will be back in prison soon enough anyway, so save yourself and the rest of the family. This is miserable and will be a horrible strain.

Vehicles

It is absolutely essential that offenders on release have no contact with police, because an arrest for any reason will violate them back into prison. The most frequent cause of police contact is traffic stops. Have offenders run licenses through the state online database or visit the driver's license bureau and check for outstanding tickets and suspensions. Get tickets paid, suspensions lifted, licenses renewed, insurance paid, and tags updated *as your first order of business*. Make sure the vehicle is titled in the offender's name. Get all the lights in working order. I cannot emphasize how important these precautions are. Offenders must drive lawfully in street-legal vehicles in order to stay free. Crapola cars with broken lights, smoking tailpipes, and bald tires are cop bait.

Regardless of the precautions, police have computers in their cruisers and routinely run license tags to check for outstanding tickets, warrants, and detainers. They will immediately see that offenders have a criminal record and will give the car extra scrutiny and look for a reason to make a stop, a search, and an arrest. Offenders must keep their vehicles street legal and squeaky clean. No drugs, no guns, and no thug buddies. They should sit up straight and avoid the "thug slouch," which attracts police. They should drive like grannies. Keeping those hands at the 10-and-2 position also is a great idea.*

---

* During my 40s, I went through a knucklehead period of maniac driving. After numerous tickets and suspensions, several thousand dollars in fines, ruinous insurance rates, and some near arrests, I finally got the memo. Now I drive like a little old lady. It makes my family and friends nuts. Cops like it, though. They like it a lot.

Here's another great idea. Put photocopies of the following items together in a large envelope:

► Receipts for ticket payments

► Suspension waivers

► Insurance cards

► Vehicle registration

► Offender's driver's license

Keep these copies in the car. If stopped by police, offenders can simply hand over the entire envelope without fumbling in the glove compartment and storage bins. This is important for four reasons. First, the state may not update its databases in a timely fashion, so the police computers might not report that tickets have been paid and suspensions lifted. Second, if cops see offenders bend down out of sight as they grope around for their license and registration, the cops may assume they are reaching for a weapon. This will have unfortunate consequences. Third, many offenders on release are poorly organized and apt to dash out to the car and drive away without their wallets. Copies of licenses and registrations kept in the vehicle can be verified by police, who can check motor vehicle databases on their computers. This means that police can see that the driver is licensed and the vehicle registered and insured. They will be less likely to make an arrest. Fourth, cops demand paperwork, but they hate to read it. A mass of paperwork is like roach spray for cops. They can't wait to shove it all right back and bark, "Get out of here!" See my book *Arrest-Proof Yourself* for more details.

You should also insist, over and over again like a broken record, that your offender never ride in other peoples' cars except in absolute emergencies. In offender world, other peoples' cars contain drugs, drug residue, guns, stolen merchandise, fugitives with outstanding warrants, and obnoxious, loud passengers and drivers, who will attract the police. Other peoples' cars are often stolen and on police watch lists. Your offender will be found to be in constructive possession of any contraband discovered and will be immediately violated back to prison.

Offenders should never, ever, loan vehicles to anyone for any reason. Loaned vehicles come back scratched, dented, and smeared with drug residue or containing partially filled dope baggies and the occasional gun that was stuffed under the seat and forgotten during a tense brush with police.* Sometimes vehicles don't come back at all. They're in the junkyard or the police impound lot.

---

* When cars are stopped by police, driver and passengers immediately stuff their guns and dope under the seats. When police do not make a search, people in the car are so relieved that they typically fire up some spliffs and get wasted. Modern dope contains so much tetrahydrocannabinol that after a few tokes, passengers can't remember their names, much less their guns.

Offenders should never rent a car using their, or *your*, credit card and loan it to someone else. Because of vehicle seizure laws, drug dealers prefer rental cars. They pay fools to rent them and take the heat when cops swoop.

ARREST PROOFING

I've mentioned my first book, *Arrest-Proof Yourself*, several times, but it's an especially important resource for probationers and parolees, who need to avoid *all* unnecessary contact with police. This book gives advice from an absolute expert—my coauthor, Dale Carson, a former cop and FBI agent who is now one of Jacksonville's top criminal defense attorneys. It features charts to measure the arrestability quotient, or likelihood of being arrested. It explains why cops behave like they do and shows why they target some people, and not others, for stops, interrogations, and arrests. And it explains how to dress, drive, walk, and talk so as *not* to attract police.

Cops can always find a reason to make an arrest. A friend of mine in his 20s has been busted three times when cops showed up at the loud parties he's fond of. The third time, cops were at a loss for a reason to arrest him until one of them noticed that my buddy was standing *on the grass of a private lawn* rather than in the public right-of-way. They arrested him for "prowling." So far he's beaten every rap, at great financial cost to his family. One day, however, one of those bullshit busts will stick and he'll cop a felony that will end his college or professional career. For probationers and parolees, things are even tougher. Even a bullshit bust is enough to send them back to prison.

When offenders do come in contact with police, they should not conceal the fact that they're on probation or parole. They should not lie, which can get them violated. They should be brief; they should not volunteer statements or tell long, convoluted stories that lead to lies. Cops can check statements with their computers and cell phones. Offenders should be polite. They should keep their hands at their sides and ignore all provocations.

Every day of probation and parole is not a day of freedom—it is a day spent serving a criminal sentence in outdoor jail. Offenders should never forget this. Not for a minute.

You can help, though. You can help a lot.

24

TO SNITCH IS A BITCH
Cooperating with Police and Prosecutors

For defendants charged with murder, armed robbery, rape, gun crimes, narcotics trafficking, or acts of violence, and for habitual offenders, probation is not an option. The only choice for lessening their sentences is to cooperate with law enforcement officers and prosecutors—in a word, to become snitches. Cooperation can lessen sentences dramatically and in some cases result in charges being dropped. Nonetheless, this is a risky decision, both for defendants and their families, who may be at risk of violent retaliation from "no-snitch" hit squads.

When making the decision, offenders and their families and attorneys need to gauge whether cooperation is possible. This will depend on several factors:

1. The importance and timeliness of the information offered

2. Whether the information is of interest to law enforcement

3. The level of truthfulness and cooperation that an offender can offer

Let's examine these criteria. First, the information must be timely. Crime tips spoil faster than tuna fish in hot sun. Offenders have to decide quickly. Most wait too long, until their information is out of date and worthless.

Second, contrary to common belief, law enforcement is not interested in all crimes all the time. Law enforcement personnel and money are limited. Police, for example, are not interested in crime outside their jurisdictions. Federal law enforcement agencies, such as the FBI, will investigate only violations of federal law of a certain magnitude. If you offer the feds information that a certain person took a lunchbox full of dope across a state line, they're likely to yawn.

The same will happen when defendants offer to tell local police about street-level drug trade. For example, let's say a defendant wants to tell cops that his buddies No-Nuts, Stone, and Dweezle are slinging rock on a certain street corner. T-Bone is their connection and drives by in a rental car every afternoon to re-up the stash. Think the cops will light up over this?

Nope. These are just corner boys and the re-up guy. In every big city, there are so many corner boys in the drug trade that police don't bother keeping track of them, which would be about as useful as inventorying fleas. Whenever jails are not stuffed to the rooftops, cops can catch all the corner boys they want by using an undercover officer who wears a buttonhole camera that photographs the dope, the suspect, the cash, and the sale.

Information worthy of a proffer concerns big crimes like terrorism, major drug dealing, murder, armed robbery, kidnapping, child molestation, white slavery, kiddie porn, snuff flicks, racial and hate crimes, and racketeering in labor unions, construction, loan sharking, and protection.

Finally, once offenders decide to cooperate, they have to be absolutely truthful about what they know, and they must admit to *all* the crimes they have committed. This is a huge stumbling block. Most offenders have spent their lives lying about their activities. Coming clean is, for many, a psychological impossibility.

Recently I went to a federal prison in Georgia to work as a Spanish interpreter for a defense attorney. The client had serious drug charges pending from the FBI, which had done its usual thorough investigation. Without a deal, this guy was going to vanish into the hole for decades. He was, however, an excellent candidate for a proffer. He had information about a drug ring operating from the Caribbean and supplying a major U.S. city. In addition, he had information about a counterfeit ID operation that employed corrupt government employees to plug phony numbers into government computers so that the bad IDs appeared legit during traffic stops and airport security checks. This latter operation would be of special interest to the Department of Homeland Security.

Unfortunately, this defendant simply could not tell the truth. During hours of interviews, I watched him hem and haw, tremble and sweat, and stutter out lie after lie to his own defense attorney. He had had his fingertips surgically altered, and I'm not sure that anyone knows his real name, much less whether his story contains even a few nuggets of truth. The FBI, of course, doesn't care. They have no problem locking up yet another Juan Doe. He'll be able to ponder his decision at length and at leisure in the depths of some supermax* far, far away.

WHAT THE POPO WANT

The cops and the feds want total cooperation. They want it for years, until the offender, like a lemon, is squeezed dry. Once a proffer is negotiated, the length of cooperation required is completely at the government's discretion. No judge will intervene. Lies, screwups, and new crimes will end the deal and get the offender tossed back into prison for the full sentence. Once in prison, snitches have a short life expectancy.

---

* Supermax, a contraction of "super-maximum," refers to ultrasecure state and federal prisons. All supermax prisoners stay in solitary confinement in total lockdown. There are no windows; there is no hope. These places make Alcatraz look like a Holiday Inn.

Law enforcement officers may require the offender to testify against criminal associates in court. They may insert the offender back into a criminal organization and run him as a confidential informant (CI). They may ask him (usually it's a him) to wear a wire or a concealed video camera. Is this a high-wire act? It's worse. This is skating on a razor blade! Fall off one way, and back you go to prison for the full sentence. Fall off the other way, and you get a bullet through the head from your criminal associates.

When cooperation isn't dangerous, it's humiliating. Informers have to stand bitch to the cops and the feds. They have to rat out former friends and associates. To stay the course, and get a sentence reduction or unconditional release, offenders need to make the cops and the feds *like* them. They have to be charming, helpful, and friendly. They have to remember to send birthday cards—seriously!—and to buy the occasional small gift of a soda and a sandwich for their benefactor/tormentors. They have to stifle larcenous, even murderous, impulses, and knuckle under completely for the duration. They have to banish "authentic" behavior and saying what they really feel—which is to tell the cops and the feds to take a flying flip backwards and f#*@ themselves on the way down.

HIP-POCKET INFORMANTS

Police and the FBI are notorious for recruiting offenders as "hip-pocket" informants. This is the practice of bracing up offenders and threatening to arrest them on new charges unless the offenders cooperate. Because the offenders are not actually arrested, their cooperation is unofficial, undocumented, and unrewarded.

For local cops, this is an unethical but not illegal practice—in fact, it's standard operating procedure. Many of the informers are drug addicts. For a few dollars and a hamburger, they'll chirp like crickets. Do not allow your defendant to be pressured into unrewarded assistance.

For federal agents, maintaining hip-pocket informants is currently prohibited, but I suspect the practice continues. If your offender is trapped in a hip-pocket squeeze play by federal agents, inform defense counsel. FBI agents are required to register informants and to formalize and document the terms and conditions of informants' services. If caught recruiting hip-pocket snitches, they face disciplinary action up to and including dismissal from service. It may be possible to trap the feds in a hip-pocket squeeze and to pressure them to formalize the relationship and agree to reduction and dismissal of charges. This will require a defense attorney with large stones and a taste for intrigue.

THE PROFFER

Offenders should *never, ever* agree to an informal informant cooperation arrangement or sign a proffer formally agreeing to cooperate without the assistance of legal counsel. All terms and conditions need to be negotiated, including witness protection and relocation.

Federal law enforcement agencies have more resources for this than local police, for whom "witness relocation" may mean nothing more than a bus ticket and a box of cold fried chicken.

Make sure that you, the family, are included in the protection offers if you feel threatened. This is no joke. Cooperation is tricky, risky, and dangerous. It needs to be negotiated, documented, formalized, signed, sealed, and delivered for judicial review. Anything less is lunacy.

Defendants will look to you to help make this huge decision. In advising whether to take a proffer, keep in mind the following: In federal prosecutions resulting from investigations by agencies like the FBI and the Department of Alcohol, Tobacco, Firearms and Explosives, the conviction rate is nearly 90 percent. There is no parole in the federal system. All time is served; all time is hard. In a state prosecution, the outlook is grim if the case is strong, if there are credible eyewitnesses, or if there is forensic evidence or surveillance audio and video. Also grim is any prosecution in which the defendant is charged as a repeat offender or being prosecuted in a tough-as-nails sentencing state such as Florida.

Cooperation is a hard road, but it's the only road for serous offenders. The alternative is long, tough prison time and emergence from prison, decades later, middle-aged and crazed.

Or dead.

YOUR PERSONAL
WITNESS PROTECTION PROGRAM
Blowing the 'Hood

FLEE FIRST.

When you receive a violent threat, leave the neighborhood at once. Don't wait, don't wail and moan on the phone, don't walk in circles wringing your hands. Round up the family, load the car, and scram! vamoose! vanish!

Do not expect the police, attorneys, or government agencies to help you. There isn't time. It only takes minutes for bad guys to load their weapons and roll the death wagon. Perhaps you were planning to testify against a violent criminal as part of a plea deal. Perhaps your defendant accepted a proffer of cooperation. Perhaps the bad guys only *think* you or your defendant snitched them out. When bad guys are coming for you, what they think doesn't matter. Avoiding a hail of bullets does.

Every year, witnesses, cooperating defendants, and their family members are injured or killed by hoodlums. In most cases, they received a threat but didn't act. They diddled; they dawdled; now they're dead. Some of the bad guys pack so much artillery and ammo they can practically saw a house apart. When babies, visitors, and relatives get killed, they don't care, as long as their "snitch and die" message gets delivered.

Stick 'Em Up!

GETAWAY INSTRUCTIONS,
Page 1

1. **Do not** argue with someone making a threat over the telephone. Do not waste time attempting to explain that you and the defendant are not snitches. The bad guys may be keeping you on the phone while they drive over to kill you.

2. Grab checkbook, prescription meds, toiletries, a change of clothes, and cash and credit cards. Kill the power at the main box, which saves you money and prevents fires from stoves and hot water heaters left unattended in vacant homes, and also discourages squatters. Lock the door. Hop in the car and drive. Any direction will do. Once you clear the neighborhood, there will be time to think, plan, and act.

3. Before you shelter with friends or relatives, ask yourself how reliable and discreet they are. Will they take you in quietly? Or will they get on the phone the minute you arrive and start gabbing with people *back in your neighborhood*? "Omigod! Guess who showed up!"

4. Will your presence put friends and relatives at risk?

5. Are your family members and children disciplined enough to stay off the phone and stay out of their old neighborhood? Bad guys can easily post lookouts or simply offer money and make threats so that neighbors will rat you out if they see you.

6. Inform defense counsel of the threat. Follow his or her suggestions.

7. If your defendant is at risk and is still in jail, inform jail administrators of the threat. If the threat occurs on nights or weekends, telephone and ask for the watch commander. Well-managed jails have established procedures in place for protecting threatened inmates. Follow up with a letter addressed to the jail administrator, sent certified mail, return receipt requested. If your defendant is injured or killed and jail staff did not act swiftly to secure the defendant's safety, a letter will help in a lawsuit for damages.

8. Report the threat to police. Ask if your state has a witness protection program and get the telephone number and Web address—but don't get your hopes up. The Federal Witness Protection Program, made famous in TV shows and movies, is used only for high-profile cooperators in federal prosecutions. Too often state programs are heavily publicized but lightly funded.

Stick `Em Up!

GETAWAY INSTRUCTIONS,
Page 2

9. Do not reveal your hideout to jailed defendants. They can be beaten and made to talk.

10. Be careful of jail visits, especially if you are required to visit only on a certain day. Do not drive your own car. Bad guys may post lookouts in the jail parking lot and lobby.

11. Get a cell phone with a GPS chip so cops can locate you quickly if you have to call for help.

12. If your state allows it, get a weapon and a concealed weapons permit. Don't get squeamish about this. If you have to blast a bad guy, do it. Even if you are prosecuted later, would you rather face a jury and await a verdict or face a killer and await a bullet?

Err on the side of caution. If you flee unnecessarily, you can laugh about it later, but if your suspicions are well founded, when a strange car pulls up in front of your house and AK-47s start to chatter, you won't be there.

26

THE FAMILY MANAGEMENT PLAN
Making a Difference for Your Defendant

THROUGHOUT THE BOOK, I'VE urged you to create a family management plan that will make the case for leniency, guide defendants toward an ordered middle-class mindset, and thereby enable them to live peacefully and lawfully. Is family management a magical solution to crime? Of course not. Crime is not a problem to be solved but a condition to be managed downward over time. Family management works only for offenders who have family who care for them and are willing to make efforts to socialize them. Offenders who don't are "managed" in jails and prisons.

Nonetheless, by devising a plan, you are taking control of a situation that all too often has seemed a bewildering confrontation with the titanic forces of the state. When defendants work with their families in devising the plan, they are showing initiative and willingness to change. Already, in doing this, they are vastly different from the majority of defendants, who lie around in jail and wait for their families to do all the work and pay up so they can get out and start a life of crime all over again.

FORMULATING THE PLAN

The family management plan is a document, with supporting letters and educational, employment, and military records, that tells the court what offenders and their families are willing to do in return for leniency. On p. 213 is a sample plan. Tear it out and copy it, or customize one of your own. If you don't own a computer, you can always handwrite your plan.

Your plan will be, in effect, a report of the middle-class values and behaviors that your defendant has or is in the process of acquiring. Most defendants and their families get this, but they think that the time to acquire these desirable traits is *after* defendants are released. To be legally significant in petitioning for leniency, however, defendants need to begin to acquire middle-class values, and to plan to obtain middle-class accomplishments, *before* their sentencing. When defendants are free on bond, this is easier than when they are in jail. In jail, middle-classification is difficult but not impossible. When defendants are in jail, family members do most of the legwork. Defendants, nonetheless, have to do the following:

1. Think about their lives

2. Make choices

3. Plan for a future

Working on a family management plan keeps inmates concentrating on freedom and prevents their becoming engrossed in, and adapted to, jail and prison life. In the outside world, knowing how to do time in prison is like being good at tiddlywinks—an interesting but useless accomplishment.

The Ultimate Defendant Test

Formulating the plan requires the *active* participation of defendants. It tests their willingness to become socialized and to work toward freedom. If your defendant is willing to work with you on the plan, that's your way of knowing that he or she is worth saving and worth the extraordinary investment of your time and money.

The plan helps defendants and their loved ones to be specific about each step along the path to socialization. On the next page is a chart illustrating the difference between specific plans and the usual mumbled promises, mixed with lies and evasions, that judges routinely ignore. You will need to be practical about these matters. Do not let affection or a sense of obligation lead you into wishful thinking or into reading more into defendant promises than is actually there. When you hear the sounds of vagueness and BS, prod defendants, over and over, to get specific:

▶ "Exactly what school will you attend?"

▶ "How much can you pay in child support?"

▶ "What 12-step meeting do you plan to attend? When does it meet?"

▶ "What job can you find when released?"

And so on. Expect this to be tedious and painful. For defendants who have been doing whatever they pleased most of their lives, planning the work and working the plan are extremely difficult. If defendants are free, they should hit the phones and the Internet and pound the pavements gathering relevant information for court appearances. If incarcerated, they will ask for your help. When this happens, it's a good sign.

All this, of course, puts you in the position of bossing around defendants. When they're adults, and especially if they're not your children, this is hard. You can take solace, however, in one fact. Society does not tolerate unsocialized individuals. *Somebody* is going to boss them around eventually. If not you, then police, judges, and corrections officers. This is a law of nature.

Like gravity.

BULLSHIT DETECTOR

BS	TRUTH
1. Yeah, I'll go back to school.	**1.** I will enroll in the Community College GED program. The semester begins on _____ .
2. I'm thinking about the military.	**2.** I've spoken with the Marine Corps recruiter and have been advised as to my eligibility. Upon completion of sentence, I will enlist at once.
3. I know I need to get off drugs.	**3.** I will make an appointment with Dr. _____ to get injections of an opioid receptor blocker. I will attend a Narcotics Anonymous meeting every Monday night.
4. Yeah, I'll get a job.	**4.** I have prepared a resume. I have registered with the state employment service and also with a temp staffing agency.
5. I'll take care of the kid.	**5.** My plan contains a budget that shows how I will pay child care.
6. I'll start going to church.	**6.** I've contacted pastor _____ about joining the _____ church located at _____ .

SUPPORTING DOCUMENTS

It is important to gather supporting documents and attach them to the plan. Examples include employment verification, military service records, educational records, diplomas, job skill certifications, and special licenses—such as CDL (commercial driver's license), real estate sales license, and barber and cosmetology licenses. Don't forget certificates attesting that the defendant has completed in-house training or apprenticeship in things like restaurant management, spray painting, welding, heavy equipment operation, brick laying, carpentry, etc. If the defendant is a member of a union, photocopy the union membership card and attach it.

Character reference letters from religious leaders, teachers, and coaches also are important. You have to give a judge reasons to grant leniency. Some people may find it inconvenient to write a letter. In that case, offer to write one for them if they will agree to sign it. Add photos, with captions, showing family members, and the schools, workplaces, churches, synagogues, and mosques that defendants will attend.

RENDER UNTO CAESAR . . .

Speaking of churches, temples, and mosques, if at all possible, your defendant needs to get some religion. Most inmates, unfortunately, have no religion. If they think about religion at all, they consider it a form of craziness for little old ladies and goofy girls.

Some inmates do get religion. Usually they get too much of it and run around jails and courtrooms loaded down with crosses, crescents, Bibles, Korans, Torahs, skullcaps, and so forth. Every other word is "Praise Jesus!" or "As Mohammed says, peace and blessings be upon Him. . . ." When defendants are recent and enthusiastic converts, advise them to tone it down in court. The criminal justice system is secular. Judges are not interested in defendants' religious beliefs, only in their civilized behavior or future possibility thereof.

From a practical standpoint, any religion will do. All the major faiths teach ethical behavior and restraint of violent urges and appetites. All combat the mental habits that lead to crime. I do, however, suggest that you nudge defendants into the *mainstream* version of their religion of choice. All religions have exotic variants. Christianity has its anchorites and snake handlers and Islam its mystics and whirling dervishes. Mormonism has its wacko polygamists, and Judaism its numerologists and mystic parsers of the Zohar. Hinduism has wandering sadhus. I don't begrudge anyone the opportunity to seek an experience of God while living in this Vale of Sorrows, but the time for the most intense religious experiences is *outside* the courtroom! Best not to appear too pious, or too nutty, before His or Her Honor.

> Render unto Caesar the things which are Caesar's
> And unto God the things that are God's.
> —Matthew 22:21

WORKING THE PLAN

Once the plan is completed and its supporting material collected, a large challenge is to make it legally significant. You are, in essence, attempting to butt in on a criminal proceeding in which you have no statutory standing. You have to inform defense counsel, whether public or private, about the plan. Ask their suggestions. Then ask how they propose to *use* the plan. This is critical.

Some private attorneys, alas, use a family plan only as a form of client voodoo. They keep the family busy formulating the plan. This gives everyone who is paying the fee

FAMILY MANAGEMENT PLAN, Page 1

Defendant _____

Case Number _____

Jail Number _____

The following members of the defendant's family will assist the defendant in completing the terms and conditions necessary for reduction of bond and/or supervised release:

Name _____ Relationship _____

Name _____ Relationship _____

Name _____ Relationship _____

Name _____ Relationship _____

PROPOSED COUNSELING AND TREATMENT

Both the defendant and family believe that to become a contributing member of society, the defendant requires the following:

☐ Drug treatment   ☐ Psychological counseling

☐ Anger management courses   ☐ Parenting courses

☐ Other _____

EDUCATION

The defendant has completed _____ years of education and has the following diplomas:

☐ High school   ☐ GED

☐ Associate's degree   ☐ Bachelor's degree

☐ Technical school _____

☐ Professional certificates _____

The defendant will pursue further education as follows:

Educational institution _____

Contact name and telephone _____

Proposed enrollment date _____

Degree or certification sought _____

Defendant ☐ will   ☐ will not   take instruction in English as a second language.

FAMILY MANAGEMENT PLAN, Page 2

EMPLOYMENT

The defendant was ☐ employed ☐ unemployed at the time of arrest.

The defendant has the following job skills: _____

_____

The defendant, if granted leniency, will pursue employment as follows:

☐ Return to current employer _____

☐ Interview with the following employers/job placement agencies, which have job openings for which the defendant is qualified:

Employer/Job Placement Agency _____

Job description sought _____

Contact name and telephone _____

_____

Employer/Job Placement Agency _____

Job description sought _____

Contact name and telephone _____

_____

Employer/Job Placement Agency _____

Job description sought _____

Contact name and telephone _____

_____

FAMILY MANAGEMENT PLAN, Page 3

ENLISTMENT IN THE ARMED SERVICES

The defendant, if released, will enlist in the following service:

☐ Marine Corps　　☐ Army　　☐ Navy　　☐ Air Force　　☐ Coast Guard

Proposed enlistment date: _____

PRIOR MILITARY SERVICE

☐ Marine Corps　　☐ Army　　☐ Navy　　☐ Air Force　　☐ Coast Guard

☐ Active duty　　☐ Reserves　　☐ National Guard

☐ Honorable discharge　　☐ General discharge　　☐ Dishonorable discharge

Rank _____

Decorations _____

(Discharge or duty status papers are attached.)

RELIGIOUS OBSERVANCE

The defendant will attend religious services weekly at:

Church, mosque, temple _____

Pastor/priest/imam/rabbi _____ Telephone _____

COMMUNITY SERVICE

The defendant will volunteer in the following organization upon release:

Organization _____

Type of service _____

Contact name and telephone _____

_____

FAMILY MANAGEMENT PLAN, Page 4

LIVING ARRANGEMENTS

The defendant will live at the following address: _____

_____

This dwelling is a ☐ private home ☐ rented house ☐ rented apartment

The following family members will live with the defendant:

Name _____ Relationship _____

Name _____ Relationship _____

Name _____ Relationship _____

REQUIRED APPEARANCES

These family members will supervise the defendant to ensure timely appearances before this court and before probation officers and to ensure participation in required counseling, education, therapy, community service, and job training:

Name _____ Relationship _____

Name _____ Relationship _____

Name _____ Relationship _____

PERMANENT ADDRESS

The defendant's permanent address will be: _____

_____

The following family members will assist defendant in understanding legal notices, completing and returning required forms on time, and issuing required change-of-employment and change-of-address notices:

Name _____ Relationship _____

Name _____ Relationship _____

FAMILY MANAGEMENT PLAN, Page 5

FINANCIAL SUPPORT

These family members have agreed to guarantee the defendant's payment of the costs of probation, child support, fines, restitution, and therapy:

Name _____ Relationship _____

Name _____ Relationship _____

Name _____ Relationship _____

BUDGET

Fines _____

Restitution _____

Court costs _____

Jail costs _____

Probation costs _____

Counseling/treatment _____

Drug tests _____

Tuition _____

Child support _____

VEHICLE

The defendant will drive the following vehicle. _____

Tag no.: _____ Name on title _____

The following family members will assist the defendant to maintain the vehicle in street-legal operating condition and will supervise the maintenance of valid licenses, registration, and insurance and the registration of the defendant as an approved and insured driver:

Name _____ Relationship _____

Name _____ Relationship _____

FAMILY MANAGEMENT PLAN, Page 6

DRUGS AND ALCOHOL

The defendant ☐ is addicted to drugs ☐ has used drugs ☐ has never used drugs.

The defendant ☐ is an alcoholic ☐ is not an alcoholic

If released, the defendant will attend the following:

☐ 12-step program or other rehabilitation program

    Contact name and telephone _____

☐ Treatment at the following facility _____

    Contact name and telephone _____

Defendant signature _____ Date _____

Family member signature _____ Date _____

Family member signature _____ Date _____

the idea that something important is going on and that they are actually helping their defendant. Then the attorney merely mails the plan to the prosecutor! This accomplishes nothing. Prosecutors, already choked with paperwork, do not appreciate receiving yet another document to file. Of course, in busy offices, excess paper can always be used to hold coffee cups, doughnuts, and nail polish or to swat flies.

A good attorney, however, can use your offer at preliminary hearings and during plea bargaining and sentencing. Attorneys may ask you to appear at these hearings and stand up to let the judge see you. You know the attorney is working the plan when you hear statements like these:

► "Because the defendant has family support and a place to live, bail bond should be reduced."

► "Because the defendant has agreed to enlist in the armed services upon completion of sentence, felony charges should be reduced to misdemeanors."

► "Because the defendant has a plan of action to continue education, get drug treatment, obtain work, and live with members of his family, he should be sentenced directly to probation."

Your goal is to put a human face on things. You want your defendant, who by now has a neat haircut and is freshly washed, to stand out from the pack of slouchy, stinky, mumbling defendants in crowded courtrooms. You want to show the court that your defendant can become a citizen. He or she has family backup!

You are working to transform a defendant into a citizen. It's tough, and it's expensive. When you are successful, you will have done your defendant, and your family, a great service. You will have done society an even bigger favor. Government, police, judges, jails, and prisons can't create citizens.

Only family can.

27

WHY ARE SO MANY PEOPLE IN JAIL?
Juking the Stats in the Crime-Crazed U.S.A.

BY THIS POINT, YOU have made the big decisions regarding the criminal defense of your loved one. You have worked through the lists, consulted www.wesdenham.net, and spent your money. I fervently hope I have assisted you in obtaining the best result for your defendant. In this last chapter, I'll step back from the tactics of individual defense and discuss larger issues; specifically, why so many people are being arrested and why jails and prisons are filled to bursting. A discussion of a well-publicized report will make things clear.

On February 28, 2008, a media-gasm occurred. As the sun rose across the fruited plain, faxes hummed, e-mail boxes tinged, and in the offices of the Associated Press, the *New York Times*, and CBS, the rewrite weenies pounded the keys. The cause of the commotion? A report from the Pew Charitable Trusts that announced, in stentorian tones and 120-point type:

> **One in 100:**
> **Behind Bars* in America 2008**

I downloaded the full report from Pew, then plunged manfully into snappy graphics, howling headlines, bar graphs, and ominous lines squiggling across the X- and Y-axes of the graphical universe. The result?

The Pew report has the wrong emphasis. It actually *understates* the problem.

The Pew figure, which shows that more than 1 in 100 adult Americans is incarcerated, is actually a tally of jail and prison inmates on a single day, January 1, 2008. Of course, on New Year's Day, the drunk tanks are fuller than usual, but what about the rest of the year? For more relevant numbers, let's descend from the think tank to the street. From my townhouse, built in a hopeful moment on the edge of the urban hellzone, I can see, on a clear day, the Jacksonville jail rising above the waterfront and hear the inmates howl. Research from my hometown presents a more relevant way to view incarceration numbers. These figures are derived from 2006 statistics of the Jacksonville Sheriff's Office and the U.S. Census Bureau:

---

* FYI, not all jail cell doors are constructed with *bars*, through which, as any correctional officer will tell you, punches can be thrown, kicks launched, strangleholds initiated, and spit, blood, urine, sperm, and feces hurled. Most modern cells and dormitories have solid steel doors with slots for food, air, and handcuffs.

Jacksonville in Jail 2006

Jacksonville population	837,964
Less minors under 18	−217,870
Less senior citizens over 65	−87,148
Total Adults	532,946
Arrests by Jacksonville Sheriff's Office	50,318
÷ Total Adults	532,946
Percentage of adults arrested *yearly*:	**9.44%**

In regard to Jacksonville statistics, our sheriff is entirely typical of urban police chiefs in his "zero-tolerance" tactics. Our pretrial detention facilities are well managed, and less violent than most city jails, but with zero-tolerance policing being practiced with a vengeance, the jails are packed to the ceilings.

In most cities, between 8 and 10 percent of the population are arrested *each year*. This means that over a 5- to 10-year period, an extraordinarily large percentage of the population get arrested and spend at least one day in jail. And how many people have been arrested at least once in their lifetime? No one has ever researched this important number. My gut says it is huge. I believe that an astonishingly large fraction of the American population have, at some point in their lives, been arrested and dragged down to the local pokey for at least one meal of mystery meat and mashed potatoes followed by a fitful snooze on steel shelves.

If jail and prison populations are soaring, what about crime? Guess what? *It's going down and has been for years.* Let's consult the experts at the FBI, which publishes a famous, annual uniform crime report entitled, in dramatic G-man style, "Crime in the United States."

> Preliminary figures indicate that, as a whole, law enforcement agencies throughout the Nation reported a decrease of 1.4 percent in the number of violent crimes brought to their attention in 2007 when compared with figures reported for 2006. The violent crime category includes murder, forcible rape, robbery, and aggravated assault. The number of property crimes in the United States from January to December of 2007 decreased 2.1 percent when compared with data from the same time period in 2006. Property crimes include burglary, larceny-theft, and motor vehicle theft. Arson is also a property crime, but data for arson are not included in property crime totals. Figures for 2007 indicate that arson decreased 7.0 percent in 2007 when compared to 2006 figures.

VIOLENT CRIME RATES

Adjusted victimization rate
per 1,000 persons age 12 and over

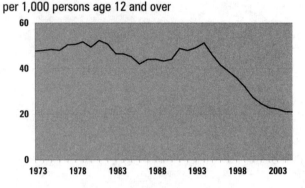

PROPERTY CRIME RATES

Adjusted victimization rate per 1,000 households

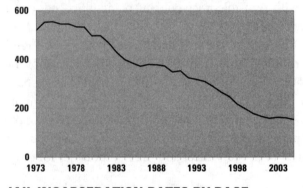

JAIL INCARCERATION RATES BY RACE AND ETHNICITY

Number of jail inmates per 100,000 U.S. residents

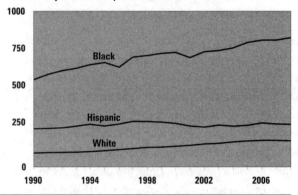

Crime and incarceration trends as of 2008, courtesy U.S. Department of Justice, Bureau of Justice Statistics.

But is this reduction in crime a blip or a trend? The Department of Justice knows all and says it best in the charts on the left. Note that both violent and property crimes have been falling for years, while at the same time incarceration has been rising. Black incarceration increased over 50 percent in 16 years. No wonder African Americans are paranoid about police!

The message of these charts and "Crime in the United States" is clear. Crime is down; jail and prison admissions are up. Before my life meandered into criminal justice, I used to think that crime and incarceration were causally related: "Of course crime is down! All the crooks are in jail!" They're not—not all of them, and not many of the worst. After years of crime-rate decline, prison and jail populations should have started to decline also. They have not.

That's because the increase in incarceration has nothing to do with the crime rate. Instead, it's entirely attributable to administrative and political trends. This chapter will examine those trends to explain why so many people, including your defendant, are in jail and prison.

CRIMINAL DATABASES: REVOLUTION UNDER THE RADAR

In the precomputer era, records of arrests and convictions existed on paper and were kept in filing cabinets. So, for example, if you got arrested in my mother's hometown of Cuthbert, Georgia, and did time in the local sneezer, the records stayed there. If prosecutors and judges in other cities wanted to know about your criminal record, they'd have to a) know that you got busted in Cuthbert, then b) send a request for records, which the clerk of the court of Randolph County might act on, or might not.*

Nowadays, all arrests and most convictions are maintained in online databases, which are instantly accessible by law enforcement officers and court personnel anywhere in the territorial United States. Defendants' rap sheets follow them everywhere. This increases their risk of being tried as habitual offenders with longer sentences. Even when defendants have never been convicted, they may have multiple arrests. It's unethical for judges to consider arrests without convictions in pronouncing sentence; nonetheless, they do. The defendants were arrested multiple times, so they must have been doing *something*, right?

Wrong!

To get a better understanding of how arrests do not always indicate criminality, listen to actual defendants on the Crime City blog on my Web site (www.wesdenham.net). You'll be astounded.

ZERO-TOLERANCE POLICING

Zero tolerance is the practice of arresting and jailing offenders for all crimes, no matter how minor. Made famous by Harvard University social theorist James Q. Wilson, zero tolerance is now the predominant policing strategy in the United States. To say that this theory is controversial is an understatement. It's hotter than plutonium at meltdown.

But zero tolerance must work, right? Crime's going down! So says the FBI—but crime was going down *before* zero-tolerance policing begat mass arrests and incarcerations. In his book *Freakonomics*, University of Chicago economist Steven Levitt makes a compelling case that the reduction in crime is due primarily to a reduction in the number of males age 18–24, which began almost 20 years to the day after the widespread legalization of abortion. Street crime is a young man's game; fewer rapscallions means fewer crimes.

Zero-tolerance policing expends most of its efforts on street crime. Zero-tolerance arrests are made by patrol officers driving around in police cruisers. They use the following techniques to locate potential arrestees:

---

* Small towns are refreshingly different. When we buried my mother in Cuthbert in 1987, we were unable to file the death certificate right away because the courthouse was closed. A sign hanging on the doorknob informed us that bass were biting down at the reservoir and that the courthouse was closed for the duration of this blessed event.

- ▶ Response to citizen calls

- ▶ Traffic stops

- ▶ Street stops of pedestrians and loiterers

For nearly a year, I scrutinized the Jacksonville perp parade, the 100 to 150 inmates who are arrested every day. An attorney arranged for me to see the names on the daily intake, and I perused the charge sheets on the sheriff's Web site. It took me months to realize what I *wasn't seeing*—professional crooks. Pros make a full-time living from criminal enterprise. Examples include pimps, madams, professional car thieves, truck hijackers, port thieves, railroad thieves, professional burglars, white slavers, immigration coyotes, labor and protection racketeers, con artists, and mid- to high-level drug dealers.

Everyone will, of course, object to my argument that drug dealers are an infrequently arrested category of professional crook. Aren't there plenty of them in U.S. jails? I reply that there are thousands of people *charged* with felony possession and intent to sell, but how high on the food chain are they? Consider, for example, drug distribution in my hometown. My calculation is that Jacksonville residents each day consume a quantity of illegal drugs that would fill a tractor-trailer. (Mercifully, I exclude the walking dead who huff glue and gasoline and chug cough syrup.) Here is my formula, based on estimates that approximately 10 percent of the adult and juvenile population use illegal drugs. It is rough but revealing:

10% of adults and juveniles (60,000) x 3 joints daily = 180,000 joints
Crack, heroin, X, tweak, cocaine, blue bombers, etc. = 40,000 hits

= A Whole Lot of Dope

As in every city, dope rolls in on the roads, motors up the rivers, and lands on airstrips *every single day*. Periodically, police and the FBI capture a good-sized load, but do they capture good-sized crooks?

Mostly they round up "mules," low-level haulers who are hired as day labor. In chapter 17, I mentioned a federal drug bust on which I'd worked as an interpreter: the FBI crowed to newspapers that it had broken up a Major Narcotics Ring—but the defendants actually were illiterate Otomí Indians from Mexico who had been paid $3,000 to drive a load of crank (methamphetamine) from the Rio Grande Valley to Jacksonville and deliver it to dealers in a Wal-Mart parking lot. They never even met the local drug distributors, who were just voices on the end of "burner" cell phones.

Distributors, with reason, worry more about other drug dealers than cops. The kingpins, the ones with mansions, yachts, and helicopters, don't worry at all. For years, the big boys have lived outside the United States, ever since enforcement of the Racketeer

Influenced and Corrupt Organizations (RICO) Act allowed government to seize their mansions and toys.

Also rarely encountered in municipal jails is another subset of professional crooks who make more money than all the rest—white-collar criminals. These include perpetrators of mortgage, insurance, and bank frauds; embezzlers; forgers; corrupt public officials; attorneys who steal client funds; thieves of corporate secrets and intellectual property; movie and music pirates; and the perpetrators of the numberless scams involving investments and securities. Topping this list are cybercriminals who use computers and the Internet to burgle bank and credit card accounts and to steal personal identification information.

Why are professional crooks arrested and prosecuted so rarely? The reasons are simple: Arresting professional crooks requires painstaking investigation using wiretaps, search warrants, video and audio surveillance, informants, crime scene analysis, and wholesale quantities of shoe leather–pounding by detectives. White-collar criminal arrests require even more specialized staff—forensic accountants, document examiners, information technologists, and prosecutors expert in the laws of corporations, banking, securities, and real estate. Is this expensive? You bet, and excruciatingly time consuming. After months of work, maybe one or two guys get arrested. Lousy stats.

White-collar crime is mostly ignored. To get justice, the victims, such as banks and insurance companies, have to do their own investigations. They have to present prosecutors with cases prepped, documented, and wrapped up in a neat package with a bright bow on top. Otherwise, they get no justice. The only cybercrime routinely investigated by local police is the use of the Internet for the solicitation of children for sex. This disgusting crime happens to be inexpensive to investigate. All it takes is a PC connected to the Internet and a cop who can mimic kid slang and type with more than two fingers. The cop replies to Chester the Molester's e-mails, lures the creep to a stakeout, and then makes a bust amid the whir of cameras and the roar of applause.

Otherwise, cops focus exclusively on street crime. Zero-tolerance is effective against petty street criminals and violent criminals but ineffective against professional criminals. Pro crooks are not committing crimes on the street in plain view where cops can see, stop, question, search, and arrest them. They do their crimes indoors. They drive carefully in street-legal cars and rarely get pulled over for traffic stops.

Notice how often you hear elected officials vowing to raise taxes to *put more police on the streets*. Next time you hear this, cringe. This is just more zero-tolerance vacuuming of petty offenders. When elected officials get serious about fighting crime, they'll fund more detectives and the expensive technicians who support them. These guys don't roll around the streets. They sit at desks poring over records, listening to wiretaps, and debriefing confidential informants. They go to jails to interview snitches. They testify in courts to convince judges to grant them wiretaps and search warrants. To catch big rats, you need a different breed of cat.

STAT MADNESS, UPCHARGING, AND ADD-ONS

Stat Madness

In my first book, *Arrest-Proof Yourself*, my coauthor and I revealed a cop secret: police officers are evaluated, promoted, and paid almost exclusively on arrest statistics derived from monthly arrest reports. Throughout America, police sergeants, like manic sales managers, flog the troops daily to make more arrests.*

Legally speaking, "arrest" means simply to halt, to stop the action. You're technically under arrest during a traffic stop. For cops, however, arrests don't count unless somebody gets carted off to jail and a tick is placed on the tally sheet. When officers' arrest counts are low and they get zinged for "low police activity," enormities occur. Cops start using legal but unethical tactics, such as scream-outs** and whispered insults, to provoke people into arrestable behaviors. (This is called "putting a suspect in the trick box.") Police officers may make willy-nilly traffic stops in a frantic search for *someone* to bust. Last year, for example, police announced a "crime crackdown" in my neighborhood. For three days they stopped and searched hundreds of cars. They arrested 283 people, mostly for misdemeanor drug possession. Now is this crime busting, or simply a roundup of goofy stoners and pathetic crackheads? Whether the public got served and protected is debatable; what's certain is that departmental arrest stats got a shot of steroids for the month.

Upcharging

To get more felony arrests—misdemeanors are considered bullshit busts—police and prosecutors engage in the practice of upcharging. This means accusing the defendant of the most serious charges that can be adduced from the illegal behavior. Interpretations matter. Here's an example. A guy slaps his wife. She shrieks. Neighbors dial up some law, and the perp is duly arrested. This happens every day and everywhere. But was the slap simple battery, a misdemeanor? Or aggravated assault and battery, a felony? Usually, officers decide it's the latter.

---

* But let's cut the boys and girls in blue some slack. They get *told* to work the way they do by elected officials. Many police officers find zero-tolerance policing boring and arresting petty perps day after day futile. Good officers—real police—would much rather get their teeth into big criminals. Cops are idealistic this way. Like all skilled hunters, they prefer dangerous game.

** Scream-outs occur when cops put their face right up to yours, often nose-to-nose, then bellow into your face until you are covered with spit. This causes you to push off the cop, which justifies felony arrests for battery on a law enforcement officer, fleeing and eluding, and resisting arrest. See *Arrest-Proof Yourself* for information on how to resist these tactics and avoid arrest.

Add-Ons

These are another noxious police and prosecutorial practice—extra charges brought after the fact when prosecutors, or more likely the booking officers at the jail, read the arrest report and slice, dice, and parse the offense into as many crimes as possible. Here's a common example. You've probably seen it on local television news. If you watch the show *COPS*, you've seen it many times, in all its flavors and colors.

Police stop a suspect driving at night. "License and registration, please!" After duly perusing these sacred documents, one of the cops asks in a friendly way, "Hey, by the way, you don't happen to have any guns or narcotics in that car, do you?"

The suspect, who has joints in his jeans, panics. He bails, pushes the cops, and makes like a rabbit for the nearest alley. The cops hit the radios, and the squeal goes out. Within minutes more cruisers are careening into the neighborhood, sirens whooping. A police helicopter spins up, hovers overhead, and aims the floodlight. Nothing! But the pilots have more tricks. They fire up the FLIR (forward-looking infrared) technology, and now they've got the suspect on the screen! He's a green dot hiding in a garage. A K-9 is unleashed. The pooch wriggles through a loose board and pounces. The police apply some "reasonable force" by letting the dog chomp on the suspect's arms and legs for a while before making an arrest.

A search turns up, alas, only a few scraggly joints. No charges are possible so far except misdemeanor possession. There's fleeing and eluding, of course, and resisting arrest, but these are bullshit busts. But recall that the perp actually *pushed* a police officer. Aha! That's "assault and battery on a LEO."* This is an effective and exceedingly common add-on *felony* charge that, in the eyes of law enforcement, justifies the expense of apprehending the suspect, and in our example, the ghastly cost of aviation fuel, and a doggy treat for the Rottweiler.

Within the justice system, however, no one gets upset by all this upcharging and adding on, since 9 times out of 10, charges get bargained down or tossed out as part of a plea bargain. If you've ever listened to attorneys dickering over a plea, you'll begin to look at justice as they do—as a legal rug bazaar.

Upcharging and add-ons are unconscionable. They add to the cost and confusion of the criminal justice system. Even when bargained down or tossed out, the upcharges and add-ons remain on defendants' arrest records for the rest of their lives. In the future, these multiple charges will make for awkward interviews both with police officers who pull up arrest records on their laptops at every traffic stop and with employers who have access to the NCIC database. In the computer age, add-on charges stick for life, regardless of whether judges and juries convict.

---

* LEO stands for Law Enforcement Officer. In criminal justice, everybody pronounces LEO phonetically, as in "Leo the Lion."

Upcharges. Add-ons. They're hell for defendants and their families but great stats for cops and prosecutors. They're the mud that sticks. They cost a fortune to unstick.

NEW CRIMES FOR NEW TIMES

Jails are filled with defendants charged with behaviors that once were noncriminal or were classed as civil or nonarrestable infractions. Here's a list of the most important:

Driving Under the Influence (DUI)

Back in the day, drunk driving earned you a ride home in a cruiser. Not anymore. In many states, DUI merits mandatory jail time, no exceptions. There is broad agreement as to the wisdom of this policy. State legislators have had it with the carnage wrought by drunk drivers, not to mention the unpaid medical bills from public hospitals that have to be picked up by the taxpayers.

Probation and Parole Infractions

Petty probation and parole infractions, such as failing to telephone probation and parole officers, failing to attend meetings, or failing to report changes of address and employment, have been criminalized. This is not trivial. Nationwide, according to the United States Department of Justice,* the percentage of prison admissions for parole and probation violations in 2005 was 34 percent. In Florida and California, prison admissions of probation and parole violators have created crises. There are not enough prisons or money to deal with these offenders.

Legislators would sooner contract leprosy than appear soft on crime, and they have been loath to mandate non-prison punishments for these peccadilloes. They don't want to fund new prisons either. This is an impossible contradiction.

Probationers and parolees who use drugs, commit new crimes, pose a danger to society, or flee the state merit prison. But to face hard time for not mailing a change-of-address postcard?

Madness!

Domestic Disturbance

In many states, new laws require police to *always* make an arrest when they respond to a domestic disturbance. Granted, legislators want to protect women—and increasingly men—from spousal or partner battering. But there's a lot of gray area here. Do you know a couple who don't argue? Most cops are excellent judges of human behavior and are good at determining whether a situation is dangerous. The new laws, however,

---

* William J. Sabol, Todd D. Minton, and Paige M. Harrison, *Prison and Jail Inmates at Midyear 2006*, U.S. Department of Justice, Bureau of Justice Statistics, June 2007, www.ojp.usdoj.gov/bjs/pub/pdf/pjim06.pdf.

limit their discretion. Jails are packed with men and women whose crime was *yelling at their spouse*.

Rape

Society has chosen to criminalize unwanted sex, even in cases where the sex may have been wanted at the time but later, on mature reflection, not. I believe that in strengthening women's legal rights and recourse, courts and legislators have overreacted. They have encouraged felony arrests and long sentences in too many cases in which it is not clear that what happened was rape.

I worked extensively on a case where a navy seaman was charged with rape by his former lover, with whom he had had a passionate, adulterous affair. The case was a heartbreaker. This guy had terrible judgment and a drinking problem. The sex occurred in a motel room in front of witnesses. But the defendant, his accuser, and the witnesses were all *blind drunk*. The witnesses, all of whom had passed out, could say nothing. The accuser and the defendant also fell unconscious until the next morning from too much drink. Sex occurred. But was it rape? A judge thought so and found him guilty. He was dishonorably discharged from the navy only four months short of 20 years' service and a pension. He's now serving time in a Florida prison.

If your family member is charged in similar circumstances, you will want to consider a stout defense. The charge of rape is now applied in circumstances in which no violence occurred and no one can say whether the sex was or was not coerced.

In addition, unscrupulous people, both male and female, are not above having consensual sex and then claiming rape. I interviewed a defendant in a case in which his sex partner, after an evening of wild and apparently enjoyable sex, charged her lover with rape. Outside the house, she banged her head on a tree to produce cuts and bruises, then drove calmly to a hospital emergency room for photos and a rape kit. Fortunately, there were eyewitnesses to this chicanery, so the defendant was freed. It is noteworthy that the woman was not charged with making false statements to police.

ARREST BY SAY-SO

A frightening development in law enforcement is the extent to which police will make arrests based on complainant statements, *without* corroborating evidence, *without* probable cause, and *without* direct knowledge of, or investigation by, a police officer. Not all of these cases involve vengeful former lovers like the one above. In an earlier chapter, I mentioned an armed robbery where five eyewitnesses described the assailant as a black male. The police, nonetheless, arrested a red-headed, blue-eyed Lithuanian, because someone in the neighborhood fingered him. That's all it took. Someone simply declared, "He's the one," and—*badda bing*—he's in jail.

I myself have had experience with this travesty of justice. Several years ago, a personal enemy of mine mailed an anonymous letter to the sheriff. In the letter, this scumbag declared that I was making false police reports by telephone and, somehow, intended to use these reports to support the sheriff's opponent in the upcoming election. For two weeks, a police detective badgered me every day attempting to question me. He admitted that I had filed no police reports, but he simply had to question me about alleged political skullduggery. Had I allowed this detective to interrogate me, I have no doubt I would have been arrested. Of course, I wrote the book about how *not* to be interrogated. My attorney gave the detective an ass-chewing that ended these police shenanigans.

Since then, I have indeed called police on one or two occasions. Because caller ID blocking doesn't work with police, and to protect myself, I make such calls with an untraceable "burner" phone, which I buy at Wal-Mart like all the other bad guys. What kind of world do we live in where personal enemies can attempt to have you arrested and jailed with whispers, innuendoes, and anonymous letters?

One of the enormities of zero-tolerance policing is that it encourages officers not to use common sense in evaluating criminality but simply to make arrests and let prosecutors, judges, and courts sort out the issue of whether, in fact, a crime actually occurred. This produces the huge numbers of arrests on petty charges and the large percentage of jailed inmates who are immediately released or have charges dismissed or nol-prossed. This isn't law enforcement. This is madness!

JAILS AS PSYCHO WARDS

Nothing is more disgusting than seeing mentally ill people in jail. I do not refer to inmates who are depressed or neurotic or who have behavior problems. I refer to psychotics, people who are howling, babbling, shrieking *insane*. I'm talking about people who don't know what planet they're on, who beg Jesus to stop whispering in their ear and implore Satan to stop pricking them in the fanny with his pitchfork. They drool, they twitch, they snatch imaginary flies from the air.

The Bureau of Justice Statistics puts the number of psychotics in local jails at 24 percent.* This is a national disgrace. Mentally ill inmates are likely to do violence to themselves, to other inmates, and when they're released, to citizens. They can't help it; they're crazy. So why are they in jail? Simple. There's no place else to put them. In the past 50 years, the number of state mental hospitals has decreased by 90 percent. Released mental patients are supposed to be "mainstreamed" into society via less expensive group homes and outpatient treatment. All too often, they are "main-streeted" into homeless shelters and jails, from which to be loosed in due course upon an innocent and unsus-

---

* Doris J. James and Lauren E. Glaze, *Mental Health Problems of Prison and Jail Inmates*, U.S. Department of Justice, Bureau of Justice Statistics, September 2006, www.ojp.usdoj.gov/bjs/pub/pdf/mhppji.pdf.

pecting America. The irony is that mental hospitals were first built, beginning in the 1840s, precisely to get the mentally ill *out* of jails and poor houses. In 170 years, we've come full circle.

The closure of state mental hospitals was precipitated by media frenzies over documentaries such as 1967's *Titicut Follies* that showed the mistreatment of mental patients. Activists rose up before TV cameras and in courtrooms to declare that involuntary incarceration of the mentally ill was a violation of their civil rights. There were howls of protest. State governments, offered the chance to drastically reduce their budgets and at the same time appear high-minded, couldn't padlock mental hospitals fast enough. In the present century, state mental hospitals are still grim institutions, but instances of gross abuse are unusual. To ordinary people, a mental hospital looks dreadful, but if you're living on the street in a cardboard box, an institution that offers three hots and a flop, a shower, and some pills to quiet the demons looks very warm and fuzzy.

The oft-repeated statement that mentally ill people are more often victims than perpetrators is fiction. The truth is worse. They're both victims *and* perpetrators. Jason C. Matejkowski and associates at the University of Pennsylvania estimate that 16 percent of homicides are committed by psychotics. They summarize the all-too-common scenario as follows:

> Rage or anger was the most frequently mentioned motive for murder, and this emotion was overwhelmingly directed toward intimate or familial relations via firearm or sharp object. In general, the offenders were raised in households with significant family dysfunction, had extensive histories of substance abuse and criminal activity before their murder conviction, and received a paucity of treatment for their mental and substance use disorders.[*]

Behind the dusty, academic prose one descries the high school shooters, the college killers, the company employees "going postal," and the nutcases barricading themselves in houses and committing "suicide by cop" on your evening news.

How often have I sat across the steel interview table from these pathetic, dangerous creatures? Even when you shout from inches away, they can scarcely hear you, so exigent are their inner voices. As long as the insane rotate in and out of the criminal justice system, both they and society are in danger.

In chapter 7, I advised you what to do when your family member is mentally ill. Getting treatment, obtaining the proper driver's license restrictions, and retaining medical records are indispensable. Keeping your mentally ill family member out of jail and in treatment will also keep you safe.

---

[*] Jason C. Matejkowski, Sara W. Cullen, and Phyllis L. Solomon, "Characteristics of Persons with Severe Mental Illness Who Have Been Incarcerated for Murder," *Journal of the American Academy of Psychiatry and the Law* 36, no. 1 (2008): 81.

DRUGS, DRUGS, DRUGS

Oyez! Oyez! Drugs are everywhere! Be it so stipulated. Nonetheless, you may not be aware that as society's attitudes toward drug consumption have loosened, laws have tightened. This began with New York's notorious Rockefeller drug laws of 1973, which mandated a sentence of 15 years to life for selling 2 or more ounces, or possessing 4 or more ounces, of heroin, morphine, opium, cocaine, or marijuana. Possessing more than 1.45 pounds (a kilo is 2.2 pounds) brought a mandatory sentence of life without parole, which made such possession equivalent to first-degree murder. A murder one ticket? For less than a kilo? Kids walk by my porch every day with more dope than that in their backpacks. This injustice was reformed only in 2004, at which time New York's prison population plummeted like a stone.

Florida was not to be outdone. With the exception of marijuana, where possession of 20 grams, or about two joints, not too tightly stuffed, is still a misdemeanor, the threshold for felony charges for all other Schedule I, II, and III drugs is—get ready—one molecule! Any amount detectable by chemical indicator (or if The Man really wants to get you, by mass spectrometer) is a felony. This merits one year or more in one of Florida's 137 prison facilities, all located in picturesque rural areas. Hurricanes are occasional; mosquitoes are eternal.

Nationwide, a quarter of all inmates face drug charges. About 70 percent of inmates have Schedule I, II, or III drugs in their system at jail admission. Include alcohol, and the number of zonked arrestees would be close to 100 percent.

Penalties for drug possession are inhumanly harsh. If you decide your family member can kick the habit, then defend to the max. Society has not yet devised sufficient non-prison alternatives for drug users. Drug treatment and drug courts are still in their infancy, and draconian laws are daily enforced.

The increased use of illegal drugs has occurred *at the same time* as the criminalization of drug use and possession. No one knows whether the two trends are causally related or coincidental. The age when jails were not filled with drug users is a fading memory. Sometimes when I see drug-addled idiots zigzagging on the sidewalks outside my home, I despair. I think that surely potheads and crackheads will follow us all the days of our lives, and dwell in the House of The Man forever.

THE DEATH OF DISCRETION

Life is untidy; justice is worse. The riotous bazaar of prosecutors piling on charges and defense attorneys bargaining them down, with judges signing who-knows-what orders as fast as pen can move, is upsetting to the administrative psyche. Government prefers to proceed methodically, and inexorably, in the manner of planets or vegetables. To bring bureaucratic calm to this judicial mayhem, and to join sheriffs and police chiefs worshipping at the altar of zero tolerance, legislatures and Congress have limited the discretion that can be exercised by police, prosecutors, and judges:

► Many states and the federal government have enacted mandatory sentences. Do the crime, you do the time. No wiggle room for judges. Many states have repeat offender courts (ROC) or habitual offender (HO) courts, where felons with long rap sheets get hammered with double and triple sentences.

► Many states have restricted parole boards by mandating that a large portion, often 85 percent, of a sentence be served before parole can be granted.

► States have also decreed that most violations of probation and parole, no matter how trivial, require rearrest and reincarceration. Politicians want convicted criminals in prison, out of town, and out of mind.

The results are not unexpected. Crime is down, prison admissions are up—and the two *may not* be related. The bill for all this has arrived. Legislators now regard criminal justice as a vortex that whirls tax dollars into oblivion. As for the justice flea market, it's more frenzied than ever, since the only way to get around mandatory sentences is to toss out or downgrade the charges, which, of course, were multiplied and upgraded at the time of arrest. This produces a system that is impossibly opaque to defendants and their families. It's a lawyers' paradise, as, perhaps, it was intended to be.

FRYING UP THE SMALL FRY AND THE CLOGGED ARTERIES OF JUSTICE

Policing and prosecuting for the numbers—"juking the stats," to use a cop term—fill jails with petty offenders. Imagine what it costs government to process these myriad arrestees who are jailed for a night then released. First, there's the cost of the jail—building, staff, chow, jumpsuit, flip-flops, toothbrush, and razor. For each arrest, both a prosecutor and public defender must be assigned. Files get created. Computers whir. Court calendars fill. Within 48 hours, judges have to arraign the blinking miscreants.

Now, if the purpose of jailing people is to *detain* them to appear at future hearings and trials, why do judges *free* so many so quickly? Obviously, with first-time and petty offenders, judges are not concerned that defendants will flee. By and large these gorks show up in court when required. So why were they arrested and tossed in jail in the first place? Because jail jukes the stats. It creates full employment for cops, attorneys, clerks, guards, judges, bailiffs, and their numerous supportive minions. It also satisfies the public's desire to administer pretrial punishment.

These are the reasons, and they're an outrage.

Overnight incarceration of petty and first-time offenders is counterproductive. Like fried food, it fills the judicial arteries with sludge—human sludge. Every cop in America has the means to "arrest"—that is, stop—suspects and compel their appearance in court *without* hauling them to jail. This is a citation called a Notice to Appear, "NTA" in the trade. Most people know these summonses as the got-to-go-to-court type of traffic ticket.* Few outside the system realize that NTAs can also be issued for criminal misdemeanors. With NTAs, the accused appear before a judge without the expensive wheel spinning occasioned by incarceration. Most importantly, if the judge levies a fine and does not order jail or prison time, inmates are not arrested and booked. They avoid not only a conviction record but also an arrest record.

What fascinates me is that researchers, such as those at Pew, always emphasize what incarceration costs government. Nobody studies what it costs families. I often ponder what my city would be like if, say, 5,000 families each year bought new cars and new homes instead of flushing their cash down the criminal justice system. Car dealers and realtors would weep for joy.

Naturally, I have made a few suggestions to governments regarding the high cost of jails. In Miami, I suggested that instead of building new jails, the city could, at far lower cost, buy a cruise ship, feed inmates six fabulous meals a day including cocktails, and float the bad boys on the high seas. Escape would be impossible, since the perps would be too fat to swim. In Jacksonville, I appeared before the city council and told them that with more NTAs for petty offenders, the taxpayers might not have to shell out $350 million for a new courthouse.

Among municipal officials, I'm about as popular as a cockroach on angel food.

HEAR, O GODDESS, THE RAGE OF A TRICK

Sometimes the numbing caseload created by zero tolerance makes for sloppy police work and slapdash prosecutions that allow killers to go free. Just recently an accused murderer, whom I'll call X so the rat won't sue me for defamation, was exonerated in the county adjacent to mine. X is the kind of person who was born angry. When he wakes up any other way, he conjures rage with alcohol. Naturally he has no friends and has to pay for sex. He's nothing to anybody, just a whore's trick.

He frequently called police to complain that prostitutes were taking his money. He seemed perpetually surprised that whores actually get paid to get laid. One day X had a howling argument with a prostitute, then emptied his gun into her. She died on a hospital gurney, but not before naming her killer. X was arrested in a pool of her blood.

---

* Most traffic violations are civil, not criminal, infractions, an important distinction. Drunk driving is the exception.

X declared that the prostitute was trying to kidnap and rob him and claimed self-defense. During the long trial, police made unauthorized changes in official reports, and this forced prosecutors to drop the charges. It makes you cringe to see such things. Too much time is spent on petty criminals, and too little on the worst. The only justice X will see, if he sees any at all, will be street justice administered by a pissed-off pimp.

Government, peculiarly, is resistant to change yet subject to fads. These become encased in bureaucracy, which values the perfection of procedure over useful work. When a Harvard professor propounds a theory of urban policing that has a snappy name and rings some political bells, chiefs around the country venerate the notion as if it were doctrine blasted into rock by the almighty hand of God. In zero-tolerance policing, they have erected an idol of justice, a fiery Moloch that devours defendants in every city in America.

Zero-tolerance policing and the arrest and jailing of petty offenders are the practice of the land and will be so for years to come. For the families of the accused, this means that too many Americans will continue to be arrested for minor offenses. They will continue to make those hideous, nighttime phone calls begging for your help. This is the Horror.

The justice system is collapsing under the burden of mass arrests of petty offenders. At the same time, it does not arrest enough professional and white-collar crooks. And that, ladies and gentlemen, is why so many defendants desperately need your help. Their loved ones, their families, are all they have. Families are all there is.

APPENDIX A
Library of Forms and Letters

I include standard documents in this appendix for several reasons. First, in my experience, only about half the families of defendants have good Internet service and are familiar with downloading and printing documents. Second, most jails, prisons, and police departments do not provide forms such as medical and financial powers of attorney and medical information sheets, which may be necessary to protect your inmate's health and prevent financial losses.

Tear these forms out of the book, or use them as templates for forms you handwrite or type on your computer. The main thing is to get needed forms signed, notarized, and delivered quickly. Additional forms are available on the *Arrested* page of www.wesdenham.net.

LIMITED POWER OF ATTORNEY FOR MEDICAL INFORMATION

I, _____,

grant to _____, the power to act in my

behalf only in the below listed capacities:

a. To receive from health care providers, including physicians, nurses, hospitals, pharmacies, insurance companies, home health care services, psychologists, and counselors, the following: health care information, prescriptions, and medical records, including X-rays and diagnostic test results.

b. To submit the above health care information to attorneys, to other health care providers, to jail and prison administrators, and to jail and prison health care contractors.

I have signed and sealed this Power of Attorney this _____ day of _____, _____.
                                                                      day   month   year

_____ (SEAL)
Signature

STATE OF _____

COUNTY OF _____

On this _____ day of _____ , _____,

personally appeared before me the said named _____ ,

to me known, and known to me to be, the person described herein and who executed the foregoing instrument. The signer verified his or her identity with a jail or prison identification bracelet, which I accept as a valid, state-issued form of identification, or with the following identifying license or document: _____.

The signer acknowledged that signer executed the same, and being duly sworn by me, made oath that the statements in the foregoing instrument are true.

_____

Notary Public—State of _____

My Commission Expires: _____ (SEAL)

INMATE MEDICAL AND PSYCHIATRIC INFORMATION FORM, Page 1

INMATE INFORMATION

Inmate's full legal name _____

Street address _____

City _____ State _____ Zip _____

DOB _____ Jail number _____ Location _____

FAMILY INFORMATION

Family contact name _____ Relationship _____

Street address _____

City _____ State _____ Zip _____

Daytime telephone _____ Evening telephone _____

Family contact signature _____

PSYCHIATRIC INFORMATION

Psychiatrist/psychologist/treatment facility _____

Street address _____

City _____ State _____ Zip _____

Telephone _____ Fax _____

INMATE MEDICAL AND PSYCHIATRIC INFORMATION FORM, Page 2

MEDICAL INFORMATION

Diagnoses _____

Day medications & dosages _____

Night medications and dosages _____

Side effects _____ Allergies _____

Is the inmate suicidal? ☐ No ☐ Yes If yes, explain_____

_____

_____

_____

Other medical conditions_____

_____

_____

_____

Doctor's name_____

Street address _____

City _____ State _____ Zip _____

Office telephone _____ Emergency telephone _____

CONFIDENTIALITY WAIVER/MEDICAL POWER OF ATTORNEY

I ☐ have ☐ do not have a signed, written waiver of confidentiality or medical power of attorney that allows jail medical staff to disclose medical information to me.

☐ Waiver/Medical POA is attached   ☐ Waiver/Medical POA is not attached

LIMITED POWER OF ATTORNEY,
Page 1

I, _____ , currently incarcerated at
_____ , whose address is
_____ , in the city of _____ and state of
_____ , do hereby appoint _____
to be my Agent and Attorney in Fact, and to act on my behalf in the capacities listed below:

POWER	INMATE INITIALS
☐ Write checks, open and close bank accounts, receive statements.	_____
☐ Conduct any business with any financial institution.	_____
☐ Receive and deposit monies due me.	_____
☐ Pay and maintain my credit card accounts and make purchases and execute balance transfers solely to pay for my criminal defense.	_____
☐ Apply for, receive, or settle matters regarding government benefits.	_____
☐ Access my safe-deposit box.	_____
☐ Sell or lease my real property.	_____
☐ Maintain or sell my vehicle.	_____
☐ Cancel leases or sublet my apartment and other rentals.	_____
☐ Enter my residence and store or sell my personal property.	_____
☐ Purchase and maintain insurance on my behalf.	_____
☐ Operate my business.	_____
☐ Apply for and maintain professional licenses and permits.	_____
☐ Request and file documents on my behalf with any government agency.	_____
☐ Prepare and file my tax returns.	_____
☐ Employ attorneys, detectives, and other professionals on my behalf.	_____
☐ Settle any matter with the Armed Forces of the United States.	_____

LIMITED POWER OF ATTORNEY,
Page 2

My Agent and Attorney in Fact shall indemnify and hold harmless third parties who accept and act pursuant to this Power. This Power shall be effective upon the date of execution. It shall revoke other general or limited Powers signed by me. It shall be durable and last until my death or until revoked in writing.

I have signed and sealed this Power of Attorney this _____ day of _____, _____.

_____   _____
Signature   Jail or prison number

STATE OF _____

COUNTY OF _____

On this _____ day of _____ , _____ ,

personally appeared before me the said named _____ ,

to me known, and known to me to be, the person described herein and who executed the foregoing instrument. The signer acknowledged that signer executed the same, and being duly sworn by me, made oath that the statements in the foregoing instrument are true.

I accept the jail or prison identification bracelet, badge, or insignia issued by this state's Department of Corrections, or by the Federal Bureau of Prisons, as proof of the signer's identity.

_____

Notary Public—State of _____

My Commission Expires: _____ (SEAL)

APPENDIX B
How to Dispute Attorney Credit Card Charges

First, a word of warning. Do not dispute credit card charges by attorneys because you are mad at them or angry at the sentence imposed on your defendant by the judge. In starting a groundless dispute, you will only deluge yourself in paperwork and lose the dispute anyway. To be successful, your dispute must have a solid factual basis. In the case of attorneys' fees, the dispute must be initiated because of either failure to perform specified services in the contract or for gross, and difficult-to-prove, negligence.

Credit card disputes are governed by the Fair Credit Billing Act. The key to disputes is documentation. Verbal agreements, unless confirmed by letter, are valueless. You must follow the rules. Here's the procedure:

1. You are required by law to contact the attorney and attempt to negotiate an adjustment or refund *before* you initiate the dispute with the credit card company. Any agreement you reach regarding refunds or changes in fees should be documented. A simple letter will do, such as one beginning with, "As we agreed by telephone today . . ."

2. If you cannot reach agreement with the attorney, *document your attempt to do so* with a letter. This can be simple, such as "Pursuant to my telephone call today, we are unable to resolve the dispute over fees." Call your credit card issuer and initiate a dispute. The customer service rep will lead you through the process. At the end, you will receive a dispute number. Write it down. Many banks will issue a conditional credit equal to the amount of the dispute so that you do not have to pay unless you lose the dispute.

3. You will receive a dispute form. This can obtained by mail, downloaded from the bank Web site, or copied from the back of the credit card statement. On the dispute form, state why the charge is in dispute and why you think you do not owe the money. You can use additional pages for your statement and are not limited to the space in the form.

4. Attach copies of the attorney contract and all receipts and documents. Also attach letters showing that you attempted in good faith to work out the situation with the attorney prior to initiating the dispute. Write your credit card number *only* on the bank dispute form. Write the *dispute number* on all other documents you attach.

5. Make sure you dispute a fair amount. You can dispute part of a charge. For example, if the attorney agreed to four motions and filed only three, you should dispute one-fourth of the amount. Thus, if the fee for the motions was $1,000, you should dispute $250.

6. You must file the dispute within 60 days of the charge, and return dispute paperwork promptly, in order to preserve your dispute rights.

7. Send dispute paperwork to the dispute department address listed on the dispute form. *Do not* send the dispute documents to credit card payment centers, which will cause delays and possible document loss. *Do not* include dispute paperwork in envelopes containing checks for credit card payment. Payment centers use high-speed check-scanning and -clearing equipment to send payment to banks. They are not equipped to handle dispute forms.

8. Send dispute paperwork via certified mail, return receipt requested, in order to document the dates of mailing and the bank's receipt of your dispute. Keep copies of everything.

9. Once the dispute is initiated, do not discuss the dispute further with the attorney. Let the credit card–issuing banks handle everything.

APPENDIX C
The Dictionary of Crime and Punishment

American English is rich in police and prison slang. The criminal jargon of the 1930s and '40s has passed into general usage to such an extent that people rarely realize that it came from jails, prisons, and mean streets. Modern police and prison slang, on the other hand, may not be so familiar. But with the help of this glossary, you can learn crook slang, as well as basic legal terminology. You will get hip fast and figure out what everyone's talking about. For example, if your loved one is charged with agg assault after a raid on a Beavis and Butthead lab, draws ad seg time in the hole, then gets consigned to a cell with some *pinche hue* fatback daddy, you'll want to look it up. Otherwise, *ese*, you're a bunny.

A
ad seg. Administrative segregation.
AFIS. Automated fingerprint identification system.
agg assault. Aggravated assault.
arraignment. A preliminary hearing at which a defendant enters a plea of guilty, not guilty, or *nolo contendere.*

B
bail. 1. Property consigned to the court to assure a defendant's appearances. 2. Jump out of a vehicle and run from police, an excellent way to catch add-on charges of fleeing and eluding, resisting arrest, and assault and battery on a law enforcement officer.
balling. Making money in criminal enterprise.
banging. Fighting.
Beavis and Butthead. Refers to dumb crooks and crimes. "Beavis and Butthead labs" are stovetop operations to cook up methamphetamine in the home. They often explode.
beef. Crime.
bim. Bimbo.
blue bombers. Tranquilizers.
the Blue Horde. Rush of uniformed corrections officers who subdue inmates with batons, TASERs, and pepper spray.
BOLO. A police call meaning "Be on the lookout (for)."
bong. 1. A prison food-cooking pot. Made with a can surrounded by toilet paper that is set on fire. 2. A dope pipe of glass or metal.

booty bandit. Sexual predator who engages in forcible sex with young inmates.

BOSS. Once prison slang meant to stand for the first letters of "sorry son of a bitch," arranged backward. Now it means simply "boss."

box. A jail cell.

bunny. A fool.

burner. A prepaid cell phone that is untraceable to the buyer. Burners are paid for in cash and frequently changed. Burners show no subscriber identity, because there's no subscriber.

bus. An ambulance.

butt scanner. A magnetic scanner that checks incoming inmates for metal secreted in rectums, mouths, and shoes.

buzzer. Police badge.

C

capo de tutti capi. "Boss of bosses," a mafia and movie term.

carnales. Chicano slang for "homies."

catch a squeal. Receive a call on a police radio.

cheesy whore. An inmate who will trade anal sex for a deck of smokes or a commissary snack. Refers to anal discharges of pus that congeal into something akin to cottage cheese. Generally indicative of anal gonorrhea.

chingaso. Hard blow with fist, foot, or baseball bat. After a few *chingasos*, you're *chingado*, or all messed up.

cholo. Low-level thug in Mexican Spanish; also a mestizo, someone of mixed Spanish and Indian blood.

chota. Chicano slang for police officer.

CI. Confidential informant. Police term for snitch.

clique up. In state and federal prisons, the practice of prisoners to hang out with those of similar race or ethnicity.

CO. Corrections officer.

CODIS. Combined DNA Index System, used to match DNA from evidence to people.

constructive possession laws. Laws that ascribe ownership and possession of illegal firearms, drugs, and stolen merchandise to everyone in a vehicle in which the contraband was discovered, regardless of whether he or she was aware of the contraband's presence.

cool. Calm (someone) down. Screaming, out-of-control inmates are "cooled" in a restraint chair or by force.

coyote. A guide who arranges for immigrants to enter the United States illegally.

crank. Methamphetamine.

creds. Credentials. Law enforcement agents always carry creds.

D

daddy. A sexual predator. After a few thrusts, he yells, "Who's your daddy!"

dangle. Beat it, as in "Go dangle."

deck. Pack of smokes.

deuce. Two-year sentence.

discovery. The prosecution's evidence, which should be examined by both defense counsel and the defendant.

double sawbuck. 20-year sentence.

drop a dime. Call the cops to rat somebody out. You have to be of a certain age to remember when pay phone calls actually cost a dime.

dry cell. Cell with no running water. Used by jails and prisons without a fanny scanner to make inmates excrete contraband hidden in their rectums.

E

ese. Literally, "that guy." In jail, a Chicano inmate. On the street, "Yo, ese," means "Hey you!"

exculpatory evidence. Evidence that would tend to exonerate a defendant. Withholding exculpatory evidence is a frequent, and illegal, practice of prosecutors.

F

fatback. An obese inmate.

fin. Five-year sentence.

frequent flyer. Cop slang for a repeat offender.

G

garbagehead. A hopeless addict hooked on multiple drugs.

gate out. Be released from jail or prison.

grab some air. "Hands up."

grift. Swindle; con game.

gumshoe. Private detective.

H

hashish. Trichomes (hairlike protrusions) of the marijuana plant that are rolled by hand and pressed into blocks held together by marijuana sap. Trichomes contain a higher percentage of tetrahydrocannabinol than the leaves. Hash, often cut with dung and other disgusting substances, has lost its mystique, since marijuana itself now packs enough punch to drop a bull moose.

high-hat. To snub or treat with condescension. Also used as a noun, as in "give 'em the high hat." The term derives from the period in which snobs wore top hats.

HO. Habitual offender. Special courts that try habitual offenders are called HO courts.

the hole. Isolation cell; solitary confinement.

home. "Homeboy," a buddy or gang member.

hooped. Carrying contraband in the rectum or vagina.

hop head. Drug addict.

'hound. Greyhound bus.

hue. *Huevo*, Spanish for "egg"—and also "testicle." Chicano guys often refer to one another as *hue*. Sometimes they say *"pinche hue,"* which means fucked-up testicle. Weirdly, this is a term of affection.

hump and dump. To rape and kill in jail or prison.

I

IAFIS. Integrated Automated Fingerprint Identification System.

ink. Tattoos.

in limine. A motion *in limine*, which is Latin for "within the boundary," is a motion to exclude certain evidence, usually made at the beginning of a trial or in a separate hearing.

J

jacket. Cop and jail slang for file or records. Jail administrators can and will release a "hot jacket" of inmate disciplinary infractions to a prosecutor to speed up sentencing and get the inmate out of his or her jail and into a prison. Cops are said to have a hot jacket when their personnel files reveal frequent disciplinary violations and repeated instances of beating and shooting.

jail wine. Wine made from fruit juice or Kool-Aid fermented with urine.

jit. A crazed, unpredictable kid high on methamphetamine or crack.

juking the stats. Police tactics that produce high arrest statistics.

K

kief. Hand-rubbed, powdered trichomes (hairlike protrusions) of the marijuana plant that contain a higher concentration of tetrahydrocannabinol than the leaves.

K-9. A police dog trained to sniff drugs or subdue suspects. A "K-9 unit" is a police officer, dog, and cage-equipped cruiser.

kite. Written note tossed from cell to cell.

L

la Migra. Spanish slang for agents of the U.S. Immigration and Naturalization Service (INS).

L & L. Acronym for a charge of lewd and lascivious conduct. Refers to public flashing, masturbation, unwanted touching, squeezing, and anal and oral sex.

la placa. The police. *Placa* is Spanish for "badge." It also refers to a license plate.

la poli. Spanish slang for "police."

law. Collectively, cops. "Time for some law" means call the cops.

LEO. Law enforcement officer. Pronounced phonetically, as in "Leo the Lion."

M

mouthpiece. Lawyer. Refers to the extraordinary privileges that attorneys have when talking to police on behalf of clients.

N

nap. Sentence. "Take a nap" means to do time.

NCIC. National Crime Information Center.

nolo contendere. A plea of "no contest," offered instead of a guilty or not-guilty plea. A Latin phrase meaning "I do not wish to contest."

nol-pross. Short for *nolle prosequi*, Latin for a decision not to proceed. When a case is nol-prossed, it means that the prosecution chooses not to proceed. The defendant will be freed; however, the prosecution reserves the right to bring charges in the future, subject to statutes of limitations.

O

omertà. Sicilian dialect for "or death." Refers to the code of silence among members of the mafia and their associates.

op. Operative, or operation, as in "black ops."

P

paper handcuffs. Probation.

perp. Perpetrator.

pick. Prison-made knife.

pig. Correctional officer, police officer. Also known as "hack," "screw," "turnkey," etc.

pig sticker. Prison-made knife.

pimp roll. Wide-legged, macho swagger that rolls the shoulders up and down.

pinche hue. See "*hue*."

pop a cap. Shoot a bullet into.

posse. Gang members who go everywhere together. Also refers to entourages of athletes and entertainers.

protect and serve. 1. What police officers do—often painted on their cruisers. 2. A slang term, as in, "I'm gonna protect and serve your ass right into jail."

punk. Weak inmate used as the "catcher" for anal sex. Usually a younger man or boy; almost never a "fatback."

R

rat. Informant.

real police. Term of admiration among cops. Real police make clean busts that stand up in court.

recognizance. A bail arrangement that requires no guaranty of cash or bond, only the defendant's signature on a written promise to appear for hearings and trial. Such defendants are said to be "RORed," or Released On Recognizance.

respond. The all-purpose verb used in police reports. Police never walk, run, or drive. They "respond." They will, for example, respond to an address, respond through the front door, respond up the stairs, etc.

restraint chair. Metal or plastic chair with heavy arm and leg restraints used to manage unruly or crazed inmates. Most jails keep these in soundproof cells.

re-up. Daily delivery of drugs to the boys working the street corners controlled by a drug dealer.

ROC. Repeat offender court. These are special courts with fast calendars, top-flight prosecutors, and tough judges who mete out long sentences to "frequent flyers."

rollies. Hand-rolled cigarettes or joints.

S

SAR. Suspicious Activity Report filed by banks with the U.S. Department of the Treasury. SARs record suspicious transfers of cash and cash equivalents in amounts as low as $3,000. These reports identify money laundering and the financing of terrorism.

sawbuck. Ten-year sentence.

Schedule I. Illegal drugs for which there is no medical use.

Schedule II and III. Habit-forming prescription drugs as defined by the U.S. Controlled Substances Act.

shank. Prison-made knife.

shine. Jail booze made from fruit juice, sugar, and urine.

shiv. Prison-made knife. Usually used for stabbing, since most shivs are made of plastic or wood and have points but no sharp edges.

show out. To challenge corrections officers.

six, or six up. To warn when correctional officers, lawyers, or police officers approach. The term is derived from military pilot slang where "12 o'clock" means "dead ahead" and "six o'clock" means "directly behind." "Get your six" means back up a buddy.

skel. New York prison slang for "skeleton." What drug users become.

snitch. Informant.

SODDI. Some Other Dude Did It. What every suspect says when arrested.

spliff. Jamaican slang for a fat marijuana joint. Some are as big as small cabbages!

stare party. Giving other inmates, or guards, the evil eye.

stool pigeon. Snitch.

strawberry. Inmate who will sell sex for drugs. Refers to bright red fannies inflamed by infection.

suitcase. Rectum.

T

'tard police. "Retarded police."

tatts. Tattoos. Jail tatts are often made with staples pulled from legal documents and inserted into a plastic razor handle. The ink is made by melting plastic chess pieces, checkers, or razor handles into black goo.

three hots and a flop. Three hot meals and a bed.

throwdown. Evidence, usually a weapon, illegally placed at a crime scene by police to convict a suspect or justify force.

toughen up. To shout insults or administer beatings to improve an inmate's attitude, as in "The sergeant was just toughening you up."

trick box. 1. A defendant's situation when being interrogated by two police officers. Officers know the tricks; defendants don't. When questioned by skilled interrogators, defendants in the trick box will contradict themselves, lie, confess, or implicate others. 2. "Putting a suspect in the trick box" means using legal but unethical inciters, such as racial or ethnic epithets, touching, or crowding, to get a suspect to shove police officers or flee during roadside questioning.

tweak. Methamphetamine.

twink. Young inmate used for sex.

U

upcharging. The practice of multiplying and adding on all possible charges during an arrest.

V

vic. Crime victim. Many states give victims a statutory role in prosecutions.
vigorish, or vig. Usurious interest on illegal loans.
VIN. Vehicle identification number.

W

white-bread America. Middle-class values despised, or feared, by inmates.

XYZ

X. Ecstasy.
Xed out. Killed.

INDEX

Abbott, Jack Henry, 85–86
acquittal, 143
active supervision, 190–191
add-ons, 227–228
administrative violations, 195. *See also* parole; probation
affidavits to dismiss judge, 164
alcohol
  attorneys and, 150
  vs. drugs, 75
  jail wine, 46–47
  military service and, 96
appeals, 149
Arpaio, Joe, 53
arrest reports
  description of, 24
  sample, 25, 26
Arrest-Proof Yourself (Carson & Denham), 7, 34, 51, 96, 200, 201, 226
atemporality, 81–83
attorneys. *See also* attorneys, private; public defenders
  arrest reports and, 24–25
  budgets and, 180, 183
  contingent-fee, 53
  contracts and, 170–172
  cost of, 14–15
  deciding on, 168
  disbarred, 136, 139–140
  drugs and, 35
  evaluation of, 146, 148–151
  family management plan and, 212, 219
  guns and, 35–36
  hearings and procedures and, 162–163
  information checklist for, 145
  information on, 27
  interviewing, 144, 147, 148–151, 154, 155
  law enforcement experience and, 150
  lawsuits against, 156
  payment of, 153–154, 170–172, 183–185
  presence of, 2, 3
  price quotations and, 152–153
  proffer of cooperation and, 204
  self-representation, 169
  unprepared, 140
  waiving right to, 2, 3
attorneys, private. *See also* attorneys; public defenders
  choosing, 133–134
  issues regarding, 14–15
  vs. public defenders, 15, 125, 129–131, 134–135, 142, 153
  types of, 135–140

bail
  commercial, 118
  conditions of, 117–118
  drug addicts and, 77
  reduction hearing, 118–119, 121
  when to pay, 1, 119–120

bail bonds
  business of, 120–121
  caution on, 14
  charge sheet and, 24
  description of, 118
  mortgages and, 186
  sample arrest report and, 26
  scams and, 121–123
balance transfers, 183–184. *See also* loans
banks, 183, 185, 188. *See also* finances;
  loans
bar associations, 132
bar number, 148
behavior
  in jail, 3–4
  unsocialized, 80–85
  during visitations, 40–41
Bergman, Paul, 7
Berman, Sara J., 7
bill of particulars, 159
body cavity searches, 2, 5
bond. *See* bail; bail bonds
bond reduction, 143, 156
bounty hunters, 121
brutality, police, 107
budgets. *See also* fees; finances
  government, 60
  importance of, 179
  inmates and, 180
  preparation of, 180, 183
  probation and parole and, 198
  worksheet for, 181–182
Bureau of Justice Statistics, 230
burner phones, 64, 224, 230. *See also* cell
  phones

caffeine withdrawal,
  3, 77, 89

cars
  contesting seizure of, 159, 167
  defendant's, 188
  driving under the influence and,
    228
  ignition interlocks and, 194
  military service and, 96
  parking, 22, 39
  probation and parole and, 199–201
  searching, 34–35
  street legal, 107
  title loans and, 186. *see also* loans
  visitations and, 39
Carson, Dale, 7, 201
case numbers, 26, 27
caseload
  challenges and, 142–143
  public defenders and, 126–127
cell phones, 61, 62, 193. *See also* burner
  phones
cell stores, 46
change
  jail as impetus for, 10
  readiness for, 89–92
character. *See also* defendant evaluations;
  morals; values; virtues
  assessment of, 108–109, 111
  indications of, 109–110, 112
  references, 211–212
  success stories, 110, 113
charge sheet
  description of, 22, 24
  sample, 23
charges, dismissal of, 9
children
  bail and, 120
  military service and, 95–96
  probation and parole and, 198
  state custody and, 108

citizen
  criminal vs., 13
  description of, 8
  military service and, 97
  transformation into, 219
clerks of the court, 24
collateral, 118, 122
commissary, 3–4, 46, 51, 62
communication
  attorneys and, 162–163
  mail and, 12
community service, 193
compelling discovery, 160
complainant statements, 229–230
computers. *See also* Internet
  criminal databases and, 223
  records checks in, 198–199
  searching, 36
  security and, 63–64
condoms, 70. *See also* sex; sexually
  transmitted diseases
confessions, false, 82
confidential informants. *See*
  informants
constructive possession, 194, 200
contesting seizure of property or vehicle,
  159
contractors and legal subcontracting,
  135–137, 148
conviction rates, 129–130
convicts, definition of, 11
cooperation, proffer of. *See* proffer of
  cooperation
corrections officers. *See also* police
  abuse by, 44
  corrupt, 46
  interacting with, 3–4
  rape and, 69, 70
  scams and, 66

  spitting and, 45
  sympathy for, 29
corruption, 46, 140
costs of defense. *See* budgets; fees;
  finances
court dates, 24
courts, factors considered by, 7
credit, letters of, 185. *See also* loans
credit cards, 183–185, 188
crime, study of, 17–18
crime scene, visit to, 164
criminal databases, 223
criminal defense, books on, 7
criminal justice system
  as market, 126–128
  minorities in, 7
Criminal Law Handbook, The (Bergman
  & Berman), 7
crooks, 140
curfew, 192

death, in custody, 53–54
defendant evaluations. *See also* character
  checklist for, 105–106
  description of, 104, 107–108
  self-evaluation, 104
  support and, 103
  true vs. false statements, 211
defendants. *See also* inmates
  change and, 10
  educating, on law, 168
  family management plan and,
   209–211
  finances of, 188–189
  financial contributions from, 187
  helping in defense, 173–174
  instructions for, 2, 3–4, 44–48
  interests of, 8

preparation of, 163
vampire, 115–116
defense attorneys. *See* attorneys;
   attorneys, private; public defenders
Department of Justice statistics, 222, 228
detainees, definition of, 11
detectives, private, 150
direct sentence to probation, 144
disbarred attorneys, 136, 139–140
discovery
   defendant review of, 176
   motion to compel, 160
discretion, limitations on, 232–233
dismissal
   of charges, 143
   of judge, 164
   motion for, 156
diversion into treatment, 58, 143–144
documents, forms for, 187
dodo birds, 139
dogs/K-9s, 107, 149, 159
domestic disturbances, 228–229
driving. *See* cars
driving under the influence (DUI), 228
drug trade, 81–82, 224–225
drugs
   addicts and, 76–78
   arrests for, 224–225
   bail and, 117–118
   disposal of, 35, 37
   incarceration rates and, 232
   military service and, 94
   nonaddicts and, 74–76
   probation and parole and, 191, 195
   smuggling of, 56
   tests and, 78–79, 191
   visitations and, 39
drunk driving, 228

education, 193
educational records, 27
employment, 27, 193
equity loans, 185. *See also* loans
escapes, 29, 48
evaluations
   of character, 108–110, 111–112
   of defendants, 104–108
   of self, 113–115
evidence
   destruction of, 37
   exculpatory, 159–160
   forensic, 163–164
   investigation of, 163
   motions regarding, 159, 161
   subpoenas of, 164
   suppression of, 164
exhibit preparation, 164
expert witnesses, 150, 164

Fair Credit Billing Act, 183
families
   importance of, 9, 110, 113, 235
   interests of, 8–9
   intervention of, 17, 41–42
   military service and, 95–96
   plea bargains and, 129
family management plan
   bail and, 119, 120, 156
   description of, 88, 209
   formulating, 209–210
   intervention and, 17
   parole hearings and, 192
   probation reports and, 28, 168, 195
   supporting documents, 210–211
   use of, 211, 219
   worksheet for, 213–218

Federal Bureau of Investigation (FBI), 28–29, 140, 149, 204, 221
federal cases, 149
fee mills, 138–139
fee whores, 135
fees. *See also* budgets; finances
    attorneys', 152–153
    for incarceration, 62
    for initial attorney interview, 147
    probation and parole and, 193
fights, avoiding, 3–4, 45
finances. *See also* budgets; fees; loans
    attorneys and, 14–15, 131, 134–135, 150–151, 168
    bail bonds and, 119–120
    commissary and, 62
    defendant's, 188–189
    freedom and, 8
    getting money, 183–185
    incentive pay, 171–172
    jail currency, 47
    jail phones and, 61–62
    military service and, 95–96
    money orders vs. personal checks, 29
    plea bargains and, 140–141
    probation and parole and, 193–194, 198
    quarters, 22
    scams and, 62–66
    security and, 64
    strain on, 9
    structured payments, 170–171
    toxic loans and, 186
    trial quotations, 163–165, 167–168
fines, probation and parole and. *See* fees
fingerprints, 29–30, 35
flash incarceration, 196
flip-flops, 2, 5

food in jail, 50–51
forensic and scientific analysis, 163–164
Fortas, Abe, 125
Fourteenth Amendment, 125
fraud, bond, 122
Freakonomics (Levitt), 223
fugitives, harboring, 122–123
future
    character and, 112
    focus on, 43–44
    lack of concern for, 81–82
    military service and, 97
    planning for, 210

gambling, 47
geographical restriction, 192
Gideon, Clarence Earl, 124–125, 131
Gideon v. Wainwright, 124–125
guns
    attorneys and, 150
    disposal of, 35–36
    military service and, 96
    probation and parole and, 194
    visitations and, 39

habitual/repeat offenders, 115–116, 160, 233
harboring fugitives, 122–123
health
    care, 55–57
    maintaining, 3
hearings
    bail reduction, 118–119, 121
    to contest seizure of vehicle of property, 167
    to dismiss judge, 164

family management plan and, 219
jury selection and, 167
parole, 192
right to, 168
hip-pocket informants, 204. *See also*
informants
Homo chaoticus, 80–85, 109
houses, searching, 32–34
housing, 188, 199
hygiene, personal, 3, 112

ignition interlocks, 194
in limine, motions, 164
In the Belly of the Beast (Abbott), 86
incarceration
flash, 196
of mentally ill, 230–231
statistics on, 220–221
incentive pay, 171–172
informants
attorneys and, 149–150
confidential, 204
dangers of, 16
decisions regarding, 202–203
hip-pocket, 204
motion to disclose identity of
government, 161
probation and parole and, 193
threats and, 206, 207–208
information
gathering, 11, 22
Internet and, 21
inmates. *See also* defendants
character tests and, 109–110, 112. *see
also* character; defendant evaluations
ploys of, 45–46
respect for, 44

snitching and, 2
innocence, three degrees of, 104
instructions for detainee, 2, 3–4, 44–48
Internet
bookmarking and, 30
payments via, 185
probation and parole and, 192
scams and, 63–64
searches, 21
interrogations
attorneys and, 162–163
deception during, 2
preventing police, 37–38
interventions, 41–42

Jail Mail. *See also* mail
Character Witnesses, 178
description of, 12
Discovery Review, 176
Stay Safe, 3–4
What Happened, 175
Witnesses, 177
jail number
first call and, 1
mail and, 2, 22
jails
alcohol in, 46–47
daily life in, 12, 43–45
definition of, 11
food in, 50–51
good vs. bad, 53
hard vs. soft, 52–53
locations of, 51–52
phone calls from, 61–62
rules of, 27
scams in, 62–66
visits to, 39–41

judges
   dismissal of, 164
   factors considered by, 7
   interests of, 8
juries
   challenges and, 167
   consultants for, 164
   instructions to, 167
   selection of, 167
   sympathy of, 129
juvenile justice system, 7–8

K-9 alerts, 149, 159

law, regulation of practice of, 132
lawyers. *See* attorneys; attorneys, private;
  public defenders
legal advice, lack of, 6
leniency, 17, 19, 28, 140, 167
letters of credit, 185. *See also* loans
Levitt, Steven, 223
lies
   abundance of, 10–11
   defendants and, 144, 147
   police and, 37
   probation and parole and, 201
   proffer of cooperation and, 203
   truth-checking and, 24
lineups, 162
loans. *See also* budgets; fees; finances
   bank account security, 183
   car title, 186
   credit cards and, 183–184
   defendant's, 188
   equity, 185
   payday, 186

   tax refunds and, 186
   toxic, 186

mail. *See also* Jail Mail
   establishing address for, 30
   first letter, 2
   probation and parole and, 197
   suggestions for, 51
   supplies for, 22
mandatory sentencing, 233
marijuana, 75–76. *See also* drugs
Marine Corps, 98–99. *See also* military
  service
Matejkowski, Jason C., 231
Medal of Honor, 99–100
media, avoiding, 30–31, 53
mental hang-ups, 89–91
mental illness, 57–58, 230–231
military service
   advantages of, 95–96
   defendant evaluation and, 106, 108
   disadvantages of, 95
   discussing with defendants, 93–95
   enlistment checklist, 101
   families and, 95–96
   records of, 27
   socialization and, 97–100
   women in, 98
minorities, 7
momma's boys, 113–115
money. *See* budgets; fees; finances;
  loans
morals. *See also* character; values;
  virtues
   military service and, 94
   premorality and, 13, 84
mortgages, bail bond, 186. *See also* loans

motions
mailing of, 148
types of, 155–156, 159–162, 164

National Crime Information Center (NCIC), 28–29
Navy SEALs, 97–98, 99–100. *See also* military service
Nifong, Michael, 159
nolle prosequi (nol-pross), 9, 119, 143
notaries, 57, 187
notice of appearance, 156
notices to appear (NTAs), 234

offenders, definition of, 11

parking, 22, 39. *See also* cars
parole
conditions of, 192–194
costs of, 15, 181–182
demands of, 16
description of, 191–192, 195–197
family assistance and, 197–201
violations of, 195–197, 228, 233
pawnbrokers, 186
payday loans, 186. *See also* loans
payment plans, 150–151, 170–171. *See also* budgets; fees; finances
people avoidance, 193
Pew Charitable Trusts report, 220
photography, 164
plea bargains
criminal justice system and, 128–129
family and, 129
fee mills and, 138–139

as free good, 140–141
improving, 142–143
preliminary work for, 142–143
private attorneys and, 134
public defenders and, 15, 125–126
quotation for, 157–158
vs. trials, 129
police. *See also* corrections officers
brutality, 107
motion regarding, 161
preventing searches by, 37–38
polygraph operators, 150
pornography, illegal, 36, 37
possession, constructive, 194, 200
posting bond, 119–120. *See also* bail; bail bonds
power of attorney, 57, 187
premorality, 13, 84
preparation for trial, 163–164
prescriptions, 56. *See also* health
prisons, definition of, 11
private detectives, 150
probation
conditions of, 192–194
costs of, 15, 181–182
demands of, 16
description of, 190–191, 195–197
direct sentence to, 144
drug use and, 74–75
family assistance and, 197–201
marijuana and, 76
terms and conditions of, 162
violations of, 195–197, 228, 233
probation reports
description of, 28
family management plan and, 168, 194–195

sentencing and, 167–168
professional criminals, 224–225
proffer of cooperation
    dangers of, 174, 204
    deciding on, 202–203
    description of, 160
    negotiating, 204–205
property, contesting seizure of, 167
protection racket, 45–46
public defenders. *See also* attorneys;
  attorneys, private
    caseload and, 126–127
    experience of, 129–130
    information on, 27
    in noncapital cases, 124–125
    vs. private attorneys, 15, 125, 129–
        131, 134–135, 142, 153
punishment, pretrial, 12

quotations, price, 154–155

racism, 7
Racketeer Influenced and Corrupt
  Organizations (RICO) Act, 224–225
rap sheets, 28–30
rape
    avoiding, 68–69
    charges of, 229
    corrections officers and, 69, 70
    psychological care and, 70
recognizance, release on (ROR), 118,
    143
records, personal, 27
records check, 198–199
red flags, 105–106, 107

reduction of charges, 144
reform. *See* change
release on recognizance (ROR), 118, 143
religion, 212
repeat/habitual offenders, 115–116, 160,
    233
restitution, 168, 193
rights waiver, 193
rumors, jail, 48

scams
    bail bonds and, 121–123
    dangers of perpetrating, 67
    types of, 62–66
searches
    body cavity, 2, 5
    of cars, 34–35
    of computers, 36
    disposal of items found during,
        35–36, 37
    of houses, 32–34
    of own property, 19, 32
    preventing police, 37–38
    probation and parole and, 191, 193
seizure of vehicle or property,
    contesting, 167
self-representation, 169
sentencing
    arrests and, 223
    plea bargains and, 125–126
    probation reports and, 167–168
    witnesses at, 167
severing counts or defendants, 160
sex
    assault and, 68–69
    avoiding, 3, 4

corrections officers and, 70
infections and, 68–72
sexual preference, 73
sexually transmitted diseases, 69–70,
71–72
signature, providing, 2
Sixth Amendment, 124–125, 127
smoking, 75
snitches, identifying, 46. *See also*
informants; proffer of cooperation
social security, 183
social structure, 83
socialization
family and, 87–88
family management plan and, 210
importance of, 13–14
military service and, 97–100
probation and parole and, 193
probation reports and, 195
unsocialized man and, 80–85
solicitation, bail bondsmen and, 122
speedy trial, motion for, 156
spitting, 3, 45
Standard Deal, 125, 130, 134, 140–141,
154
standard supervision, 191
statistics
arrests and, 226
on crime rates, 221–222
on drug charges, 232
on incarceration rates, 220–222
juking of, 233
on mental illness and crime, 230–231
stimulus-response decision making, 13,
85
stolen goods, disposal of, 36, 37
striking counts, 159
striking priors, 160

subcontracting, legal, 135–137, 148
subpoenas, 156, 164, 193
sucker fish, 139
suicide threats, 59
supplies, 21–22
supply and demand
attorneys and, 132–133
Standard Deal and, 126
support
deciding on, 103–104, 107–110
denying, 113
suppression
of evidence, 159, 164
of identification by a witness, 161
of testimony, 164
supreme court cases, 149
surety, 118

tattoos, 3, 47
tax refund anticipation loans, 186. *See
also* loans
taxes, defendant's, 189
telephone calls
burner phones and, 64, 224, 230
call forwarding, 63
cell phones and, 49, 61, 62
initial, 1–2, 5
responsible use of, 112
scams and, 62–63
three-way calls, 62
telephone numbers, importance of, 27
threats
media attention and, 31
proffer of cooperation and, 205
of rape, 68–69
response to, 206, 207–208
warning regarding, 49–50

three degrees of innocence, 104, 107
time
    abundance of, in jail, 5
    lack of concern for, 81
tobacco, 75
toxic loans, 186. *See also* loans
trials
    attorneys and, 148
    preparation for, 167
    quotation for, 163–165, 167–168

unprepared attorneys, 140
unsupervised probation, 191
upcharging, 226, 227–228

values. *See also* character; morals;
  virtues
    budgeting and, 180
    check, 84–86
    defendants and, 80
    middle-class, 86–87, 209
    obtaining, 90
vampire defendants, 115–116
victim restitution, 168, 193
video, 164
violations of parole and probation, 195–
    197, 228, 233
virtual account numbers, 184–185
virtues, 109, 111. *See also* character;
  morals; values
visitations
    attorneys and, 148
    communication and, 12, 24

pointers for, 39–41
voodoo doctors, 137–138

warrants, 19
weapons. *See* guns
Web sites. *See also* Internet
    bookmarking, 30
    searches and, 21
white-collar criminals, 225
Wilson, James Q., 223
wiretaps, 149
withdrawal, drug, 77–78
witness protection, 50, 204–205, 206,
    207
witnesses
    character, 178
    dangers of being, 16
    defendants and, 173–174, 177
    expert, 150, 164
    interviewing, 163
    investigation of, 163
    preparation of, 163
    at sentencing, 167
    subpoenas of, 164
    suppression of, 161, 164
women, military service and, 98

zero-tolerance policing
    caseload and, 128
    description of, 223–225
    example of, 138
    impact of, 153, 221, 230, 234–235
    supply and demand and, 132–133